OVER THE FALLS

Sdok^{w}albix^w Survivance Surrounding Seattle

Jay Miller, PhD

© 2019

contents

contents

1   Intro   3 Territory   4 Sense of Place

6   ~ 1 ~ *Rally Round The Falls*   11 Lake Sammamish Sources   11 Snoqualmie Sources
        12 Snoqualmie Villages   13 Sammamish River & Lake Shore   14 River

20 ~ 2 ~ *Saduwa & Upper Sdok^{w}albix^w*   22 Slahal family network

27 ~ 3 ~ *Patkadəb & Lower Sdok^{w}albix^w*   31 Kittitas Crux

36 ~ 4 ~ *Lakes*   37 d^{z}ak^{w}us   38 Owl and His Wife Frog   42 Siddles

44 ~ 5 ~ *Culture Constituents*   44 Communal   45 Riverines   48 Drainage   49 Rank
        50 Personnel   50 Genders   53 Man   53 Woman   54 Age   54 Chief   55 Warrior
        55 Doctor   55 Prophet   56 Ceremonial   56 1st Salmon   56 Growlers   56 *spədak*
        57 *Syowin*   58 Potlatch   59 Seasonal   60 Subsistence   60 Calendar   65 Harvesting
        65 Fish   67 Shellfish   68 Game   69 Berries

70 ~ 6 ~ *Kinscape*   71 Twin Kindreds   72 Household   73 Intersept   75 Comparisons
        78 Components

80 ~ 7 ~ *Decedence*

87 ~ 8 ~ *Survivance*   90   2 maps

        Appendices 91
92   ~ A ~   Star Child and Diaper Boy + Star 94
99   ~ B ~   Snoqualmie 20 April 1856 Census ~   Nathan Hill @ Holmes Harbor
101 ~ C ~   James Teit 1910 Letter to Franz Boas
104 ~ D ~   *Tacoma Sunday News Ledger* 24 December 1916: page 6 ~ Duwamish Indians
                 name Agent Roblin ~ "Qua-Whad," After Title of Old Wise Man ~
                 Roblin Background & Work
113 ~ E ~   1933 Land Claims Sdok^{w}albix^w Testimonies
115 ~ F ~   Lushootseed ~ dx^{w}ləšucid ~ (t)x^{w}əlšucid   118 Chinuk Wawa
119 ~ G ~   Kin Terms by AC Ballard & Zalmai Zahir
125 ~ H ~   BAR 7 Criteria

Bibliography   127 = 150

Thanks   151

Index   152-156

INTRODUCTION

TRI-TRIBE

Sdoqʷalbixʷ are a study in contrasts over centuries, with twists, turns and contested present. Their casino draws in millions of dollars for a federally recognized tribe without a valid membership list in any kind of accord with their constitution, which recognizes crucial roles for elected intergenerational "traditional" chiefs, real threats of banishment, but ignores the regionally significant network of their ancient hereditary chief.

In central Puget Sound east of Seattle, three rivers flowing out of the Cascade Mountains form a wishbone. The Snoqualmie River is its southern branch, Skykomish is the north one, and Snohomish is the end prong flowing into the Sound. Residents of these last two drainages speak Northern Lushootseed (Appendix F), while Snoqualmie speaks the southern dialect. Of especial note, their river plummets over a landmark 300-feet waterfall that both centers the tribe even as it distinguished upper prairie and lower tidal communities. For much of written history, however, emphasis has been given to Lower Sdokʷalbixʷ, to the virtual erasure of the Upper, who had more area, more towns and houses, higher incomes, and far reaching ties of kinship, trade, and elite status. Moreover, Sdokʷalbixʷ, like ancient Gaul, has three divisions: upper, lower, and lakes, who also have been seriously overlooked because they overlapped with Duwamish on the large lakes near Seattle now known as Sammamish, Washington (formerly Duwampsh), and Union, as well as many smaller ones.

With the majestic Falls at their hub, the Upriver ~ Upper Sdokʷalbixʷ under the distinguished name title of Saduwa ~ Saniwa ~ Sanawa are enmeshed within a vast network among elite families tracing their own kinship pedigrees to peaceful competition expressed by a gambling game now known as Slahal that promotes friendly interactions. Such gambling with fate also figures in creation stories where animals play it against humans to set up today's conditions, such as who eats whom. Saduwa moved across both sides of the Cascades, then his heirs settled along the Skagit, out of harm's way, far from Seattle's orbit.

When Watson Martin (1933), Saduwa in the early 1900s, testified for tribal land claims, he named the towns of "Skashia, Toquiki, Yetsk, located at Falls City now, Yahakabulch, Schwalp, Toquill, Skwut, now located at Snoqualmie Falls; Bokwab, a prairie, Tswodum, Sotsoks" in all comprising 58 houses. (Appendix D matches these names with known numbers).

Downriver ~ Lower Sdokʷalbixʷ forged a political system like a chiefdom dominated by the Kanim family drawn to the coast from the regional crossroads of Kittitas about 1800 in reaction to devastating pandemics in the late 1700s, local battles, and keen advice from emigrants from Eastern tribes like Delaware, Iroquois, and Cherokee who had already borne the brunt of European invasion and devastation.

Drawn into the global market by the fur trade from ships, then forts like that built at Nisqually in 1833, Sdokʷalbixʷ ceded their land to the US at the 1855 Pt Elliott Treaty when Patkanim signed second after Seattle himself. They were supposed to move to the Tulalip Reservation, the largest on Puget Sound because it was intended to contain "dwindling" last survivors. But there was neither room nor welcome on these traditional

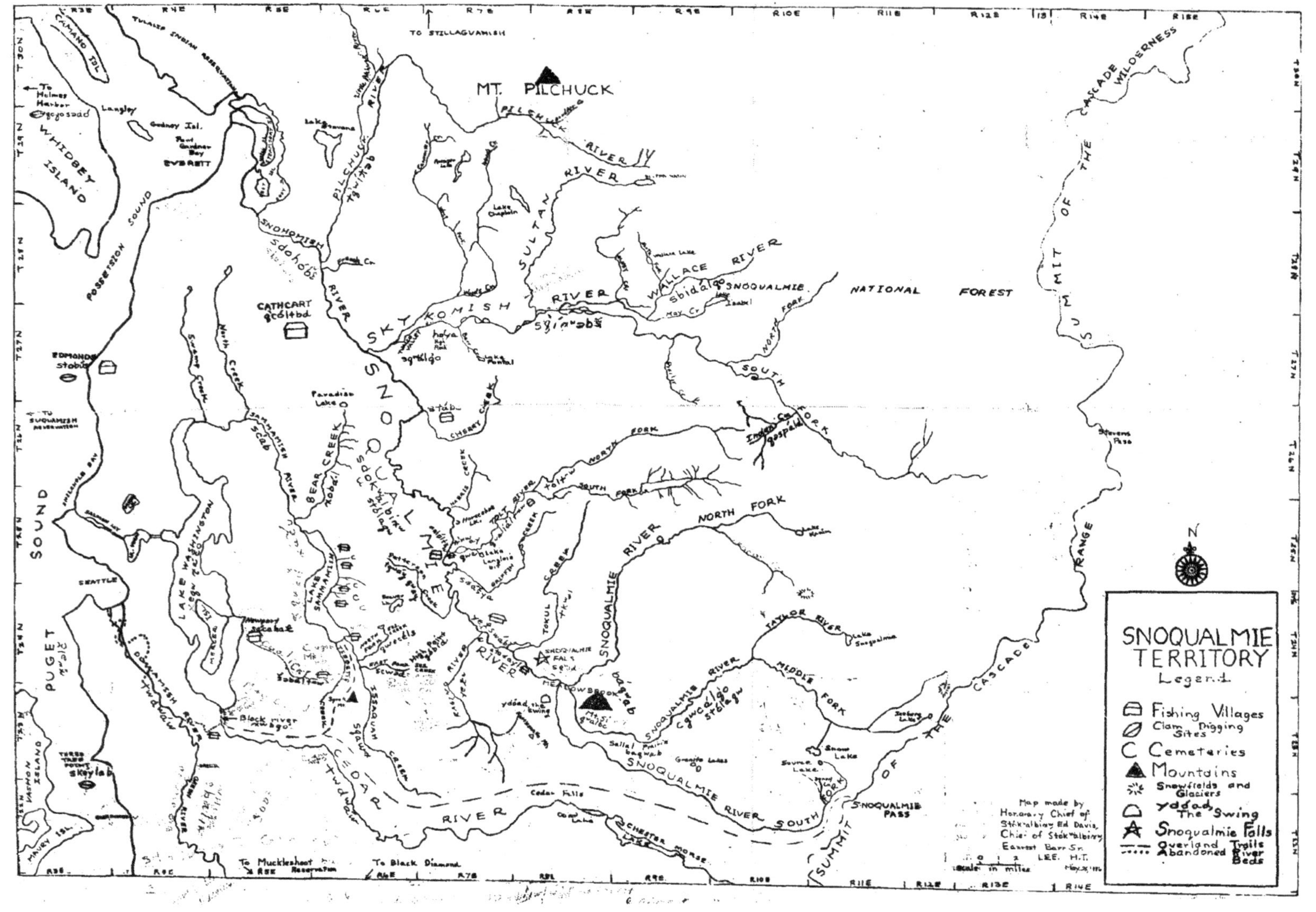
TO STILLAGUAMISH
MT. PILCHUCK
PILCHUCK RIVER
WHIDBEY ISLAND
CAMANO ISL.
Langley
To Holmes Harbor
Gedney Isl.
Port Gardner Bay
EVERETT
POSSESSION SOUND
SULTAN RIVER
WALLACE RIVER
SNOHOMISH RIVER
sdohobs
CATHCART
EDMONDS
Stobo
To Suquamish Reservation
SKYKOMISH RIVER
sbidalgo Snoqualmie
NATIONAL FOREST
SUMMIT OF THE CASCADE WILDERNESS
SOUTH FORK
Stevens Pass
Paradise Lake
BEAR CREEK
North Creek
Sammamish Scab
CHERRY CREEK
NORTH FORK
SOUTH FORK
Indian Co.
gospels
PUGET SOUND
LAKE WASHINGTON
SEATTLE
LAKE SAMMAMISH
Snoqualmie
TOKUL CREEK
SNOQUALMIE FALLS
SNOQUALMIE RIVER
NORTH FORK
TAYLOR RIVER
MIDDLE FORK
Black river
CEDAR RIVER
Cedar Falls
SNOQUALMIE RIVER SOUTH
SNOQUALMIE PASS
SUMMIT OF THE CASCADE RANGE
Granite Lakes
MANLEY ISL.
THREE TREE POINT
Skaylab
To Muckleshoot Reservation
To Black Diamond
Map made by
Honorary Chief of
Stkxalbing Ed Davis,
Chief of Stkxalbing
Earnest Barr Sr.
LEE. H.T.
scale in miles
N
SNOQUALMIE TERRITORY
Legend
Fishing Villages
Clam Digging Sites
C Cemeteries
Mountains
Snowfields and Glaciers
yddad The Swing
Snoqualmie Falls
Overland Trails
Abandoned River Beds

Sdohobsh lands. Some like Snuqualmie Jim did settle there at Mission Beach, but others stayed in the foothills, working in the growing hops industry. Some homesteaded, with all the irony of dispossessed natives reclaiming a bit of their ancestral lands by officially "severing all ties to their tribe" as witnessed by merchants and farmers who relied on their sales and stoop labor.

Sdokʷalbixʷ Territory

Because Sdokʷalbixʷ maintained a coherent community at Tolt,[1] now corporatized as Carnation in recognition of the dairy company that runs a model facility there, long under the leadership of elders and of Jerry Kanim, though continuing that family name without any known proof that he was more of a descendant than a fosterage claiming helpful ties to treaty signer Pat Kanim. The BIA continued to deal with him and them as an off reservation, landless community, making recurrent promises for a reservation that never happened. Instead, members lived on their own homesteads and hop farms until hop lice aphids destroyed this industry in western Washington, and the agent at Tulalip encouraged many Sdokʷalbixʷ to move to the Muckleshoot reservation where there were jobs in a sawmill.

Motivated by political awakenings before WWI, local tribes agitated for a BIA review of landless native communities in preparation for a federal lawsuit to gain compensation for treaty violations and thwarted land claims. At the start of 1919, Charles Roblin submitted his roll of landless tribes of western Washington, which in time became the constitutional basis for several tribal roles, including Sdokʷalbixʷ.

In 1953, in anticipation of getting the US government "out of the Indien[2] business," a list was drawn up of local tribes to be terminated, including the Seattle Duwamish, despite the fact their name leads the preamble of the Pt Elliott Treaty, and the Sdokʷalbixʷ at Tolt. Thus, without due process, consultation, or any goodwill, the BIA stopped dealing with these tribes, throwing them into legal limbo. Yet dogged elders and young leaders recruited local academics at religious schools to help research and write a petition for reinstatement. Opposed by Tulalip millions and ill will in claiming rightful succession to Sdokʷalbixʷ assets and claims via Patkanim's mark on the treaty, Sdokʷalbixʷ eventually prevailed in 1999. Duwamish has yet to succeed, largely because Seattle, Bellevue, and other municipalities now occupy and dominate their valuable territory. Simultaneously, rural Cowlitz and urban Chinook have also been seeking federal acknowledgement, with only Cowlitz succeeding, building clinics first and finally a huge casino with aid and advice from the Mohegan Sun casino of Connecticut.

Of note, Sdokʷalbixʷ have satisfied only six of the seven criteria for approval by BIA's BAR ~ Bureau of Acknowledgement and Research (Appendix H). The last is an approved official membership roll, which has now been postponed for two decades. Meanwhile their casino, near Seattle and prime outlet malls, brings in millions. They continue to hold elections, usually with police and security guarding the door, and report results to the Everett BIA. They also make huge contributions to favorable candidates in local elections and to town, state, and federal officials, as well as for aid and cleanup after local disasters. Yet the membership impasse

---

[1] Tolt derives from the remarkable "Demarked House" with a blue wave across the front.
[2] Throughout, Indien, of the West Indies, is my preferred spelling of the more confusing Indian.

continues, with present councilors on record decrying the corruption and disarray of purported tribal rolls, none of them in accord with their constitution.

In all, by ever playing the US system against itself, Sdok^{w}albix^w exemplified survivance, exalting Native America's own triumphs. Originally a 1700s legal term for survivorship while grantor and heir are both living, French Canadiens revived it as "*La Survivance*," and Jacques Derrida uses it for a spectral existence neither life nor death. In particular, Gerald Vizenor (2008), Anishinaabe cultural theorist and goad, exalts it as "active sense of presence, the continuing native stories, not mere reaction, to be renunciations of dominance, tragedy and victimry" as exemplified by the later urban life of Ishi. Deliberately imprecise, it can be a portmanteau of "survival + endurance" ~ "survival + resistance" ~ "survival + connivance" deriving from sur = beyond, in excess (of survival) + vivance = vitality ~ vibrance."

It has been exemplified in the emerald Puget Sound Basin, 40 miles wide and 170 miles long, was originally a dense evergreen forest of hemlock, fir, and cedar, setting the Northwest apart, along with deciduous trees such as red alder, big leaf maple, and cottonwood. Alpine zones, parklands, prairies, and extensive intertidal zones also provide resource habitats. Parklands and prairies interspersed through these forests were culturally maintained by regular burning (Boyd 1999; Suttles 1987; White 1980: 20). Traditional territories were carefully tended by fires set when the weather was right for a safe contained burn, maintaining open grasslands as hunting grounds and as crop fields of many root foods. Thousand miles of shoreline have such ecologically diverse habitats as islands, deltas, tide flats, marshes, estuaries, shallow bays, and beaches. Away from shore, terrain is hilly, interspersed with lakes, and dense with undergrowth.

Plentiful game varied from marine mammals (porpoise, seal, sea lion) and birds (waterfowl) to land mammals (deer, elk, bear, otter, raccoon, beaver, mountain goat). Edible plants ranged from a host of berries to clover, cow parsnip, ferns, nettles, willows, and camas.[3] Wapato (wild potato) grew in shallow water bodies and cranberries were harvested from bogs. Lakes and rivers contained freshwater fish and shellfish. Diverse microenvironments comprised shellfish, ocean fish, porpoise, seal, sea lion, waterfowl, deer, elk, bear, otter, raccoon, beaver, mountain goat, and the seasonal runs of five salmon species, smelt, and herring (Nelson 1990: 481). Marine foods included species of shellfish, ocean fish, river fish, and anadromous fish (migrating between salt and fresh water).

Sense of Place

The Puget Sound basin, with Seattle at its center, was and is the home of the Lushootseed Coast Salish.[4] Cascading down its rim of mountains, each river was dotted with winter towns,

---

[3] Early settlers did not recognize that native people were cultivating their lands and beaches because they assumed the plants were "wild" and the primary goal of pioneer farming was "to get the land subdued and the wilde nature out of it" (White 1980:35).

[4] Lushootseed derives from the word stem *ləsh* meaning specifically the sheltered saltwater of Puget Sound, with *-ucid* ~ -utsid for 'river, mouth, language.'

villages, hamlets, and seasonal camps (resorts) of a distinct tribal community, which fully interacted with all neighbors to give order and meaning to Lushootseed culture.[5]

Salishans of the outer coast emphasized class, while those of the inland, upriver, and southern Sound held Plateau ideals of a kin-based society. "Southern Puget Sound culture emphasized spirit quests and had a lesser emphasis on inherited privileges than the Northerners" (Roberts 1975: 32, 35, 77). Each "tribe" occupied an entire drainage, whose flow provided cohesion and identity to an otherwise diverse collection of communities and camps.

River systems draining into Puget Sound originate in the mountain ranges to the east or west. Distinct tribal communities occupied towns, villages, hamlets, and seasonal camps along each river system and were named in reference to the location where they lived. Families in each of these communities fully interacted with neighbors near and far, through visits, marriages, and gatherings to give coherence, order, and meaning to overall culture (Miller 1999: 15-17). The Mid-Sound area of Puget Sound was inhabited by people who spoke Whulshootseed Southern Lushootseed as their primary language, although many also spoke other languages as well.

The people who traditionally occupied the area now known as Seattle and Lake Washington were collectively called the Duwamish in the early literature and documents. In the late 1880s, many Duwamish were driven out of Seattle and found refuge among intermingled Lakes kin. Other Duwamish families became affiliated with two federally recognized tribal governments, the Muckleshoot Indian Tribe and the Suquamish Tribe.

The Muckleshoot Reservation, snared between two treaties – Medicine Creek for signers & Pt Elliott for lands, was established for hostiles and those living along the Duwamish, Green, White, and upper Puyallup Rivers (Indian Claims Commission 1974b: 101-132), including Stkamish (St-kah-mish, stqabš), Yilalkoamish (yilal'q^{w}u'abš), Skopamish (Skope-ahmish, sq^{w}əpabš), Smulkamish (Smalhkamish, sbal<u>x</u>q^{w}u'abš), and Tkwakwamish (dx^{w}x^{w}aq̓^{w}əbš) (Indian Claims Commission 1974b: 101-132; Suttles and Lane 1990: 486-488). Many Sdok^{w}albix^w and some Duwamish families settled with relatives and enrolled at Muckleshoot.

Throughout our focus is native names, especially name-titles, the very essence of a native perspective on these places and events. These names have endured, and natives upholding them exalt survivance. Pitfalls of using only the English alphabet to write Lushootseed names (needing triple the letters, Appendix F) is shown here by widely varied English spellings.

Survivance balanced dualities: exchanges of Uppers with Lowers, camas for salmon, old Slahal family with new chiefdom, stem with nodal kindreds; all swirling around the lethal Falls where ancestors emerged and kinship blossomed, foiling the death of parents with decedence kin term shifts. More recently, whims of USA, BIA, and BAR, delisting the tribe in 1953, were trumped by restoration in 1999, though continuing petitions to postpone a final membership roll combined with a casino providing millions of dollars keep them in a triumphant limbo frustrating detractors.

Throughout, my comments are between {curley brackets}.

---

[5] Though the seasonal contrast between towns and camps is ingrained in the literature, elders speak of summer camps as more like resorts. Of course, this may be more a reflection of their young age, with hard work done by adults, but the image is telling. Similarly, native settlements themselves require more suitable English terms, such as variously hamlet, haven, town.

1 ~ RALLY ROUND THE FALLS

At the actual and symbolic heart of the Sdok^{w}albix^w is *sq^{w}əd* = Snoqualmie Falls (45-KI-508) just east of Seattle. Plummeting 268 feet, the Falls divided Upper and Lower Sdok^{w}albix^w, while also marking the place of their founding ancestors as a tribe. Extensive root prairies, later hop farms, characterized upper communities, and river resources, especially salmon runs, those below, with much sharing, trading, and exchange between these ecozones. A third branch x̱ačuʔabš ~ x̱achu'absh occupied lakes near saltwater.[6]

Moon (Ballard 1999a), the Transformer ~ Changer of this region actively remade this landscape at the beginning of time, stretching a former fish weir into the present Falls as a rebuke to ungenerous humans, who were thereby denied salmon runs. The epic of Star Child ~ Star Husband (Appendix A), which sets the origins of chiefly families throughout Puget Sound, begins with two Sdok^{w}albix^w sisters from Tolt (now Carnation) of the lower Snoqualmie River camping in the upper Snoqualmie prairie to dig fern roots. Sleeping outside, looking up at the sky, each girl wishfully selected a star to be her husband. These Star beings heard and raised the girls up into the sky country, where each awoke lying beside a man, one very old and the other young. Resentful of her aged choice, the elder sister soon became pregnant by her more astute and powerful husband with the child who would become Moon. Secretly making a rope ladder, she escaped from the sky and gave birth on earth, only to have her baby stolen and raised by Salmon Women. Profoundly sad, another son, twisted from a diaper, miraculously came to her, but their lives were miserable. When fully grown, the twin brothers met, changed the world, and became Sun and Moon in the sky, rejoining their Star fathers. Along the way, Moon changed many species, one by one, into their present forms, and, most dramatically changed a large, productive fish weir into the present blocking Falls. In each river valley, he placed a married man and woman, giving them particular fish and wild game to feed them forever. The escape rope hanging in the air became a "swing" = *yiʔduʔad* between Mt Si and Rattlesnake Mt until Rat, angered for being pushed aside, chewed through it so it crashed to the earth, becoming a local landmark now badly chewed up as a rock quarry on one side.

The Falls remains the home of powerful spirits, where those of prairie and river meet, in addition to one that lives within the deep plunge pool. Natives continue to pray, seek visions, and ask for help there. The water itself is holy, and used for cleansing, healing, and religious applications. Most especially, the bowl of the Falls – rim, cliffs, basin, pool – concentrate mists that rise up into the sky, carrying the prayers and hopes to Heaven.

At the Falls, moreover, change and appropriation is constant. An electric generating station, the first built entirely underground, intruded: Plant 1, 1898 ~ expanded 1905, within a

---

[6] While those who lived along the Snoqualmie river were politically distinct by villages, Arthur Ballard and other local authorities recognized that the Lakes people (x̱ačuʔabš ~ x̱achu'absh) blended Snoqualmie and Duwamish. Because federal guidelines are monolithic either/or, on the Roblin Roll, therefore, some Lakes people are listed as Snoqualmie and some as Duwamish but it is easy to follow a paper trail to know that Zackiuse and others were Lakes People who chose Snoqualmie enrollment.

chamber below penstock intakes on the south bank; Plant 2, 1910 ~ expanded in 1957-8, on the north bank about one-quarter mile downstream of the Falls, with a concrete and wooden dam, four penstocks, tailrace tunnel, concrete-lined tunnel, open forebay, headgate house, generator leads, transformers, and transmission lines connecting both plants to a switching station.

Yet tribal and ecumenical forces sought protections for this scenic and strategic Falls, for many years the lone place in Washington State formally determined eligible for listing in the National Register of Historic Places as a Traditional Cultural Place ~ Property (TCP)[7] because, beginning in November 1987, Christian bishops and other religious leaders across the Northwest asked officially for forgiveness from Native peoples for what their churches and missionaries had done to them:

> This is a formal apology on behalf of our churches for their long-standing participation in the destruction of traditional Native American spiritual practices. We call upon our people for recognition of and respect for your traditional ways of life and for protection of your sacred places and ceremonial objects (Church Council of Greater Seattle 1987, 1997).

In its aftermath, Sdok^{w}albix^w and other tribals came forward to ask for help improving conditions at Snoqualmie Falls, intent on placing it on the National Register of Historic Places and according it status as a TCP.[8] Soon enlisted in this cause was Rev Dr Kenneth Tollefson, an ordained minister and professor at Seattle Pacific University, a Free Methodist campus, who was already working on the petitions for federal re-recognition of Snoqualmie and Duwamish tribes, both deliberately dropped from federal listings in 1953. The Snoqualmie Indien Tribe was reinstated in 1999, though problems remain with the legitimacy of their government because it has no official membership roll yet holds regular elections. Duwamish remain in federal limbo, though they fleetingly gained status for three days between US Presidents Clinton and Bush.

The Falls has long been a famous tourist attraction throughout the Seattle region, with a gazebo viewing platform high above them much favored for outdoor weddings. An overview restaurant, selling its famous pancake mix, draws crowds.[9] Yet their tremendous spiritual significance for the Snoqualmie Tribe was ignored and, occasionally, maligned. Made aware of this disrespect, taking up the words of their apology for "recognition, respect, and protection of

---

[7] The registration form was prepared by Leonard Garfield (staff member at what was then the state Office of Archaeology and Historic Preservation) "from a 1/2/92 draft nomination by Dr. Kenneth Tollefson." While the Falls was determined eligible in 1994, it was not formally listed in the National Register until 9/2/2009; nominated under Criterion A, as a "Property associated with events that have made a significant contribution to the broad patterns of our history ~ Ethnic Heritage."

[8] Conflicts intensified because federal guidelines require community consultations prior to reliscencing. The Federal Energy Regulatory Commission (FERC), formerly Federal Power Commission, issued the initial license until 31 December 1993 for Snoqualmie Falls (Project # 2493) on 13 May 1975, retroactive to 1 March 1956.

[9] Salish Lodge ~ Snoqualmie Falls restaurant is now owned by the Muckleshoot Indian Tribe, ironically.

your sacred places," the Church Council joined in the tribe's efforts to change how the Falls were managed. Dr Tollefson, already involved in justice for tribes, now added the Falls to his research concerns, aided by Council lawyers.

Bullying and insensitive, Puget Power (now Puget Sound Energy ~ PSE), the public utility generating electricity from the Falls, tried to overawe and impress concerned protestors by giving them tours of underground facilities, feeding them a fancy lunch, and having all the VPs talk all day about what a great job they were doing in the "public interest," totally oblivious that they could not sustain their privileged white agenda. At the end of that day, a Sdok^{w}albix^{w} Indien Shaker stood up with her mother and daughter to insist "We are really real and you are deaf to our pleas!" Stunned silence ended this long day.

The especial offense by the power company was the apparent turning off of the water flow at night, then turning it on again during the day, "like it was their own private fountain" as apparently arrogant bigots sacrilegiously interrupting the flow and mist carrying prayers upward. (Actually, they were diverting full flow into the penstocks at night.)

Local clergy scheduled meetings and gatherings, sometimes at the Falls itself, often in local parks to accommodate large numbers. Tollefson undertook surveys and interviews to gather hard data in support of their cause. As momentum grew, the large Tulalip Reservation intruded, citing their 1855 Point Elliott Treaty rights assigning Sdok^{w}albix^{w} to their reservation. Since these Sdok^{w}albix^{w} holdouts had been "dropped" from lists of federally recognized tribes in 1953, they had no official standing, though literally standing on moral high ground fully supported by the Church Council.

Media support took the form of local news, colorful books on endangered places, and a visit from CNN, which included a disastrous interview with Puget Power that further revealed their arrogance. They offered to allow the tribe to have the water turned off and on, just like they were doing, oblivious to the basic fact that it was continuous flow that was vital to their traditional beliefs in spiritual wellbeing via the rising mists.

On a national level, support built to protect "sacred places." The Center for American Places, founded 1990, through Abrams and Liveoak Editions (Jake Page 2001: 82-87) produced a lush volume documenting 18 such places, including the Falls while the battle still raged but a plan was emerging for the Sdok^{w}albix^{w} to manage or buy the environs as PSE was considering a strategic shift from the generation to the distribution of energy. A letter from the Taskforce highlighted the hypocrisy of the PSE proposal to allow flows on "Native American Allocation Days (which never coincided with the Snoqualmies' ceremonial uses" (Page 2001: 86). Supporters made much use of this book's appealing photographs, insisting that any manipulation of the mists was an assault on "religious expression," including the Falls in global efforts.

Mobilized by the formal apology, the Native American Taskforce of the Church Council of Greater Seattle was formed. Their first request came from Lummi seeking protection for Madrona Point, a native cemetery on Orcas Island eventually bought by private funds. A subgroup then formed the Snoqualmie Falls Preservation Project (*Snoqualmie Valley Reporter* 11 August 1993), with local clergy leading ceremonies at the Falls, such as "A Blessing of the Waters, A Ritual of Repentance, Cleansing, and Renewal" on 12 September 1992. Lutheran pastor Rev John Magnuson also wrote articles for newspapers, quoting theological scholars such as Mircea Eliade and Joseph Campbell, on sacred places and universal beliefs so as to respect and honor indigenous faiths and places. Ron Adams next led the project. Natives from other tribes also conducted their own public and private ceremonies at the Falls, expanding intertribal support from the Northwest and Plains.

Eventually protection of the Falls became conflated with the Snoqualmie Tribe's effort to regain federal recognition. Tulalips, in particular, opposed separate Snoqualmie restoration since some Snoqualmie treaty signers, especially Patkanim, and other leaders did move to Tulalip in accord with the 1855 Treaty of Point Elliott at Mukilteo, though there was never enough land space for all of these tribes on the reservation. This tension was recognized by the Bureau of Indian Affairs in their Final Determination to Acknowledge the Snoqualmie Tribal Organization (Federal Register 1997):

> The Snoqualmie Tribal Organization was given until September 9, 1995, to respond under section 83.10(k) to third party comments. The extended period was granted because of the voluminous nature of the comments submitted by the Tulalip Tribes and because of the extended period of time that third parties had to comment on the proposed finding.... Third party comments were received on September 27, 1994, in opposition to acknowledgment from the Tulalip Tribes, Inc., and from Les Wahl and Dorothy Cohn, members of a separate petitioner called the Snoqualmoo tribe.[10] Comments were received from the Snoqualmie Tribal Organization on September 5, 1995 (Federal Register 1997).

Additionally, Tulalip lawyers argued the Falls had lost its sacred status, and they should be paid for this damage: "Although the Falls were historically important for cultural and religious uses, construction and tourism have interfered with such uses of the area," according to the Tulalip (Williams 1992). The Tulalip have noted that Indian cultural ceremonies require seclusion and an undisturbed site, with water flows minimally affected by human development. The Tulalip are seeking compensation for their loss of the Falls as a cultural site, following original Project construction in 1898 (CRMMP 1996: 38). (Yet federal guidelines insist that tribes themselves determine the "integrity' of a TCP site, not outsiders. Thus, as long as people pray, water flows, and mist rises – the Falls has integrity.)

Puget Sound Energy (formerly Puget Power), the private property owner of the Project Area, opposed listing the Falls as a TCP in the National Register of Historic Places due to unfounded concerns that the Snoqualmie would use listing as a device to deny the relicensing effort (CRMMP 1996: 40). However, the implementing regulations of the NHPA section 106 (36CFR800.4.c.2) states, "If the agency official determines any of the National Register criteria are met and the SHPO/THPO agrees, the property shall be considered eligible for the National Register for section 106 purposes." Therefore, regardless of whether the Falls are listed or not listed, once they are determined eligible, FERC has to treat the Falls the same as if it is listed.

Meanwhile momentum built through a series of concerns with religion, preservation, culture, tradition, and heritage. Throughout, Puget Power added insult by going out of their way never to refer to the Snoqualmie Indien Tribe ~ Nation by name and title, always keeping any reference very vague and apolitical. Public hearings on FERC relicensing held at Mt Si high

---

[10] Snoqualmoo descend from Tom Glasgow's marriage to Pat's daughter Julia, cf footnote #22.

school and Eastside community colleges were well attended, with outspoken testimony from church and civic leaders, righteously bristling at Puget Power's arrogance and ignorance.

Linda Dombrowski,[11] then of Small Tribes of Western Washington (STOWW), provided a telling example.

> When I first visited the falls with a tribal representative, as we walked up the steps to view the falls from above, on one of the walls was a metal installation linking the Snoqualmie Tribe to the falls. After the tribe started to voice their concerns, it was removed. All that remained were the holes. In July/August of 1989, during the time of the Good Will Games, the Snoqualmies went up to the falls on a Sunday afternoon to stage a demonstration. I told them I did not think they would get any media coverage because it was the weekend, too far from Seattle, and during the games. But it was important to them and a large group went in full regalia. Well a media team did go and they gave them at least 10 minutes on the late news on Sunday.

In the midst of these struggles, Greg Watson (1996) asked Puget Power on behalf of the local Snoqualmie Valley Historical Museum for permission to preserve discarded historic artifacts and mementos. He was allowed only a single day to do so, and, in the process of saving examples of early electrification, collected the discarded sign from the machine shop where it had been tossed aside.

Finally marshalling data and forces, the Washington State Advisory Council on Historic Preservation, meeting in Tacoma, by a unanimous nine votes, declared the Falls worthy of being a TCP, bolstering further tribal efforts for public support for social justice and fair play.

In 2008, FERC and Washington Department of Archaeology and Historic Preservation (WA DAHP) forged a Memorandum of Agreement (MOA) confirming the Falls's 1992 eligibility with the Keeper of the National Register. Subsequently in 2009, FERC and DAHP entered into a Memorandum of Agreement (MOA) with PSE as a concurring party. Stipulation A-16 of that MOA required PSE to withdraw its objection to the Falls TCP being listed on the National Register (FERC 2008). PSE then sent a letter to the Keeper certifying that PSE no longer objected to the TCP nomination of Snoqualmie Falls, and on 2 September 2009, the Snoqualmie Falls TCP was officially entered into the National Register of Historic Places (FERC 2009).

Ironically, the Indien Shaker family that first spoke out enlisting the help of local museum and cultural resources specialists to work with them and the state historic preservation office, were briefly banished, as allowed in the tribal constitution, after the tribe was restored and a brother had served as chairman. Yet their concern with the sanctity of the falls remains strong and they lead an annual thanksgiving service to its rising mists. Tribal elders have also had a special pole placed at the lip of the Falls as a further spiritual claim on their crucial sacred site.

Today, the public and members of the taskforce continue their concern for the Falls, dismayed by construction of huge housing developments nearby and increased traffic congestion

---

[11] Email, Thursday, 30 April 2015, 03:26 PM.

along I-90. Momentum toward justice and fairness has weakened. The Salish Lodge there, now especially famous from *Twin Peaks* TV show, was purchased by the Muckleshoot Indian Tribe, adding to intertribal conflicts and complexities of the area. Once Snoqualmies were restored by the BIA, they quickly started a successful casino, which uncharacteristically includes huge windows open to Mt Si and other features of their stunning landscape. But it has led to both successes and difficulties, especially with regard to issues of tribal enrollment and investment strategies, usually fought out in courts or off the record settlements.

According to their own publicity, PSE is "Washington state's oldest local energy company … serving communities and … helping make them better places to live and work" but not, apparently, worship unless pressured to do so by churches, communities, and citizens lawyering up. Eventually, as noted by Raelene Gold,[12] a vital member of the Taskforce, Puget Power became "very sensitive to their public image and wanted to maintain a positive public image and this issue was giving them a black eye."

Lastly, during this struggle, the brand new National Park Service Bulletin 38 ~ Guidelines for Evaluating and Documenting Traditional Cultural Properties ~ Places (1990) set fresh guidelines, and SHPO, DAHP, and ACHP did not want the state's first nomination to go down in flames, or else it would be a long, long time before there was a second nomination. This is exactly what happened, until Mt St Helens ~ *Lawetlat'la* ~ *Loowit* ~ "Smoker" became the state's second TCP in 2015, proposed by the Cowlitz Indian Tribe, itself recently federally recognized (as Chinook was not) and intent on reclaiming its cultural patrimony, building clinics years before its huge 2017 casino, and honoring the forces of nature released by its eruption on 18 May 1980 and 10 July 2008.

The integrity of homelands was documented by Thomas T Waterman during his faculty position at the University of Washington, 1916-18, leaving an unpublished manuscript of place names around Puget Sound. As a Franz Boas student, TTW was careful to provide the names of his instructors as well as brief descriptions of these people and places. Here are his remarks for Sdok^walbix^w locales.

Lake Sammamish Sources

Mrs. Amelia Zakuse: Principal source here was Mrs. Amelia Zakuse, sister of Mrs Jimmy Moses of Renton, mentioned above. She lived near Monohan on the east shore of the lake. Her father was a well known shaman. Ceremonial objects of wood, used by him in the great SbEtEdakt {*spədak*} ceremony described by Haeberlin, were obtained by Dorsey and Boas many years ago. A few additional objects of like nature and excellent specimens of other kinds were obtained by TTW for the Museum of the American Indian, Heye Foundation. Information I obtained from Mrs Zakuse was supplemented by her aged mother, Lucy, one of whose parents was from Renton and the other from Seattle.

Mrs Zakuse's son-in-law, William Ross, was also a great service to me. He is a half breed. His mother's father was named Kika'ipqEd.

---

[12] Email, Thursday, 19 November 2015, 10:31AM.

Jim Graham, Hwa'la: He lives part of the time near the town of Issaquah at the upper end of the lake. His father was called Dr Bill (*Budi'yus*), a noted shaman. His sister, who raised his children, was Mary ~ Mali Louis ~ Lewey.

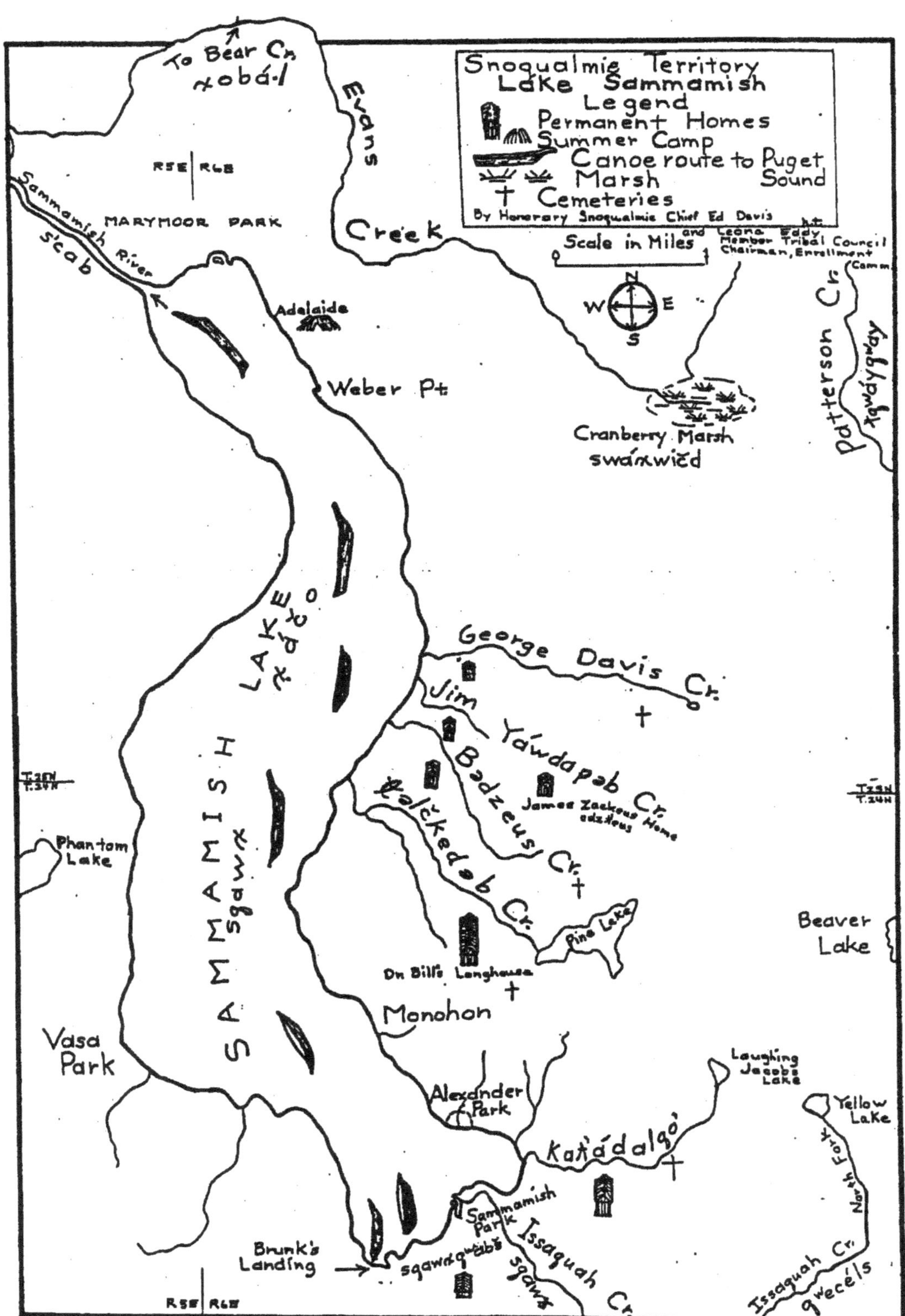

Falls

Snoqualmie ~ Sdok^walbix^w Sources

Jerry Kanim: My principal ally in this Snoqualmie region was Jerry Kanim at Tolt whose native name is Dzi'taqw³oyuks.   Unfortunately, a misunderstanding arose between us over a matter of payment for services, and we parted with mutual exasperation.   Jerry is very intelligent, quick, more or less conservative in his instincts, and full of interest for things belonging to the old times. A better informant could not be desired. His statements are marked by notable accuracy, which is partly the expression of a love for the truth, and partly quickness and clearness in seeing a point. He is an important man in the Shaker church, who later became Pentecostal.   The name Kanim is a transliteration of part of an aboriginal name.   A noted headman at Tolt in former times had the name <Patk³e'dEb> ~ "scratch head".   This was Anglicized as Pat Canim or Kenum, making two names of it. The "Kanim," also Wawa Chinuk jargon for canoe, which resulted from lopping off the Pat was adopted as a patronymic. Jerry is the son {bogus?} of this headman, who was a great fighter.   The woman he married (Jerry's mother) was named Ka'ottclt>. Jerry's wife was also a useful?

Snoqualmie Charley, <sia'txtld>:   Another excellent source, to whom Mr Ballard is especially indebted, is a blind old man called Snoqualmie Charley, Sia'txtld, who lived at Muckleshoot.

Mrs. Mary William: Mrs. Mary William, also of Tolt, gave me information on certain points.   Her father, <Xuts³ ki³e'dEb>, and her mother, <La'xtElao>, were both inhabitants of Tolt.

Jack Stillman and wife: Jack Stillman and his wife Annie, Fall City, also served as sources. They were neighbors of Jerry Kanim.

Henry Steve: A well known Indian of Marysville, who owns the hotel and other property there, also should be mentioned. He is very quick, as his success with his business shows, and he is very familiar with the old times. I received from him a good deal of information about ceremonies, which I cannot deal with in the present paper.

Ed Davis: Ed Davis, elder of the Shaker church at Fall City, also gave some information, but as he had been reared among whites instead of with his own people, his knowledge of place names etc was limited. His wife proved a more valuable, well informed by her own mother.

Snoqualmie Villages

The term Snoqualmie ~ Sdok^walbix^w <sdokwa'lbl^u>, is said to mean "Moon people." A myth recounting the adventures of Moon is localized in this country (unpublished manuscript, Waterman and Ballard, Tales of Puget Sound).[13] They existed in two "bands," one below the

---

[13] Arthur Ballard devoted his life to saving native traditions, coauthoring this collection with Dr TT Waterman while he was teaching at UW. It was never published yet provided the basis of Ballard's later collections published by UW Anthropology.

falls, and one above at Snoqualmie prairie. The principal settlement below the falls was opposite the present town of Tolt. The place was called <Xal³a'Ltx^w> ~ *xalaltx^w* ~ "Marked House" and the people, <Xal³a'ltxw-a'bc>. The most noted man here was Pat Kenum, <Patk³e'dEb>. A famous shaman was called Dr Bill <Tetcta'tctld>. He had a woman {spirit} being named Sleho'litsa for his "helper." The other group was called <Bak^wba'bc, "prairie dwellers," from <bakwob> or <baxab> "prairie" (map B 36). A well known headman here was Skade'wa {Saduwa}. I have record of another village at <Stuwe'yuq^w> on Stoessil creek …

Names on Sammamish River and the shores of Lake Sammamish

146 ?? <Xa'³palbl^u> "a lot of brush piled up" (ʔxatL³ "brush"), for a creek entering the lower Sammamish River from the south below the town of Bothell.

147 Number not used.

148 ?? <CtcEl> North Creek, entering the Sammamish River from the north flowing by Bothell.

149 ?? <Ila'huletc> for Bear Creek entering the river from the north at Woodinville.

150 ?? <Ts³Eqwsu'budup> "bubbles coming up all the time," for a place on the east bank of the Sammamish River just at Woodinville.

151 ?? <SqlulwE'lt^u> "leveling off of place" on the east bank of the river where the Hollywood farms are now.

152 Number not used.

153 šəqusaltx^w ~ 'house atop' <Ceqos-a'lt^u> "a high place with a house on it" (cEq "high" + alt^u "house" = səq + alʔtx^w) on a creek entering the river from the east below Redmond.

154 Number not used.

155 ƛ̓uq̓^w ~ 'stuff in, plug up' <TL³oq³> "crowded in, poked in" at Redmond.

156 tubalʔal ~ ' ' <Tuba'hal> "bread," for a creek entering the river below Redmond, with a number of names applied to its upper branches on ordinary maps but lacking any name for the lower course.

157 šəqid ~ čəpqid ~ 'above head, head of deep hole in river' <Ciqe'd> "head, source" of Sammamish River where it leaves the lake, also called Tsap-qed "head of Tsap," the native name for Sammamish Slough.

158 ɬapucid ~ 'throw something over mouth of it' <Laputsid> "hard to find," for the very flat and marshy outlet of Lake Sammamish draining into that river, passing through a swamp and invisible from a short distance.

159 puk^wab ~ 'a pile' <Pu'kwab> "heap, knoll" for the steep hill, with Evans Creek flowing at its base, at the north end of Lake Sammamish by the station of Adelaide.

160 ?? <Tsiya'kwlL^{tu}> for a large rounding promontory on the east shore of Lake Sammamish, with a steep hillside behind a flat point jutting out into the lake, formerly a popular place for picnics. Boys who wished to obtain shamanic power used to fast and spend two or three nights here.

161 q̇əƛ́adilq^wu? ~ 'becoming like a river' <QatL³a'dll-qo> "land otter's water," for a creek entering the lake one mile south of Monohon {Monohan}, draining out of Yellow Lake. {sq̇aƛ́}

162 sq^wax^w~ '?' <Sqwaux> Issaquah Creek emptying into Lake Sammamish at its southern end and the village somewhere on its lower course (See list of villages).

163 ?? <SiwE'dk> first stream entering Issaquah Creek from the east, its mouth about one mile north of the town of Issaquah.

164 ?? <Teqa'iob> said to mean "cougar," for the elevation known as Grand ridge associated with a story about mountain lions and certain rocks that stick up like fingers. {cougar = swawa}

165 q^wəcilc ~ 'rock for sliding' <QwEts³i'ls> "that which is left over" at the East fork of Issaquah Creek.

166 ?? <Ts³upa³lt> mountain lying east of the town of Issaquah with Tradition Lake on its plateau.

167 dx^wkayu?al?tx^w ~ 'corpse house' <TEqaiyuwa'lt^u> (possibly "corpse's house"), Sqwauk Mountain, the big hill west of the town of Issaquah, named for the Issaquah (= Sqwaux) Creek, another transliteration of this native term.

168 tx^wsq̇ilalšuɫ ~ 'canoe lookout place' <Tsqe'l^{al}cuL> "loading things on a canoe," Tibbets Creek.

169 ?asuċəq̇ ~ 'something pokes at you' <Abcusts³Eq> "tree sticking up" on a broad flat promontory opposite Monohan where some Yakima warriors who came across the mountains were changed into trees which still stand in the water decorated with red war paint.

170 bəsċəway? ~ 'shells place' <Blstc³awai> "clamshell" at the picnic grounds across the lake from Campbell's mill where supernatural fire shoots back and forth.

Names along the Snoqualmie River

1 ?? <Sts³oluls> Where the Skykomish and Snoqualmie come together.

2 q'^wəlič ~ 'cooked, roasted' <Q^wlotc> suggesting a crooked or roasted surface, for a creek entering the Snoqualmie near a high rock.

3 ?? <St³apts> Cherry creek.

4 ?? <Ts³a'gwtsEbEd> "bubbles continually rising" in the Snoqualmie River near the site of Duval.[14]

5 ?? <Sba³dita> "mountain, crag," just below the mouth of Harris Creek where the river flows past a cliff.

6 ?? <Q^ELa'dEb> at the Carnation stock farm.

7 ?? <Ts³Elalku'Ldai> Harris Creek entering the Snoqualmie from the east below the site of Tolt.

8 čəƛ̕ə? ~ 'rock' <TcE'tLa> "rock," for a great "slide," a bare scar on the mountainside below the town of Tolt.

9 xalal?tx^w ~ 'demarked house' <Xal'aLtx> suggesting "house with designs or patterns," for an old village site, the principal settlement of the Snoqualmie people, at a flat across the Snoqualmie river from the present town of Tolt. {*xal* = marked, decorated + *al'tx^w* = house along with a fort, stone pillar, and river made of melted elk tallow (Ballard 1999: 90)}

10 ?? <Tca'ltcalac> at Tolt high school.

11 dx^wtultx^w ~ 'place for portage, bringing something across water' <^Tuxutoltx^w> for Tolt River south of town.

12 ba?balucid ~ 'little levirate' <Ba³bal³utsid> Langlois creek (subject of a myth), meaning "wife of one's deceased brother" and the reciprocal relation "brother of one's deceased husband." The plural form indicates two people who stand to each other in this relation. {literally in-laws after the linking kins-man or -woman is deceased, and therefore also 'intended spouse' to safeguard surviving children}

13 bit̕ ~ 'soup' <Bit³> "salmon soup," Langlois lake, a small pond at the head of creek #12. This soup is made of pounded dry salmon mixed with certain roots. Whales "formerly" appeared in this lake to swim about, spouting. {literally, any soup}

14 ?? <Tuba'op> for a small creek flowing into Tolt river from the south.

15 ?? <Stuwe'yuq^w> "like? throat" for an old village site on Stoessel creek, the largest affluent of Tolt river. {throaty, throat-like, Elk Tallow}

16 ?? <Tute't³t^uq³> "eddy," where Griffin creek enters Tolt river opposite Snoqualmie Charley's place. Before it filled with sand, "something" like a big salmon lived in a deep "hole" in the river there. When he came to the surface, one could hear drumming in the pool, then, down in the depths, "everyone would holler."

17 ?? <Sxa'siyats> a certain kind of shrub growing at Griffin Creek.

18 ?? <T'qwai'qwai> Patterson Creek.

---

[14] Nearby is the wet site rich in perishables, especially baskets, at SN 100 ~ Biederbost.

19 qʷiʔqʷali ~ 'grass place' <Qwe'qwais> a creek entering Patterson Creek.

20 ?? <Qwutoaba'ts> another creek entering Patterson creek above the last named stream #19.

21 ?? <YeLhʷ> Raging river.

22 ?? <Stc³oq> at a trestle two miles above Fall City on the Raging river where the railroad crosses the gully where there is a big rock and cliffs are to be seen on the north side.

23 čəstədi(l) ~ 'a nail, peg' <TsE'stEde> "cedar peg," for a creek entering Raging River from the west.

24 (sə)pkʷalqʷuʔ ~ 'perch water' <Pqalqo> "perch water" for a creek entering Raging River from the east. {q̇alsəpkʷ}

25 ?? <Tuwo'lqaib> for a lake draining into Raging River.

26 ?? <Yi'hi³Lˣʷ> diminutive of that for Raging river (See # 21), for one of the two streams into which Raging River divides in its upper course.

27 stəx̣ilc ~ 'edge pushed out' <StExels> "a big rock on the edge" in a bend of Snoqualmie River.

28 dəxʷq̇al ~ 'place of soaking' <TqEl> "place for soaking things," Tokul Creek.

29 ?? <Kaqo'iyauk> on the east bank of Snoqualmie river below the falls.

30 sqʷəd ~ 'waterfall' <SqwEd Snoqualmie falls, literally "the under part to which the stream plunges" in a magnificent cascade.

31 š(ə)qaʔłdał ~ 'upper lip' <Ska'LdaL> "upper lip," where the river takes the leap at the falls.

32 ?? <Sts³o'bEls??> for a creek entering the Snoqualmie from the west. Sto'obalallLud is the word for female whistler [?] duck; while the male is called hwai'yuk.

33 ?? <Laxwe'i> at a place above the mill at Snoqualmie.

34 Number not used.

35 xačuʔ ~ 'lake' <Xa'tcu> "lake, lagoon" for the slough where the river has two channels.

36 baqʷab ~ 'prairie' <Ba'xab> "prairie" for the former village on Snoqualmie prairie.

37 yiʔduʔad ~ 'swing' <Yi³do³ad> "swing" for a detached knoll of rock on the edge of Snoqualmie prairie ... A version of Star Husband recounts, among other things, that a girl climbed down from the sky at this point hanging from a rope, which later served the myth people as a swing. They started on Rattlesnake Mountain and swung across the Snoqualmie valley to Mount Si, a half day's journey. When the swing broke loose at the top, this rope coiled up to make this knoll (see #38, #42). Another version has offended Rat chew through the rope swing.

38 daʔšədabš ~ 'footprint people' <Daxcl'dabc> "footprints," on Rattlesnake Mountain where the myth folk stood when they started to swing.

39 q̓ʷuʔalqʷuʔ ~ 'where waters merge' <Qoa'l³qo> "confluence" of the south fork of the Snoqualmie with the main stream.

40 səq̓ʷuʔqʷuʔ ~ 'by means of gathering' <Saq³oqo> above Long's place, one mile below North Bend on the west bank of the south fork. Long ago, many Indians congregated there for ceremonial performances and potlatches. {NB also crucial site where the Kittitas families settled, Appendix C}

41 ?? <Tutsuwa'dEb> now used of a person dying of tuberculosis, for a place between the south and middle forks of the Snoqualmie River.

42 q̓əlbc̓ ~ '?' <Q³Elbts> Mount Si. Somewhere on this mountain Snohomish who were watching the "swinging" were turned to stone (see #37). {They stand along the top edge.}

43 ?? <XwotstLKtw> for a little hill, wife of Mount Si.

44 Number not used.

45 ?? <Swi'tud> Fuller Mountain.

While the upper prairie (#36) and swing (#37) are topographic features duplicated elsewhere, such as the Skagit, *xalalʔtxʷ* ~ 'demarked house' (#9) is unique to the region, indicating contact with northern traditions of "objects of bright pride." A wavy blue line marked the front of this house and a stone column, like a totem pole,[15] stood nearby.

According to the first academic ethnography (Haeberlin and Gunther 1930: 11, 14, 38):

The Nisqually called the Snuqualmi snōkwalbix̱ᵘ, which means extraordinary people. They were said to be ferocious and warlike … the only tribe who … took the heads of their enemies as trophies. The Snuqualmi were also called stōkᵘwalbix̱ᵘ, which means worthless people…. The Snuqualmi were great hunters and lived principally on game and salmon. They hunted in the mountains in winter, using snow shoes ... wore a cap of a bear's head. They visited … the coast in summer, and … ate seal and sturgeon … Flint arrowheads were brought from the Snuqualmi, who were the only tribe that made them.

This more martial stance called for greater organization in their society. Moreover, according to their respected elder Ed Davis (Miller 2014: 103, 112), they had two sanctioned death penalties: by pitch fire or by water over their beloved Falls.

---

15 Indeed, the oldest "poles" among Tsimshian are upright stones, serving like the spine of a chief to transmit spiritual power into tribal territory.

You see, the Snoqualmie had 2 ways of punishing … 1) They cut a tree down even and left a stump. Then they light a little fire and keep on throwing pitch ... put that person in there … something like an electric chair … that pitch there cooks 'em.
2) Well, they'll take her and load her on a canoe, tie her up in a canoe, take the paddles, take the pole … and they shove her out. That's just like hanging 'em …

2 ~ SADUWA ~ SANƏWƏ
&
UPPER Sdok^wALBIX^w

In preparation for the 1974 Boldt Decision[16] confirming Washington state native's treaty right to fish, Barbara Lane wrote reports concerning each of the tribal fisheries, drawn from federal and state documents, historical records, and scholarly ethnographies and ethnohistories. That for the Snoqualmie was among the first public records to highlight the duality under Patkanim[17] for those below Snoqualmie Falls and under Sanawa,[18] in various forms of his name Saduwa, for the Upper Snoqualmie, who is otherwise missing from most histories. Lane wrote:

> Two of the leading men among the Snoqualmie at treaty times were Patkanim and Sonowa…. Sonowa was regarded as the leading man from Tolt River upstream along the Snoqualmie river (1975: 1).

> Nathan Hill's 30 September 1856: 6 annual report:

> "Sadahwah" the chief of those up in the neighborhood of Fort Tilton has sent me word that he wished a reservation for his tribe up on the Prairie about the Falls – he wishes to farm like the "Bostons." The place is one well qualified – good land for farming purposes – good range for stock, the fisheries close at hand and the climate warmer than down on the salt water. I would recommend his prayer to your consideration.

> Michael Simmons, Agent for all of Puget Sound, to JW Nesmith, Superintendent for Washington and Oregon.

> There is a portion of the Indians in my district whose homes are high up on the rivers, principally on the Nisqually, Puyallup, and Snoqualmie. They are nearly related to the Yakimas and Klikitats[19] by blood, and are sometimes called Klickitats.

---

[16] *United States v Washington*, 384 F Supp. 312 (WD WA 1974), aff'd, 520 F.2d 676 (9th Cir. 1975).

[17] The nickname *patkadəb* "scratch the head" is usually treated as a two part English name: Pat Kanim and his kin now use Kanim as a family last name (Appendix C).

[18] This name-title has several valid spellings: Sanawa ~ Saduwa is easiest; Lushootseed switched M to B and N to D so native pronunciation is *Sadəwa*, with a short middle vowel.

[19] Kittitas is the most likely referent since the leaders of many of the incipient chiefdoms in Washington State about 1800 had family ties to this lush region around modern Ellensburg, just west of the Columbia River. Among these were Weowich ~ Wiyawiikt of the Yakama, Split Sun of Snkyuse, and Patkanim's father.

They are a more athletic and independent race of men, but are more closely wedded to their manners and customs, and superstitions; and are less docile, and much harder to manage. They cross the Cascade mountains frequently to visit their relations, and are, to some extent, imbued with the hostile feeling that still exists among them. Part of those Indians – those living on the Nisqually and Puyallup – were the most formidable we had to contend against during the late war. The others, the Snoqualmie, were our faithful allies, particularly Son-a-wa and his band. At my instance they carried an express across into the Yakima and brought back information. They differ in appearance, in their mode of living, and in many other respects from the salt water tribes, and I do not think they can be brought to live in harmony together, at least for some years to come (1975: 7).

On the Snoqualmie river, above its falls, is a tract of prairie country supposed to contain some ten thousand acres. This is the country of Son-a-wa, an old chief nearly related to the Klikatats {Kittitas}. During our past Indian difficulties he was our firm friend, and then expressed a desire that white people should settle in his country. Until this spring no one has thought it prudent to move there. Now, however, two men have gone at his request and taken claims. Mr J H Van Bokkelin, deputy collector of customs, writes me on the subject as follows (1975: 6):

"Son-a-wa and the other Indians tell them that they want the whites to settle there; that they can take all the prairies but a small one, and he wants the 'Bostons' to reserve that for him and his family and allow no person to take it from him."

"If there is any way the small prairie can be secured to him it would be well to do so, for there are mean white men, if the country up there is settled, that would not stop a minute in driving him off."

"This old man Son-a-wa I consider one of the very best Indians in my district; you see how modest his requests are, and yet neither I nor any other person here can secure to him this patch of ground for his potatoes to grow in. He doubtless thinks he is the rightful owner of all the ten thousand acres, but is willing to claim only one; and in all probability he will be kicked off that before the crop now in the ground is ready to harvest."

"I think, sir, that humanity, that justice, and that the peace of this country demand that government should provide for a final settlement with our Indians."

In 1870 the Bureau of Indian Affairs regarded Sonowa as head chief of the Snoqualmie Tribe. The tribe itself was reported to number 301 individuals (1975: 9).

Samuel Ross, Washington Superintendent of Indian Affairs 1870:

Patkadəb

"It is reasonable to suppose that in a wild, sparsely settled country like this, at least 5 per cent of the Indians are not found."

1923 Walter F Dickens, Tulalip superintendent took depositions, including Skookum George, allotted at Tulalip, who referred to:

"John Skadawa, sub-chief … was the son and successor of Sonowa, the old chief at Snoqualmie Falls in the 1850s (1975: 15).

Land Claim depositions 27 February 1927 by lawyers Arthur Griffin and George Stormont:

"Among the Snoqualmie deponents were Watson Martin, a grandson of old chief Sonowa, and Jerry Kanim, a nephew {?!?} of Pat Kanim. Jerry Kanim testified as chief of the Snoqualmie Tribe" (1975: 17).

FA Gross, Tulalip superintendent 24 October 1949 wrote to William Martin, _AS_ Chairman of the Snoqualmie Tribal Council (1975: 23).

Of note, only Patkanim but not Sanawa is listed on the 1856 Snoque-ol-mie Roll by Nathan Hill ~ agent for Snohomish, Snoqualmie, Skykomish at Holmes Harbor, Whidbey Island (though Saduwa's son and a ward are listed, Appendix B).

While Sanawa freely moved across the Cascade Mountains, and his heirs found safely in the Upper Skagit, Patkanim stayed <u>only</u> on the west side, as indicated by a letter he dictated:

Seattle Nov 4 1853

Chas N Mason
Acting Govr of Washington Territory

    Sir

       I ?? hear that slanderous reports are in circulation regarding my actions & <u>tumtum</u> {heart ~ mind}. I therefore improve this opportunity to state facts as actually exist.

Fir<u>st</u> I will furnish 100 good men subject to your orders at the inst{ant} of your call, to fight anywhere this side of the Cascades range, but I cannot at this time consent to go onto the other side of the mountains.

Seco<u>nd</u> I will arrest any and all such as I can find within my jurisdiction who may appear as enemies to Bostons, & forthwith bring the same before you.

On consideration of the above I require that you ↓ furnish ↓ adequate means to carry the service into effect & compensate us as the other Bostons have {been??} paid.

I will see you in answer to your order without delays.
To the above I subscribe myself
Respectfully yours to serve
Patrick X Canam
Chief of Schnoqualomy Indian tribe

Attested:
DG Maynard MR Simmons AD Drake, Lieut US Navy

In 1855, when Governor Isaac Stevens called a number of Puget Sound tribes together to sign the Point Elliott Treaty with the United States government, of the two prominent Snoqualmie tribal leaders invited, only Pat Kanim (*patkadəb*) of the Lower Snoqualmie agreed to sign the document as leader of three villages on the Snoqualmie River between Tolt River and Monroe. The other, Sadəwa of the Upper Snoqualmie, however, refused to sign that treaty and chose instead to join other tribes in the defense of their homelands. He led seven villages from Tolt to the summit of the Cascade Mountains, with 58 households.

Patkanim was famed as a fierce warrior, who, in 1848, wanted to drive all whites out of Puget Sound. By 1855, though, he signed their treaty, fought against his neighbors, and, died in 1858 under suspicious circumstances. In 1855, agent Nathaniel Hill described Pat Kanim as an "obnoxious leader," who mistreated his people, and could not also count on their loyalty.

In contrast, when war broke out, Sadəwa chose mobility, joining with other tribes in the region to defend their homelands against American intrusion and unjust actions. Saduwa is an ancient hereditary name-title, inherited through a leading family. Sanawa ~ Sadəwa ~ Aeneas ~ Eneas – distinguished by his Catholic baptismal name – led during the 1855 Treaty War, frequently living east of the Cascades in relative safety. In time, the name-title passed to Eneas's grandson, Watson Martin.

The Bureau of Indian Affairs lists Martin Watson (1933 Deposition) as "Chief of the Snoqualmie Tribe" in their 1870 census (Lane 1975: 10). Martin Inyes ~ Hi-Kan-neecha ~ Aeneas, a Wenatchi, married Ka-mi-weet, Wenatchi & Snoqualmie, having five children = Watson, Lyman, Mollie, Maggie (Maggie Martin Qui-Quia), & Ida (1986: 318). The Sanawa chiefly name-title passed as follows: Martin Aeneas~Eneas~Ennius > Watson Martin > William Martin > John Martin > Ska-dul-gwas I > Ska-dul-gwas II ~ Marvin Kempf.[20] Holders of Sanawa of Snoqualmie intermarried with Kah-my-wit, sister of Kamayakin of the Yakamas (Scheurman and Clement 2005; Scheurman and Kinley 2008). In all, in the final federal determination for Snoqualmie federal recognition, one of the four key reasons was the influence, leadership, and political continuity of this Saduwa line.

As noted by Ken Tollefson, the Sanawa name featured prominently in two recent historical events. "Return to Mukle-Te-Oh" brought Point Elliott Treaty Tribes together for a reunion at the site of the original signing (Liu 2010). In the process, hereditary names reconnected treaty signer families as "cousins." Second, Snoqualmie Indian Tribe sponsored a state-wide gathering of tribal leaders at Seattle Pacific University 6 May 2012 to celebrate the ancient peace network known as "Slahal family," said to have been shared among tribal leaders for thousands of years (Mapes 2012). Bruce Miller's nephews told the story of the Slahal game between humans and animals that won humans the right to eat game meat.

Because of their more assertive and tiered organization, Snoqualmies have been called a chiefdom, though, as yet, only recent Patkadəb has been recognized but not ancestral Saduwa. Tollefson has argued for three diagnostics to qualify Snoqualmie for chiefdomry: (1) economic

---

[20] Kempf also received two other native names at the Sauk longhouse in August 2015, including a hybrid Tekumsah Sanawa. A letter from Puget Sound Agency dated 10 May 2010 confirms his eligible pedigree and blood quantum according to the constitution, making him the only tribal member to be officially vetted.

specialization, (2) political centralization, and (3) hierarchical ordering of society (Fried 1967: 113-176; Service 1962: 132-164; Sahlins 1968: 20-27; Lewellen 1983: 29-34).

When Snoqualmie federal recognition was restored, they chose to be a Non-IRA tribe, directly under a "chief" supervised by the Bureau of Indian Affairs and guided by a constitution with membership based on Roblin's 1919 rolls (Appendix D). Roblin's sixth box holding individual documents in support of enrollment, along with his own handwritten notes, contains 10 folders, the first 7 of approved families, and the last 3 of those rejected. The Martins are in folder 2:

Martin Family (Box 6, folder 2 ~ frame 0170): Watson Martin is full Snoqualmie. His Father was Hi-kan-neecha {English name = Aeneas, Enias}, full, allotted and buried at Wenatchi, died 1916. His Mother was Ka-mi-weet, who died 29 yrs ago; and Mother's Mother was Snoqualmie. His Brother was Lyman and his Sisters Kim-stan-nee (Maggie Quia-quia) married to Jim Quia-quia, Mollie Bagley married to William Bagley, and Jennie George married to Skookum George. In his usual red ink, Roblin added that Mollie (#21) and Jennie (#114) were enrolled by these numbers at Tulalip.

In his handwritten notebook pages, Roblin reported, "Neither he nor wife ever had any land anywhere. Father of Ka-mi-weet was skadewa or Sanewa – the old time chief of the Snoqualmie Indians."

According to their own ethnocentric Snoqualmie tradition, a small group of primordial Snoqualmie ancestors migrated from the interior to become one of the early groups to settle in the Puget Sound Region. Over a period of centuries, this pristine Snoqualmie settlement increased in population, reached the carrying capacity of that watershed, and sent small groups periodically to seek homes in nearby "vacant" watersheds. As these daughter communities grew, they developed into new tribes such as Duwamish, Samish, Skokomish, Skykomish, Snohomish, Suquamish, and Swinomish. Meanwhile, the original Snoqualmie community remained in place increasing in power, wealth, and rank in relation to these newer tribes and became one of the premier tribes of the Cascades.

Saduwa also expanded his sphere of influence by negotiating a marriage with the sister of the high chief of the pivotal Psk^{w}aws ~ Wenatchee Tribe, on the other side of the Cascade Mountains, and thus expanded his contacts and influence among tribes on both sides of the mountains.

Saduwa also bestowed songs and traditions on other leaders. When a new chief was installed at Lummi, a song given in 1928 by Sanawa Watson Martin began the events, returning thanks and paying tribute to his generosity.

Slahal Family

Such intertribal alliances also derive from a much more ancient reciprocity now known as Slahal, which currently refers to a lively guessing game with pounding songs and enthusiastic gestures, as well as spiritual aids. This game also features in creation stories when winning and losing had cosmic consequences (Bruce Miller 1999: 37-43).

In his monumental study of Native American games, Stewart Culin (1907: 32, 267) noted the consistency of this game across the continent. A reminder of the antiquity of this game emerged from the ground when, in 1987, a set of 14 Ice Age bone rods were discovered in an apple orchard in East Wenatchee, Washington (Gramly 2004: Part III 50-51), recalling to the minds of native leaders the modern set of gaming sticks and bones used in Slahal today. One of the long rods has a series of horizontal lines like a zipper down the middle, much like the special "kick-stick" used to start and to end each game.

An essential difference, moreover, between the East Wenatchee set and a modern one is that the Clovis one was carved out of the leg bones of a mammoth or mastodon while many contemporary sets are carved out of wood or made from deer bones, encouraging natives to now claim that this Slahal tradition is 13,000 years old, the newly calibrated age of Clovis traditions.

Early in the early 19th century, Judge Arthur Griffin (Appendix E) advised some Puget Sound tribes to organize a tribal business council in order to deal with the white community. Ed Davis, a Duwamish, invited Jerry Kanum, catcher on his baseball team, to attend their Duwamish meeting at Puyallup for the creation of their own constitutional form of government. Later, Jerry Kanum shared his information with the Snoqualmie, who subsequently made Jerry Kanum their leader "because of his knowledge of the white culture," as well as keeping him busy and sober. During this time, however, Sanawa Martin Watson led the more prestigious Snoqualmie Council of Elders.

The Snoqualmie Constitution requires all Snoqualmie members, otherwise unaffiliated elsewhere, to pass two tests: (1) descended from a ancestor on the 1919 Roblin Roll and (2) at least 1/8th blood quantum. According to red remarks in Roblin's own hand and BIA files, Jerry Kanum was enrolled at Muckleshoot (Roblin Snoqualmie Enrollment: Folder 9, 12 Files: F9, L2 ~ 0265).

Lastly, according to elder memories,

Saduwa and his people from above the Falls were not at Mukilteo when the treaty was made, and they did not receive any land from the treaty.

After the war, the Bostons gave Saduwa the promise of a reservation. It was at Olympia that he asked and obtained a government paper showing this. Afterwards Saduwa's house burned down and the paper, which he kept there, was destroyed. He received no reservation and the Bostons crowded the Indians out. [135 | 142}

Of particular note, moreover, when Arthur Denny,[21] premier Seattle pioneer, wanted to explore passes across the Cascades, his advisor and guide was Saduwa.

In August 1865, JW Borst, Wm Perkins and myself determined to make a trip over the Snoqualmie pass proper, for the purpose of finding a more favorable line for a wagon road than that by the Cedar river pack trail. At the time we could only find one Indian (Saniwa) who had ever been through. He stated that it was lower than

---

[21] Arthur A Denny, *Pioneer Days on Puget Sound* 1895.

where the trail crossed, but was hard to get through on account of brush and timber, but was good for a wagon road.

He would not undertake the trip, but gave directions to two young Indians who took us up the foot trail, with which they were acquainted, and pointed out the line of Lieut Tinkam's travels and other whites who had crossed since, but from that point through the pass where the road now runs to near the head of the lake it was a trackless wilderness, over which the [74} Indians had not traveled except on rare occasions, in fact going down by the east side of the lake it made a distance of at least fifteen miles of uneplorexd {explored} country…. We crossed the summit, and at about nine miles from the summit we reached the trail near the foot of the lake, where we found John Ross, LV Wyckoff and Saniwa camped with our horses awaiting our arrival (1895: 73).

About 1866, Jas Entwistle homesteaded at the mouth of Tolt, below Griffin's Prairie, where old Sanawau, who died about 1880, told of military prowess at the Falls (Morse 1880 File 21: 29-30).

When Sanawau was a boy, the Snoqualmie were engaged in fighting with the Klickitats, and were pursued by them. The Klickitats had come over the mountains on horseback, and on the headwaters of the Snoqualmie had attacked the camps of the Snoqualmies who fled down the river in their canoes; but who purposely left canoes behind them, for the Klickitats to pursue them with. The Snoqualmies were the more expert canoe men, and easily kept ahead of the Klickitats. When the Snoqualmie reached the Falls, they abandoned their canoes, and took to the brush. It was in the dusk of the evening. The Klickitats were not aware of the falls being so near, and urged their canoes at full speed, to overtake their intended victims. While the Snoqualmie s were hid in the timber, and watched them, all of this Klickitat war party went over the falls to their death. This supposed that from fifty to a hundred thus met their doom.

3 ~ Patkanim
&
Lower Sdok^walbix^w

Patkanim ~ Pat Kanim ~ Patkadəb has gained all the attention because he was a strong Catholic, US ally, and supported by many brothers. Their father seems to have crossed the mountains from Kittitas, a hotbed for strong leaders in the early 1800s. Among his peers were men who became heads of horse-mobile confederacies among Sahaptin Yakamas and Salishan Snkyuse on the Plateau, as well as Skagits on the wet west side of the Cascades.

A key datum is that Puyallup leader Xot's father's father ~ tšədaškət ~ tshudashkut from Kittitas Country was full brother to Pat Kanim (Ballard 1929/99: 35).

1b *tcədáckət* Paternal grandfather of {John Xot}. Was from Kittitas County, of a predominantly Sahaptin group, but where Salishan language was also spoken. A full brother of Patkanim, the well known Snuqualmi chieftain.

Like the Skagit prophet's family, the Kanims originated across the Cascades and joined Snoqualmies, encouraged by their favored access to horses, traders, and missionaries to the east, as discussed below. Outsiders, with few or any local kinship ties, serve well as more impartial leaders. More recently, Filipino men have married into native communities and their children have taken on leadership roles.

Patkadəb "scratch the head," more of a nickname than a chiefly title, first came to historic notice[22] when he led a deer drive using hunting dogs across Whidbey Island from Penn Cove to a corral with outstretched wings in direct challenge to the upstart 1848 claim of Thomas W Glasgow, both to force him away and to feed a council of Puget Sound leaders ("chiefs") on the 60 deer while discussing opposition, by arms if necessary, to expanding American settlers while they were still few in numbers. Glasgow soon abandoned his claim when he returned from Olympia and heard about the deer drive.[23] In time, others staked permanent homesteads on the island, especially sea captains.

Patkanim, who traveled with a retinue of warriors, had several large family homes strategically located throughout their territories, near various resources and seasonal sites. During winter, his longhouse was sheltered along the lower river. During summer, he had a large round house at Coupeville with three tiers of bunks: older people on the lower one nearer the hearths, and youngsters on higher one. A hide curtain ran down the middle separated men from women (1986: 75). While the river was calm, he also kept a garden at Tolt tended by slaves. He and his troops were based at Freeland during the Treaty War. In the 1856 roll by

---

[22] Edmond Meany, Chief Patkanim, *Washington Historical Quarterly* 15: 187-198 1924.

[23] Ironically, Glasgow was married 1848-58 to Patkanim's daughter Julia, and their descendants have tried for federal recognition as the Snoqualmoo of Whidbey Island. Though they rightly claim chiefly descent through GGD Helen Beall, their ties to traditional culture and bloodlines are much attenuated. Glasgow married Helen Horan on 25 July 1858, also leaving "white" pioneer descendants (Kellogg 1934: 34, 17). See #9.

Nathan Hill (Appendix B), Pat is listed as 38 years old (born 1818), 5 feet 4 inches tall, with 4 wives, 6 kids, and two male and two female slaves.[24]

His father was Whyeeka, a Colville who moved to Yakama and then to Sdok^{w}albix^w.[25] Leaders before Pat were Waywayhipie, Tweeshri, Yocalatuna (1986: 115, 128). Quesam was chief of Skykomish in the 1850, followed by Jimmicum.

One was But-ei-tsa, who died 1887, the mother of Bob & Louis Kanim, who are listed in the 1881 census as being 30 & 36. His wife Sal-Khn {sal$\underline{x}$ən} shouted Pat's battle cry from the bluff during his attack on Leschi's camp. Wife Sa-ya-ya-he was mother of his last child, Susie, who was 60 years old in 1912 and attended the unveiling of Pat's tombstone (Meany 1924).

Noted of his brothers are Sthowie (Jim Kanim) = 32, 5'7", with 3 wives, 1 child, and 1 male slave; Tah-Te-Tum (John Kanim) = 5'3", 2 wives, and 1 child;[26] Quallawort was convicted of murder and hanged, as follows.

On Tuesday 1 May 1849, Patkanim, his brothers, and other Sdok^{w}albix^w arrived at Ft Nisqually in response to a rumor their sister was being abused by her husband. In the ensuing conflict, Leander Wallace, an American, was killed and another two wounded, one mortally. US Justice was swift, instituted in North Oregon, soon to be Washington Territory, from Salem under General Joseph Lane. US troops under Captain BH Hills were ordered by Major Hathaway to set up at Ft Steilacoom, while two of Patkanim's brothers, Qualawort and Kassass, were brought to trial, convicted, and hanged, supposedly as a deterrent to native opposition.

Patkanim further reconsidered his hostilities toward settlers when he sailed to San Francisco in 1850 and was amazed by the overwhelming number of citizens. When Seattle pioneer families landed at Alki 13 November 1851, both Chief Seattle and Patkanim became especially friendly with Arthur Denny, leading him into the lush Sdok^{w}albix^w valley. Patkanim was also an early and loyal Catholic convert, a faith brought across the Cascades after contacts with Jesuits and Oblates.

At the 22 January 1855 Treaty of Point Elliott, Patkanim signed second after Seattle, before Chowitshoot of Lummi and envoy Goliah of Skagits. He led prayers, probably in Latin and Chinuk Wawa, at the start of the sessions. Later, when the Treaty War broke out 28 October 1855 with the murders of Mr and Mrs William Brannan with child, Mr and Mrs Harry Jones, Mr and Mrs George King, and Enos Cooper; Patkanim sided with the settlers. While his troop roamed freely, other natives were confined to camps in secluded locales, often on islands.

When acting governor Charles Mason and Captain Isaac Sterrett of the warship *Decatur* demanded the surrender and arrest of Patkanim and his eight-one (81) warriors, Arthur Denny rose to their defense and had Patkanim appear with gifts of mt sheep, venison, horns, and hides that reversed their negative opinion. In time, he attacked Leschi's stronghold, and accepted a

---

[24] Saduwah is not listed; John (#16) "son of Sah-da-wah," Tom (#15) "ward of Sah-da-wah."

[25] Emily Denny said Pat's mother was Sdokwalbixw and sister of Skookum George's grandmother, and his father a Soljampsh, from the lower river (1909: 124).

[26] John was once cited as the link from Jerry Kanim to this family, with Andrew Kanim was actually "a kind of foster parent."

bounty of blankets for heads he sent to Olympia packed in salt.[27] With his earnings, he bought stylish "Boston" American citizens garb clothes: Congress gaiters, white kid gloves, white shirt with collar standing to his cheeks, and a flaming red tie (Watt 1931:250). All told, Snoqualmie, Skykomish & Snohomish, commanded by Pat Kanim and John Taylor, a Sky-ko-mish Indian consisted of 82 rank & file and 80 privates, with 4118 days service and an aggregate for chiefs and men of 4,234 days or service (Morse 1880 File 14: 43).

After the war, Pat settled at Marysville, off the Tulalip Reservation, but continued traveling throughout the region. In 1858, his body was found washed up on the shore and he was buried nearby in a coffin made by Henry Yesler with lumber from his famous mill in the heart of Seattle. Later when flooding became an issue, he was finally moved to the Catholic cemetery, where in a row of chiefs his huge granite marker bears a bronze profile. Foul play has always been suspected in his death, but his brothers, children, and kin continue in high regard, most of them denying any direct relationship with Jerry Kanim.

Arthur Denny,[28] premier Seattle pioneer, noted in his memoir:

> On my arrival in the country, I early became acquainted with Pat Kanim, Chief of the Snoqualmies … [58} He seemed to have a wholesome fear of the law and the power of the government and professed friendship for the whites, the sincerity of which he afterwards proved to the fullest extent, but the whites then in the country were disposed to look upon him and his tribe with distrust on account of their early trouble.
>
> As early as the fall and winter of 1854, he gave me information of the growing dissatisfaction and feeling of hostility among the Indians east of the mountains, and by the spring of 1855, he showed such concern that I became convinced of his sincerity. I could see no motive but friendship, when he came to me privately in the night to warn me of approaching danger to the whites. When he made his last visit and communication to me in the fall of 1855, shortly before the Indians outbreak, he stated that he was going up the Steilaguamish river to hunt mountain sheep, a circumstance to which I shall again refer (1895: 57).
>
> Very fortunately for me, and probably for Pat Kanim too, he was on hand within the time agreed upon. He had his women and children with him, and also brought a cargo {of gifts} … with conclusive proof, which I had thus furnished, of the good faith and friendship of the Snoqualmies. I never heard anything more from headquarters of the hostile Snoqualmies, but Pat Kanim was very soon employed by the Governor with a party of his tribe, as scouts and did good service during the continuance of the war.… Pat Kanim and his brothers gave me the particulars of the case, as I have before stated, and professed to accept the judgment of the court as just, and expressed a wish to cultivate friendship with the whites, and I think we have

---

[27] For his efforts and heads, Patkadəb earned $10-12,000 and his troops were given supplies for some time (McConaghy 2009: 144, 328 #77).

[28] Arthur A Denny, *Pioneer Days on Puget Sound* 1895.

conclusive evidence of the sincerity of their professions, and that they were ever afterwards the friends of whites (1895: 67).

On one occasion during the winter Nelson came with a party of Green River and Muckilshoot Indians, and got into an altercation with John Kanim and the Snoqualmies. They met, and the opposing forces, amounting to thirty or forty on a side, drew up directly in front of Low's house, armed with Hudson Bay muskets, the two parties near enough together to have powder burnt each other, and were apparently in the act of opening fire, when we interposed and restored peace without bloodshed by my taking John Kanim away and keeping them apart until Nelson and his party left, and he still lives but John Kanim was killed years ago in a similar feud in Tulalip ... (1895: 14).

Of particular note, duly noting Kanim aggressiveness, when Denny wanted to explore passes across the Cascades, his advisor and guide was Saduwa.

We crossed the summit, and at about nine miles from the summit we reached the trail near the foot of the lake, where we found John Ross, LV Wyckoff and Saniwa camped with our horses awaiting our arrival (1895: 73).

As reconstructed on the basis of recent Lower Sdok^{w}albix^w reports, the Sdok^{w}albix^w chiefdom consisted of four districts: Monroe, Tolt, Fall City, and North Bend. Kanims filled most of the key positions in the chiefdom. Pat Kanim was Head Chief, his older brother, Cush Kanim, was his assistant and advisor. Four brothers presided over the districts: John Kanim at Tolt was in charge of training young leaders; Jim Kanim at Fall City was in charge of training young warriors; while Hutty at Monroe and Klamish Kanim at North Bend were in charge of guarding the upper and lower valley. As noted at the start of this chapter, brother tšədaškət married among Puyallups to raise a prominent son, John Xot.

The two principle villages of the Snoqualmie chiefdom were located at "Tolt and Fall City" (Hill 1970: 1). The administrative center at Tolt, Kanim family home, controlled the central Puget Sound trade route that connected the resources of the islands with the resources of the Plateau across the Cascade Mountains. Located in the central area of the Snoqualmie River Valley, a large garden at Tolt was tended by slaves, and defended by the Sandhill Fort, and a series of guard villages.

The symbolic center of the Snoqualmie was the *xalaltx^w* = "demarked house", with painted walls and carved posts recording historical events, serving as meeting house for the Council of Chiefs, guest quarters for visiting chiefs and elders from other tribes, and educational center of the Snoqualmie.

Fall City, located a few miles up the river from Tolt, served as the military center of the chiefdom. Promising boys in their early teens were sent to Fall City for special military training by elders in the Kanim family. Surrounded strategically by Rattlesnake Mountain to the North, Mount Si to the south, Snoqualmie Falls to the east, and the Sand Hill to the west; the military fort at Fall City was the most secure village in the valley.

Patkadəb

Warfare was common in the densely unsettled Puget Sound (Bagley 1929: 114; Costello 1895: 103-105; Whitfield 1926: 832-835). All boys received military training from an early age. Gibbs (1877: 190) depicts the Sound Indian as living in a "state of petty warfare between many different tribes." Last HBC factor Edward Huggins (1855) describes the Snoqualmie under Chief Pat Kanim as the "most warlike on Puget Sound and the terror of the other tribes. His armed bands made raids upon the other Sound Indians, and murdered, plundered, or enslaved all those taken alive."

Such violence was uncharacteristic for the area, so its motivations probably derived from across the mountains, especially conflicts among bison-hunting horsemen venturing into the Montana Plains from the Columbia River Plateau, especially from the crossroads at Kittitas.

Kittitas Crux

Located near the north-south Columbia River and the east-west trade route that became I-90 in the Ellensburg~Vantage area, Kittitas emerged as a major contact point, pivotal in the trade of local lithic materials, especially a bright pale green jade (the color of Granny Smith apples) and the exchange of Coastal and Plateau products. Its lush meadows fed large game herds, and fostered the early adoption of livestock, especially horses. Increasingly mobile, leading families visited and married far and wide, founding dynasties with lasting impacts today.

The result was a region of complex linguistics, across two culture areas and along major rivers. In addition, leading families were multilingual within vast, resourceful kinship networks. For simple barter, exchange, and trading there was also a set of words and simple grammar, such as Chinuk Wawa in historic times, that fostered "skin trade" transactions. Indeed, the study of trade, exchanges, and gifting in the archaeological[29] and ethnographic record can trace the rise of dynastic families throughout the region, as well as material shifts due to prophetic movements.

Kittitas[30] Valley was the nerve center for the founding of powerful tribal dynasties whose overall "high elite" leadership was encouraged by the greater mobility in the later 1700s provided by the recent spread of horses into the Northwest. Much earlier, rock art styles, especially rayed ark and twins, intensified around Vantage (Boreson 1998: 613), concentrating spiritual powers.

The Sahaptin name for the Kittitas people is Pshwanwapum[31] and "a considerable number ... crossed the Cascades and settled in the Snuqualmi country, on a prairie about a mile back on the north side from Snuqualmi Falls. Here the remains of a great number of lodge-sites,

---

[29] David Munsell, The Ryegrass Coulee Site (KT88), 1968. Instead of the east-west evidence of a crossroads, this site at the top of the bluff near the I-90 rest stop of the same name, built atop 13 feet of fill, "may represent a meeting place in the Plateau for assemblages having diffused both north and south" (1968: 3). An open camp site, dating 6900-3500 BP, its tools included both microblades like those to the north (Lochnore-Nesikep) and lozenge-shaped foliate points like those to the south (Snake River).

[30] This place name *k'títaas* "Kittitas" derives from Yakama k'tít = "hard, solid (thin in shape)" (Beavert and Hargus 2009: 72).

[31] Their name derives from *pshwa* = pebble, rock, stone + *-pam* "people of" (Beavert and Hargus 2009: 153).

most of them underground lodges, could be seen until very lately {1909}, about a hundred in all. The name of this place is _Soxqo'ko_ ("people gathered together") {see Chapter 1 place name #40}. After intermarrying more or less with the Snuqualmie, and becoming to some extent incorporated with them, part (or the remnants) of these people – consisting of seven families, including the chief – moved down and settled among the Snohomish about five or six generations ago" (Teit 1928: 108). A son married to the north, becoming the Skagit Prophet. A few later returned to the Pskwaws (Appendix C). The upper Nisqually Mishel spoke both Kittitas and Lushootseed, and a Yakama name for Mt Rainier ~ Takhoma is Pshwanwapum for snow-capped peak (Smith 2006: 23).

As Verne Ray (1939: 149) noted:

The linguistic boundary itself in no way corresponds to cultural transitions, even of a secondary order. The Sahaptin-speaking Kittitas, for example, have far more in common with their Salishan neighbors on the north, the Wenatchi {Pskwaws in their own Salish}, than they have with their Sahaptin neighbors, the Yakima {Yakama}, on the south.

Its dynamism was also fueled by the overlapping of Sahaptin and Salishan language families, making the area heavily bilingual. Vast trade in a local jade, ranging from waxy white to black – most especially bright pale green – tapped into continental networks. Lush pasturage encouraged large animal herds, and the quick adoption of livestock. Larger groups on horseback – venturing into the Plains to hunt bison though opposed by resident tribes – needed more protection and hence more centralized leadership. These Salishans "through disease and wars {became} mere remnants of what was once the largest of tribes ... and commanded the Snoqualmie, Yakima, and all the principal passes through the Cascades, including those to the Cowlitz country ... the first horse seen by the Coast tribes ... was brought over by Wenatchi" (Teit 1928: 95, 97, 121). Thus, horses, pasture, and an easier communication route joined at Kittitas to aid the founding of two powerful alliances.

First, it was the homeland of Wiyawiikt ~ Weowitch, the founder of the Yakama confederation. Second, along the Columbia's Big Bend just to the east was the homeland of Split Sun ~ Suktalkosum ~ səq̓talk̕ᵂusm ~ Eclipse founder of the Columbian Confederacy eventually headed for decades by his younger son, best known as Moses, also holding this hereditary Split ~ Half Sun name-title. To the immediate south were Wanapums, led by the prophet Smohalla ~ smoxala (c1815-95) and the Sohappy families, adding a religious dimension to the region.

In the 1800s, the Upper Yakama chiefly line at Kittitas included eight sons of Wiyawiikt, of whom the best known are brothers tiyayaš ~ Teias (elder), awxay ~ Owhi, and shawaway ~ Showaway.[32] Teias's daughter was wife of Kamayakin, whose own brothers were Ice ~

---

[32] Richard Scheuerman and Michael Finley, _Finding Chief Kamaiakin ~ The Life and Legacy of a Northwest Patriot_, 2008. Erroneously, Anastasio (1975: 198) refers to a "failed" unification by We-ow-wicht of Kittitas when leadership passed to his eight sons about 1800.

Showaway (named for the uncle), and youngest Shkluum ~ Skloom. These were leaders of the Lower Yakamas. Owhi and his son Qualchan, related as cousin to Leschi in Puget Sound, were killed by the US Army during the Treaty War, precipitated when Indian Agent AJ Bolon was killed and cremated by mušiil ~ Mosheel, son of the younger Showaway, and others. In 1858, Qualchan was hanged without trial on 24 September and Owhi shot 3 October.

Moses, chief of the Salish-speaking Snkyuse,[33] was married to Owhi's daughters, Quomolah and Sanclow ~ Mary. He famously had other wives and children among allied tribes (Flathead, Wanapum, Nez Perce). The family of Pat Kanim, pro-US leader of Lower Sdok^{w}albix^w during the Treaty War with many brothers, also came from this area. From the north around Nespelem, by way of Snohomish, came the family of the Skagit Prophet, whose daughter and granddaughter rose to prominence in northern Puget Sound and intermarried into local leading families. Somewhere in this mix was mid-1800s Upper Snoqualmie leader Saduwa, baptized as Aeneas, with ties to Pskwaws ~ Wenatchi. He is buried at Cashmere, along highway 2, with his wife and others.

Wanapums long lived at P'na ~ Priest Rapids, and claim perpetual residence there (Longenecker, Stapp, and Buck 2002). Their leaders included the Sohappys and, especially, Smohalla families. Prophet Smohalla ~ šmuxala was born 1815-20 at Wallula, the large village at the mouth of the Walla Walla River on the opposite side of the Columbia River. His mother was Wanapum from P'na. Rivalry at Wallula from Homlai, nephew of murdered leader piupiumoksmoks ~ Peopeomoxmox ~ Yellow Swan (Stern 1993: 268), led him to relocate about 1855 to P'na and draw in followers. Wanapums have vibrant tradition of religious leaders, with several known in the historic record (Relander 1956, Ruby and Brown 1989, Rigsby and Finley 2009), including Shuwapso ~ swapc'a = Fast Runner into old age from *waat* (spirit patron) of *yaamaš* (Mule Deer) at Saddle Mt, as youth "taken across the sea" and returned with a book, danced on his knees until challenged by Catholic priests and thereafter stood up. He is likely the person for whom Priest Rapids is named. Today, this faith is led by the Buck family.

For the neighboring Snkyuse Columbian Salish, "the only major pastoralists not in contact with a hostile area, seem to have played a stabilizing role in maintaining peaceful relations in the Plateau" (Anastasio 1975: 146). Their family of leaders, who led bison hunts into the Montana Plains once horses were adopted, peaked with the famous Chief Moses (1829-99), who carried the dynastic name of "Split Sun". Named for an 1800 eclipse, his father Split Sun ~ Half Sun ~ Eclipse ~ Sulktalthscosum led hundreds into the northern plains to hunt bison, dry the meat, and bring it back to the Columbia for winter meals. He was killed and dismembered by Blackfeet, resentful of his encroachment into their hunting territory. His short-lived sons Patshewyah and Louis Quiltenenock succeeded him, then the title was inherited by Moses, whose boyhood name was Loolowkin ~ headband and adult name was Quetalican ~ One Blue Horn (Ray 1960, Ruby and Brown 1965, Teit 1928).

Rather, it instead broadened its alliances via many intermarriages. Indeed, his affinity diagrams consistently undervalue the vital nexus of the Kittitas.

[33] Bruce Rigsby (in Beavert and Hargus 2009: xxix) derives the designation "Yakama" from the midColumbia Salish place name for the Kittitas Valley, further emphasizing its central importance across the languages and traditions.

For the interface at Vantage (Miller 1998), in terms of rivalry and cooperation by these communities, we have the report of Abbot Gerald Desmond (1952: 34, 35), in his study of Yakama gambling:

> "Chief" Moses of the Sinkaquai'ius {Snkyuse} band of the Columbia was considered not only a great athlete but also a "great race horse man" who was willing to pay almost any price for a race horse he wanted. Smoxa'la of Ghost Dance fame, the most prominent man among the Wanapam, was also considered a professional gambler on horse racing who, in a race between his champion and a white man's horse, bet ten horses, and he and his followers added a hundred dollars to the wagers on this single race.

People also mixed together at favored root grounds in the Spring:

> As the first of June drew near, the Yakima began looking forward to the high light of the year – the "big time." Certain roots of high quality in the vicinity of the former villages ... in the Kittitas area were particularly abundant at this time of year. Practically all of the Yakima from the Kittitas area and most of those from the Yakima area foregathered there since they used the roots from this site for barter. In addition many of the Sahaptin-speaking Wanapam and a goodly number from the Salish-speaking {Pskwaws} Wenatchi and Sinkaquai'ius {Snkyuse} band of the Columbia came regularly each year, and some few visitors as well from nearly any of the groups living between the Cascades and the Rockies in this region could be expected. Those living west of the Cascades were, however, prevented from coming by the snow remaining in the passes.

In addition to these obvious language differences, Anastasio and Brunton have specified cultural distinctions:

> activity was properly conducted as directed by the salmon chief {Salmon tyee} ... quite uniformly for all the Salish groups.... among the Sahaptin, the ritual control of salmon fishing was less important than it was among the Salish (Anastasio 1975: 176).

> The events themselves differ in expressed orientation from one congregation to the other, the Interior Salish congregation typically having pow-wow or encampment type gatherings while the Sahaptian one typically has the feast type. The notable exceptions to this were the Nez Perce encampment at Mud Springs and the Yakima encampment at White Swan Long House (Brunton 1968: 17).

Spiritual traditions also continue to contrast, though both had men and women always sitting separately. At winter ceremonies, Salishans look outward into the cosmos, with each visionary grasping a central pole while singing a power song. Sahaptins focus inward, seeking the wellbeing of each member in turn during a *Waashat* service. "Wanapum ... seem to be inward-facing … yet they produced Smohalla, who had a wide effect in the Plateau with his religious doctrine" (Anastasio 1975: 186).

In all, while reflexes from Kittitas took religious expression with the Skagit Prophet, among Sdok^{w}albix^w its expressions were military and political, particularly the Kanim war lords, with Patkadəb the standout among his many brothers and sisters.

Such chiefdoms were debated in the 1990s, with Miller and Boxberger (1994) objecting to Tollefson's reliance on 1840s white documents and 1920 native testimonies, sidestepping pressures from slaving raids that began in the early 1800s, followed by the fur trade's lure into capitalist world economy. Chiefdoms should be based in territory rather than kinship, as initiated by the Kanims's move from Kittitas reported a hundred years ago by James Teit (Appendix C), providing reliable older sources for the more recent situation.

4 ~ LAKES

Among the intratribal interconnections to "share in good will," Upper Sdok^{w}albix^w contributed "mountain goats, grizzly bears, black bears, mountain deer, elk, martin, beaver, trout, white fish, berries, and a variety of other animals, roots, and herbs used for food, tea, and medicine in exchange for Lower Sdok^{w}albix^w "migrating salmon, smelt, red fish, and resources from and to the saltchuck and coast." Those on the freshwater lakes were noted for red fish and grunter sculpins. More recently, they dug up potato patches, worked stoop farm labor, and harvested cranberry bogs, with that at Monohan covering 30 acres and destined for the Seattle market (1986: 51, 223).

In his list of native sources, Arthur Ballard recognized those with a distinct Lakes identity blended with ties of kin, languages, and traditions to Sdok^{w}albix^w towns:

13b *t'a'ctcIbelo* (*t'a'ctcIbelut*) was the mother of informant Dan *sile'luc* (Lake Washington, born about 1845). She was a Snuqualmi from Falls City and a stepdaughter of Patkanim. Her mother was *Xa'XcIdai ~ xa'xashədey*, a wife of Patkanim.

14a *xoxwe'tcub* was the father of informant Susie ~ *Xwai'kwolIttse* (Lake Washington, born about 1850). *xoxwe'tcub* was a Snuqualmi.

19 – Joe Bill or *le'lkaibA'L* , born about 1860, was Lake Washington (*xa'tcoabc*) and Snuqualmi on his father's side.

In historic times, Lakes people survived on wages from pioneer David Denny, who built a sawmill on Lake Union and employed many of the Lakes Duwamish people. Such jobs allowed these natives to protect their own local houses from vandalism and squatters. Lake Union, with Portage Bay, remained a haven for local natives into the early 1900s, their occupations and homes protected, to some extent, by David Denny and his family.

During the late 1800s, two Lakes families were especially prominent in the history of the Lake Union area: the family of Doctor Jim Zakuse, who went to Snoqualmie, and that of John Cheshiahud, who went to Suquamish, as told from researcher fieldnotes, family histories, and newspaper accounts.

In his writings on local history, Ezra Meeker (1980: 129) defined the institution of the 'favorite Indian,' a native so closely allied with a pioneer family that he took their family name and recruited workers for their projects. David Denny's first ally was Doctor Jim Zakuse, an ancestor of the de los Angeles family at Snoqualmie. Another close alliance also formed between the Dennys and John Cheshiahud, the 'last Lake Union Indian' who owned tracts of land along the opposite shore of Portage Bay from that of the Zakuse family.

Lakes

Zakuse ~ dᶻakʷus Family

Doctor Jim Zakuse (Zackius ~ Jackuse) was one of the best documented Indian residents of Portage Bay, with published information available about him greatly enhanced from the family records in the possession of Frances and Andrew de los Angeles, mother and son among his descendants.

An Act of Congress was passed on 20 May 1862, "to secure homesteads to actual settlers on the public domain." In the process of filing for his own homestead, David Denny may have helped Jim Zakuse to file on traditional Zakuse lands. At least, according to King County records, the Zakuse family lived on their homestead in spite of Ordinance #5, passed 7 February 1865, calling for the removal of Indians from the town of Seattle (Thrush 2002: 100-101). David Denny always worked hard to protect the lands of his employees and was likely instrumental in securing their homesteads.

The Zakuse property was located along the Montlake Indian Trail, on the northwest shore of Portage Bay. The trail crossed the Montlake isthmus through what are now the grounds of the University of Washington main campus. The Zakuse home was located at the western end of the Indian trail; at what is now the southwestern portion of the campus.

Versions of the Zakuse name appear sporadically in the King County tax records by lot, section (S), township (T), and range (R). The following list has been compiled from the King County tax record books. In some instances, the same page number is used for two large pages facing each other.

1877 Zacuse, James Indian in lot 6 S17 T25 R4, 10 acres worth $50 (page 140)

1881 Zacuse (Indian) Section 20 Township 25, Range 4 (double page 237) {this location actually belonged to John Cheshiahud, see next section)

1885 #13 James B Zecuse S17 T25 R4 {listed with 22 Indians} (double page 127)

1886 #17 Zacuse, James, part of lot 1 S17 {T}25 R4, {listed with 35 Indians} (double page 134)

TT Waterman (2001: 80, 105-6) provided the names of several places at and near the former Zakuse homestead:

37/63 – Sqwitsqs ~ sqʷicqs = down river promontory

110/137 – Sti't'tci ~ ?? = ?? Foster Island cemetery in trees

111/138 – Sta'LaL ~ stałał = fathom measure

112/139 –Sxa'tsugwlL ~ sxʷacəgʷił = lift, pull a canoe

113/140 – Sp'Lxad ~ spałx̱ad = bog, marsh, wetland

114/141 – Sxwuba'bats ~ saxʷəbabac =jump over (solid) object

115/142 – StL³Ep ~ sƛ̓əp = deep

116/143 –Cta'q^{w}c1d) ~ ča'k^{w}šəd = trail descends to water

Doctor Zakuse's Portage Bay homestead was at the mouth of a creek known as Frog Place (see above 36/62 – Waq^{3}e'q^{3}ab ('waq^{3}e'q^3 "frog" waq̇waq̇ab), a marshy area providing abundant foods.

Although most native names are so ancient that their meanings are not obvious, the Zakuse name does have a very specialized meaning in terms of shamanic practice. The literal translation of the name 'trembling face', comes from d^{z}ak^w = "shake, rock, jar, jerk, tremble" and -us = "face" (Bates, Hess, Hilbert 1994: 87, 244). The name refers to the actions of a shaman wearing flexible headgear, often of woven cedarbark, that would quiver and so provide a manifestation of its inherent power. However, d^{z}ak^w is the northern Lushootseed dialect form of this word, not the Whulshootseed dialect form, d^{z}ax^w. Because the name is consistently used in the northern form, this suggests that the origin of the name or the source for this shamanic power was to the north, not among the Whulshootseed speakers of the Lakes region. Any name that came from an area outside the drainage system would enhance family prestige.

The title 'doctor' was in recognition of Jim Zakuse's abilities as a native medical ~ religious specialist ~ shaman. Indeed, he belonged to the higher echelons of this calling because he could perform the *spədak* ceremony, possessing the ability to go to the land of the dead and recover lost souls to restore a patient to health (Miller 1988, 1999). An important locale (*Bltda'kt*) that bears the *spədak* name is at a small creek on the north shore of Salmon Bay, to the west of the Zakuse homestead, a location ideal for staging the shamanic odyssey to the afterworld since this vicinity could provided a route for reaching the land of the dead through its earthy representation at the graveyard on nearby Foster Island .

The story of Owl and his Wife Frog (Hilbert 1980: 81-82) explains the origins of such marshy regions. The following story is a close translation of the taped telling in Whulshootseed.

Owl and His Wife Frog

Owl lived there. Owl was married to Frog. (Such a frog as usually is found in swampy places, making noises, always talking, croaking.) Not long after Owl and Frog were married, Frog became pregnant and they became parents of a small child that looked like the mother Frog. She gave birth to their child.

This child of theirs cries all the time. Frog's child cries. Her child cries. The neighbors are unable to sleep because Frog's child cries. This little child of hers will not shut up!

Frog doesn't say anything. She just sits there. Her mouth just moves. Her mouth just contorts, wiggling her lips.

Now the neighbors, in exasperation, ask Owl. "What in the world is the matter with your wife that her mouth moves around {twists, contorts, twitches} but she doesn't say anything. Nothing comes out. What is the matter with her?" Owl tries to placate by explaining that his wife is just trying to soothe their child by twisting her mouth to divert the babe. Frog took the infant wrapped in a cradle board and, as she rocks it, she finally says, *swələq, swələq, swələq, swələq, swələq, swələq, swələq.*

38

Frog repeated, *swələq, swələq, swələq.* She rocked her child. She rocked it as she said *swələq, swələq, swələq, swələq, swələq.* She tries to silence this child of hers. Again she tried to speak to the baby and she said *swələq, swələq, swələq, swələq, swələq, swələq.*

Frog doesn't shut up now; she keeps uttering those sounds. Her child cries on! Frog continues to make her sounds, now she doesn't stop making those sounds until this Owl is beside himself with frustration. He observes his wife who just says *swələq, swələq, swələq, swələq.* Finally, she does soothe her child, she soothes it. She soothes her child, her infant.

Now Owl saw her. (He became aware that things were not as they should be.) He saw his wife. He turned around. He stood up from where he was trying to comfort their offspring, this infant they had created. This little Frog was their child. A little Frog.

Owl left. He was beside himself with fright about the weird situation. His wife does not shut up. {Neighbors urged,} "Stop your wife! Why does she continue to say what she says?" The neighbors implored Owl.

No! {Nothing changed. Frog continues} *swələq, swələq, swələq, swələq, swələq, swələq.*

They talked about her. Now this was during the very time that the Transformer was traveling around. He arrived there. He peeked at them, and he listened to them. Then he said, "What is the matter with Frog? What in the world?" {He was told,} "She comforts her child after much effort, but now she never ceases to make that annoying noise." They said this of her. Owl though became very frightened, and he ran away. He flew away, he flew on. It is their child who cries and cries.

She comforts her child. Frog herself doesn't cease making noises, she seems trying to speak. She is now always talking in her strange way. She is never silent.

It was thus that the Transformer made the judgment concerning her. {He thought,} I had better just throw this Frog toward the remote swamp. So the Transformer took the wife of Owl. She had her child. She had that infant. And she was thrown into the swamp lands. To where cattails grow in wet land where water stands, undrained, swampy. (As it might variously be described). Such wet areas. Frog is thrown there.

{Changer pronounced,} "There is where you will be. There is where coming generations will hear you calling. You will be heard making those sounds. You will never cease. You will say what you say when you make such noise, when you speak *swələq, swələq, swələq, swələq, swələq.* This is what you will say to coming generations. This is how they will hear you. You will be in swamp lands."

She is now thrown there along with her child. This little child that Frog had given birth to. They are thrown there. Frog made her sounds there. She talked and talked and talked, and made noises in that dank swampy water. Now she was all right. She was just a Frog talking, not bothering neighbors and other people.

"You will now be just a Frog. You will talk like that everywhere there is swampy ground with cattails growing up. That is where you will be. You will be changed now. You will be a little, insignificant animal from now on. You will talk like that forever and your offspring will also do the same!" They are thrown there.

Owl arrived. He peeked around. His wife is gone. Again he just got scared of the uncertainty, and he went away. Owl flew off. {Transformer then decreed} Owl the person will now become just an owl bird. He will no longer be a person. He will just be a little animal. He will make noise at night. If the weather will be getting better, then Owl will speak. He will talk in hoots. That will be his work."

Owl is thrown where he went, into the brushy fir trees. His wife is away where she was placed. Now the other people were satisfied. They were pleased now. They had been irritated by the wife of Owl. So had Owl.

"The children are left. The children are left." This is what Owl says. This is the language he uses there where he was thrown to live in the trees.

There is rejected Frog: *swaləq, swaləq, swaləq, swaləq, swaləq*. At the watery cattail places until whenever ....

That is what happened to Owl at the end. His wife was lost. He didn't know what to do about it, whether or not he should bring her back. The people who lived there were so annoyed, provoked, and irritated by her grimaces and unceasing sounds, by her talking. These people could not sleep. That is why Frog is the way she is now. She is just in the dank cattail places. That is where Frog makes noises, talking croaks. She will talk, and talk, and talk and talk {when the season comes for her to be heard}.

That is the way it was, when this legend was created about Frog and her husband Owl. Owl was her timid, easily baffled husband. That is the end.

Told only in northern Lushootseed by Martha Lamont,
Tulalip, 1964 (Hilbert 1996: 81-82)

Native residence within Seattle, especially as it grew, was never easy. Washington State legislature outlawed native-white marriages shortly after the treaty with local tribes was signed in 1855 (Asher 1999; Harmon 1995). The newly incorporated town of Seattle banned native urban residence in 1865, though Indians continued to live and work in the city for various concerns with a white protector (Newell 1977; Thrush 2002: 100-101).

Natives could not legally own lands on the public domain until March of 1875 (US 1875). The Indian Homestead Act allowed Indians to own land, provided that these natives renounced any and all tribal allegiance and lived like poor whites. Indian efforts to do just that had to be substantiated on forms titled Homestead Proof – Testimony of Witness. The forms were signed by such pioneer notables as David Denny, James Bush, Thomas Cherry, Martin Monohan, George Tibbetts, and Roger Green. As the city of Seattle developed to the north in the 1870s, many Lakes Duwamish people moved or were forced out. The Zakuse family moved to the Monohan area and there was able to file on a homestead. The tax records show they retained title to the original homestead for some time.

Between 1875 and 1885, affidavits were filed in support of native homesteads around Monohan and Squawk, on Lake Sammamish, at present day Issaquah (initially called Gilman)

(Township 24N, Range 6E). In a taped interview, Ed Davis, Snoqualmie Duwamish elder, indicated how the Zakuse family came to join the Snoqualmie at Monohan.

> The old man's name was Jim Zakeuse and he had a son name of Jimmy Zakeuse. Now it was on Zakeuse's land {at Monohan, Lake Sammamish} that the big pig^{w}idaltx^w {winter dance house} was built. This Zakeuse, he was in Dave Denny's place there in Lake Union, working there. Then he moved into Lake Sammamish and that's where he was called in {called home, died}. See, all them sduq^{w}albix^w, they all come together when they run out of jobs and they settled right there. Those first ones got there, they got to building houses. Yeah, they settled there on account of red fish, trout, salmon, deer, bear, pigeons, grouse (Davis 1983: 11/134).

By 1 June 1876, Bill Sbedzuse and family were living near Sqwak (now Issaquah) on Lake Sammamish, having moved, or been forced to move, out of the Seattle city limits. This formally handwritten testimony from employers who depended on native labor both inside and outside Seattle is an example of one aspect of the 'official' Indian homesteading process.

> Territory of Washington
> County of King
> We, David Denny and Luke McRedmond, do solemnly swear that we are well acquainted with Bill Sbedzuse and know that he is an Indian formerly of the Dewamish tribe – that he was born in the United States – that he has abandoned his relations with that tribe and adopted the habits and pursuits of civilized life – that he is over the age of twenty one years.
>
> David T Denny
> Luke McRedmond
>   Sworn and Subscribed
>   Before me this 15th day of June 1876
>   Waldo M York
>   Judge of the Probate Court
>   Of Said County (Zakuse family records)

The stipulation to sever tribal connections is illustrated by the homestead affidavit of Bill Sbedzuse, who did

> ...solemnly swear I am an Indian <u>formerly</u> of the Duwamish tribe; that I was born in the United States; that I have <u>abandoned</u> my relations with that tribe and have adopted the habits and pursuits of civilized life, and am married and over 21 years of age (emphasis added, Zakuse family records).

David Denny signed similar affidavits for other Indians who settled at Monohan, acknowledging that they routinely took care of business for him.

Lakes

Waterman recorded a modern settlement (#) at Monohan.

Siddles

The Siddle family had moved to the native community near Georgetown, itself the location of an ancestral village. Pioneer George Tibbetts hired Indian families to clear his land for the future town of Issaquah (Tollefson and Pennoyer 1986: 209-210), and the Siddles moved nearby, while the native community logged off the Issaquah woods and supplied the Seattle waterfront with pilings. They also created stump farms and fields for farmers. Their homes along the southeastern shore of Lake Sammamish became known as Monohan (also Monohon). The Siddles did not own their own land on Lake Sammamish, but lived on the homestead of Bill Bidu, who had Growler power, associated with saltwater-based "enforcers" so he probably once lived along the Sound before he moved inland.

> This Lyman Siddle, he built a house on Bill Bidu's claim. (Bidu was) Related to Lyman Siddle's wife. He followed {went} to his relation. He was told, "You build a house right there now." So they built a house there. Lived there for years, when we used to come. That was Lyman Siddle's family (Davis 1983: 19, 14/137, 15/138, 33/156).

In the mid-1890s, the Siddles purchased land in Tukwila (possibly near Allentown), with savings from wages for railroad work. They continued to move to the traditional fishing sites along the Duwamish, along with joining other traditional economic activities. They also grew potatoes. Increasing white settlement and hostility forced them to sell their 133.75 acre plot of land in 1901 and relocate across the road from the Muckleshoot Reservation in 1908, near the related Williams, Hamilton, Gus, and Jack families (Tollefson 1987a).

In 1910, the Siddles joined the Muckleshoot Indian Tribe and received allotment No. 43 (138.75 acres), a tract of timber along both sides of the White River some four miles southeast of Auburn. They donated some of this land for a Shaker Church. Lyman Siddle cut cottonwood into cordwood for a man named Taylor in Seattle. The wood was dried, hauled to Auburn, and shipped to Seattle. Lyman also dug wells and practiced water witching.

After Lyman's death in 1918, Julia fed her family through her own ingenuity, household industries, and marginal wages. During her widowhood, Julia's family labored smoking salmon, raising a large garden, picking hops in the Puyallup and Yakima valleys, and trading with other Indian groups. They traded clams, salmon, and venison for leather goods, camas, and pounded deer meat. The Siddles received foods from Suquamish through Jenny Davis, Julia's cousin.

Julia Siddle gathered raw materials, wove baskets, and sold them (Gunther 1930-1940). Some of her work was used by the family to carry clams, berries, or fish. Julia also knit, going to Seattle to buy raw wool from Fry's Packing Company and to collect free fish heads from a fish monger in Georgetown. Julia sold her knitted socks for $1.50 a pair to Eddie Bauer's clothing store in Seattle. The family also received spawned out salmon from local hatcheries, or caught them fresh in the White River.

Every fall, the Siddle family camped for a week in the mountains to pick a year's supply of huckleberries for food and trade. Every summer, the family hired out during the berry picking season, which began with strawberries near Auburn, or on Vashon Island. Then they followed ripening red raspberries, blackberries, blueberries, and salmon berries, as well as currants. Between harvests, some Siddle family members worked on local farms, hoeing peas, beans, and corn. The harvest season ended in the autumn, with hop picking at Orting or Toppenish and apple picking in the Yakima valley.

The Siddles became strong Indian Shakers at Muckleshoot. They donated land to the church and carried their ministry into the work fields, welcoming visitors such as Jerry and Jenny Kanum, and Ed and Louise Davis, Snoqualmie tribal leaders of the time. Eventually, David Siddle became the skipper of a tugboat for a timber company, ran a steam donkey for a logging crew, worked as a mechanic, and did some water witching like his father.

These were the xaču ʔabš x̱achu'absh Xacuabs.

5 ~ CULTURE CONSTITUENTS[34]

Throughout Puget Sound, the basic arena where gender, rank, and sanctions are most fully expressed is in the traditional communal house. The annual arrival of salmon and other foods calls for thanksgiving, and families still host feasts, potlatches, and *Syowin* (winter dancing (Amoss 1978)) in the longhouse as traditional ceremonials brought into modern times. Today, as in the past, families display both stationary and mobile insignia of their rank and family in their homes and in longhouses, built especially for the winter dancing, potlatches, and give-aways. Chiefly names, warrior powers, and doctoring continue. US military veterans are respected like famed warriors of the past. Carvers and artists continue the ancient arts, now with efficient metal tools. Age, gender, and rank remain still important.

Communal

The pattern of Mid-Sound culture and society includes ever widening units made up of the individual beings of human and other species, living in a house (Waterman and Greiner 1921; Smith 1940: 279-287; Elmendorf 1960: 150-169; Castile 1985: 64-74; Larson 1987: 2-1-2-34). The house would contain several persons acting as a group ~ al'al, -al'tx^w. Several houses – al'al'al – constituted a settlement usually located along a waterway and included seasonal settlements – dx^{w}ʔuq̇əlb – as well a permanent dwellings. All persons have to have a house or home. This includes humans and non-humans, as well as material and non-material beings.

In the social system, the large cedar plank houses were major nodes at named locations along the shoreline or at confluences near spots rich in local resources. Usually the name was descriptive or referred to an activity or a memorable event that had taken place at the location (Waterman revised in Hilbert, Miller, Zahir 2001: 16). Shoreline and riverbank house locations were especially important for access to fresh and marine water resources. Lakeshore and upriver houses gave easy access to prairies and prime hunting territory as well. House locations in the mountains had access to berry fields and high mountain game. House types included natural shelters, tents, single-family wood frame houses, multi-family cedar plank homes, and huge public buildings used for ceremonies (Waterman and Coffin 1920, Waterman and others 1921). Ceremonial events brought together the beings and forces of the world. Beyond the house node were at least three concentric rings occupied by allies, by competitors for regional status, and by strangers ignorant of what was worthy of display or dispute (Roberts 1975: 92).

Persons dwelling within a house were organized by age, by gender, and by rank (See Chapter 6 Kinship). Within each rectangular plank house, families occupied cubicle-like living spaces. Huge standing timbers served as house posts and supported a one-slope shed roof

---

[34] Improving on prior summaries for Sound Transit (Miller 2004) with excessive citations and my 1999 general ethnography, detailed citations now appear in my *Minter Bay ~ Land, Lore, Loss, and Lucre in the South Salish Sea* 2017. We continue to highlight the neglected inputs by Jerry Meeker to Alfred John Smith, and earlier elders to Herman Karl Haeberlin, cited by specific notebooks. For Smith's resulting novel, see *Leschi in Love, Old Lukh* (Miller 2016b & d).

covered by troughed planks to carry off rainwater. The exterior was covered by cedar planks sewn and braced together so as to overlap. Beside the inner walls were bleachers, risers, or wide benches made of finely adzed planks set about a yard above the ground, sometimes as two tiers of low and high bunks. The lower one was used for sitting and storage, while the higher one was layered over with cattail mats, animal skins, and woven blankets for sleeping. Rows of boxes and storage baskets divided off family compartments. The floor was hard-packed dirt. Families had fires along the sides.

In general, the owners of the largest plank houses were high class – both men and women and might hold positions such as chief, warrior, doctor (shaman), prophet, or a specialist such as a carver, gambler, wrestler, etc. They lived in the secluded and protected rear of the house. Although all people had seasonal camps, wealthy families often had several homes at different locations. Skagit and Chelan elders referred to these summer homes as their "resorts," indicating that summer encampments included fun times as well as work.

Each large plank house was initially assembled by a group of siblings who amassed the wealth, resources, and status to host and coordinate the labor needed to finish such an imposing dwelling. Its location was hereditary, usually at a sheltered and productive fishery. Large and famous families had several such houses, each built at the location of an important resource which they controlled. The family acted as host and manager for the harvesting and dispersal of the bounty, rather than keeping it exclusively for private use. During extreme cold, everyone moved into one of these wealthy homes for the greater warmth it provided.

Senior siblings, as eldest owners of a house, lauded themselves by carving and/or painting the houseposts located in the center or corners of the house with representations of their spirit partners. Such images made visible their claim to a special relationship with a specific spot, spirit, and resources. Painted houseposts were the rule, carved ones were the exception. Shamans or Indian doctors sometimes had a plank near their bed decorated with a vague image of one source of their healing ability.

Ordinary people lived in compartments along the sides within the larger houses or in smaller houses outside. In ordinary houses, plain, undecorated houseposts were draped with baskets, traplines, skins, fishing tackle, and other possessions to keep them handy (Haeberlin 1916-1917 Notebook 28: 31). Slaves, if well treated, slept near the doorway, though exposed to traffic flow and enemy attack.[35]

A strong leader might arrange for the building of an especially large house where public events took place and out-of-town guests could stay. Such a large separate building was called a potlatch house. It was the ability to accommodate large influxes of invited people that defined a central native town as a hub and its family as leaders of a river, drainage, or region. One such house described by Haeberlin (1916 Notebook 4: 8) had two posts painted with a wide black band as background to set off a pair of horizontal white crescents (half moons), one atop the other.

In addition, most houses were associated with a number of different outbuildings and structures, including a smokehouse, a seclusion house for women during menses, saunas, canoe sheds, storage cellars, and drying racks. A special feature of the Mid-Sound was a sauna.

---

[35] If badly treated, a slave had to find a different sleeping place every night, sometimes outside the house.

Culture

Wilson George called attention to special substantial sweatlodges used by the Suquamish and others along steep banks near streams

> "where there was running fresh water. They were built of fir or cedar saplings, against the wall of a bank. The earthen bank became the back wall, after they dug it out and squared it off. They stood the poles together as close as they could, about three thick, to make the walls and stuffed the cracks with moss, which eventually took hold there and grew on the walls. Split cedar was put across the top for the roof, the split side up and the bark one down. Another row was laid over the cracks with the split side down and the bark up. Then dirt was put over the roof to seal it tight. When done, the lodge had a square shape with an entrance in the middle of the front wall, open to the roof and about 18 inches wide.
>
> The door was made of split cedar, just big enough for a person to get through. Usually, there was room enough for only one or two people. The inside walls also had moss stuffed in the cracks and were about five feet high, so people had to stoop slightly in there. There were no seats, only cedar limbs on the floor.
>
> A fire was built outside to heat the rocks, which were taken inside. If you had dry bark that didn't make much smoke, you could use it to build a fire inside on top of the rocks, but you had to brush the coals off when the rocks were hot. It was cleaner to heat the rocks outside. Once they came inside, a little water was thrown on the rocks to create steam. When the steam got too {thin}, they added more water. They stayed inside for as long as they possibly could.
>
> When you had enough, you went to the creek to throw cold water on yourself. Then you could go back to sweat again. This procedure could be repeated several times during one session. When you were all done, you rubbed yourself with soft, shredded cedar bark. The used rocks were safely stored in the back against the dirt wall, ready for the next time.

Wilson denied the sweatlodge was ever used for guardian spirit quest, any ceremony, nor had any other special meaning except it was good for a person to do (Miller with Snyder 1999: 118).

Riverines

A key Puget Salish belief is that rivers are alive, demanding respect from all residents. The word for river applied to any open channel that provided access to linked waterways throughout the Sound and out to the coast. Valued elders have confirmed that they regard rivers as a kind of woman, without elaborating further. Other Northwest tribes also say that rivers are women, such as Haida Creek Women.

The river community included networks of close kin ~ q̓ʷuʔšəd, and related people ~ ʔiišəd. These communities lived along tributary rivers and creeks ~ dᶻəɫixʷ or along lakes ~ caləɫ

~ xаču? (Whulshootseed and northern Lushootseed versions respectively (Bates, Hess, Hilbert 1994: 43, 325). Each drainage included many tributary rivers, streams, and creeks as well as several large and small lakes.

Travel from one community to another was primarily by canoes appropriate to the flow. Portages allowed for transport of canoes from one waterway to another, while inland trails along ridges connected communities and emergency messengers.

Although most Puget Basin rivers, like the Snoqualmie, had a tree-like pattern, the Duwamish drainage was an exception. It originally had a trellis-like drainage system and contained other types of waterways that were culturally treated as rivers. The Duwamish drainage was the homeland of same-named Duwamish people (Indian Claims Commission 1974a: 29-51; Hilbert, Miller, Zahir 2001: 16), though each portion of the drainage had a distinct name and an associated named community. Sometimes these names referred to tribes, although the people apparently did not regard themselves as a unified whole. In other instances, the names referred to small drainages or prominent settlements.

For example, the area now drained by the Ballard Locks includes Salmon and Shilshole Bays and Lake Union. Those families living at the western terminus of this waterway were known as Shilsholabish, those on Lake Union and the heart of Seattle as Xa^{3}tcua'bc (Hilbert, Miller, Zahir 2001: 16). Thornton Creek, Ravenna Creek, and many other small rivers and creeks, Green Lake and Lake Sammamish, and several smaller lakes, all drained into Lake Washington. This waterway of several connected lakes was the home of the Lakes people of mixed Duwamish and Sdok^{w}albix^w. Lakes were called Tsa-bah-bobs {čaləł?abš ~ Whulshootseed} or xatcoabc {xаču?abš ~ Lushootseed}. Those along the eastern shore of Lake Washington were called luwitabsh {??} (Indian Claims Commission 1974a: 36, 40).

The Black River served as the original outlet for Lake Washington into the Duwamish River, fostering an important Lakes population (xаču?abs). People on the Cedar River, which flowed into the Black, were called Katilbabsh (Indian Claims Commission 1974a: 40).

Lake Washington and Duwamish River link ended when the Ballard Locks opened on 4 July 1917. After this, Lake Washington drained to the north and west. Lowering the lake by 9 feet closed the outlet of Lake Washington and drained the Black River, which was eventually covered by downtown Renton.

Most place names along the Duwamish River, its tributaries, and lakes were descriptive (e.g., "people of the logjam", identifying the section of river where the community was located. Waterways had their own names, for example, the people of the Green River were known as the Skop^{3}absh and the Soos Creek people were the Susabsh. Village communities along tributaries also had distinct names.

In the late 1880s, many Duwamish groups were driven out of Seattle and came to live along the southern and eastern shores of Lake Washington and Lake Sammamish. As Indien names ceased to be used, native people living in the Renton vicinity were called "Renton Indians" (Haeberlin and Gunther 1930: 10), carrying into English the traditional association between a named place and a group.

Culture

As reservations became established, many families also settled at the Muckleshoot and Suquamish reservations and became enrolled members of those communities. Many families settled with relatives among the Snoqualmie; others joined relatives at reservations farther away.

In all, Mid-Sound people knew – and know – their land intimately, based on both personal and ancestral experiences. They relied on cedar, salmon, and many other local resources. Initially, Puget Sound natives coped well with the presence of the Hudson Bay Company during the first half of the 1800s. They traded furs, fish, and labor for exotic goods at Fort Nisqually, built in 1833 in southern Puget Sound. Problems arose when American squatters and would-be homesteaders arrived in the mid-1800s, and spread rapidly when commercial lumber and mining operations shipping timber and minerals to California steadily took over their lands and resources.

Euro-American logging, over-fishing, and bureaucratic insensitivity took their toll on native people and places. Hand-split-plank houses were replaced by milled lumber, and communal houses were destroyed to make way to single-family homes and public halls. Grocery stores provide much of the food eaten, both on and off reservations. Waterways and canoes that once linked everyone have largely been replaced by roads, cars, trucks, and vans.

However, many families still travel and trade for traditional foods in season. Climate, tides, terrain, and winds still inform local schedules and calendars. Though Puget Sound natives have adopted the goods, clothes, boats, and housing of mainstream society; the manner in which these material goods are used continues to be traditional, informed by their cultural and religious past.

The world of the spirits and other beings continues. Shamans, both men and women, still practice among the Mid-Sound and other Salish people (Miller 1999: 57, 74). However, many of their curing functions are now shared with members of Christian religious sects such as Pentecostal Church and Indian Shaker Church. Today, members of these faiths remain friendly, recognizing that both place great emphasis on possession by the spirit, as evidence of a direct link with God, exuberantly expressed while healing the sick and afflicted (Amoss 1978: 81; Ruby and Brown 1996: 154; Buerge and Rochester 1988: 95).

Although not a river system in the strictest sense, Salmon Bay, Lake Union, Portage Bay, Union Bay, Lake Washington and their tributary streams formed a series of connected waterways that could only be entered from Puget Sound at Shilshole, along a very meandering course through fresh water lakes and overland portages of Lakes people. Their territory extended north at least to Thornton Creek, south to downtown Seattle, and along the shores of Lake Washington. Lakes territory includes many place names, especially around Salmon Bay, West Point, Smith Cove, and eastern Lake Washington.

Stories and legends still inform place names. Where appropriate, stories or legends from similar landscapes are included herein because ecologically similar areas are often evoke the same myth actors and events.

The anthropologists who recorded the most information about the Seattle area are JP Harrington and TT Waterman, while teaching at University of Washington and working with elders to record place-name data on maps. Waterman's place-names have been reanalyzed by Hilbert, Miller, Zahir (2001), relying on his single map of the Seattle region published in 1922.

Additionally, where possible correct Whulshootseed orthography is added between { } curly brackets. Material from other sources, with orthography used by those sources, also sometime appears below.

In particular, relying on fieldwork in the Puget Sound region in the 1930s, Marian Smith (1940: 7) provided a spatial model for these cultures, recognizing seven components of community allegiance and loyalty moving outward from within a household, with the largest community loyalty coinciding with a particular drainage or watershed.

Puget Salish terms applicable to her seven components were checked with elders and Lushootseed dictionaries (Hess 1976; Bates, Hess, Hilbert 1994). Within each component, personal affiliations became more expansive moving outward from (a) family group (Smith 1940: 7) or hearth mates eating together – *hudali* ("fire place"); to (b) house group, those within a cedar plank household – *ʔalʔal, -ʔaltxʷ*; (c) village group (Smith 1940: 7) ~ birthright locals, those born at the settlement in contrast to in-laws, visitors, and foreigners ~ *gʷədᶻʔali*; (d) village site ~ houses of all residents in a settlement ~ *al'al'al*, including all seasonal settlements, towns, resorts, and camps ~ *dxʷʔuq̇əlb* ; (e) village of community networks of close kin ~ *q̇ʷuʔšəd*, and one's own people ~ *ʔiišəd* living along the same tributary; (f) village drainage ~ settlements and houses along creeks ~ *dᶻəɫixʷ* of tributary drainages; and (g) drainage system including all settlements within the entire drainage of a watershed ~ *bəqʷ stuləkʷ*.

Drainage

Each river within the Puget Sound drainage basin constituted a community of common interests in the sense that its inhabitants more frequently and easily interacted with each other within the entire drainage or watershed ~ *bəqʷ stuləkʷ*. Thus, the Duwamish watershed included Lake Sammamish, which flows into Lake Washington, which flowed into the Black River, which flowed into the Duwamish River, and the Green River which also flows into the Duwamish River, and all their tributaries.

Community relations involved economic, social, kinship, political, and, above all, religious considerations. Rather than constituting a tribe in the usual political sense of those sharing a leader, language, and locale; the people living along a river represented more of a religious congregation attuned to the same localized spirits. In the Mid-Sound languages, the greater cohesion of the downriver towns was indicated by the *-bsh* ending (meaning tribe), while the looser organization of the upriver communities was reflected in the *-bixʷ* ending for "bunch" ~ bloodline.

Traditionally, all classes were affected by terrain and location along the drainage. While everyone living along the same river shared a common identity, those who lived downriver were distinguished from those who lived inland. Generally, downriver communities, especially those at river mouths, were more populous, diversified, and prosperous than those upriver. The high born were more numerous and visible downriver, where they had greater interactions with other foreign communities. Though Smith (1940: 7) did not state it explicitly, native towns near the river mouth were more cosmopolitan, with more frequent visitors and larger gatherings. They also could expect a greater likelihood of attack and so included famous warriors.

Communities in the mountains were more egalitarian. They lived a more arduous life, which gave them a certain prestige derived from admiration of their fortitude and diligence. They also gained prestige due to access to and knowledge about certain resources, such as mountain goat wool and horn, valued by high class persons, and medicinal plants or paint acquired in the high mountain areas.

Overall, relying on Smith's (1940: 6-7) model led to a simplified, fourfold model emphasizing communal, seasonal, ceremonial, and personnel aspects. Further, in reverse order, the person combines gender, body, mind, and soul with spirit allies; communal includes house and settlement of hearth mates, households, settlements, and most kin; seasonal alternates economic with religious activities; and ceremonial emphasizes grateful relations with other beings transported across time and space, including forest, prairie, river, or sea. In most cases, community focus is their own river, such as the Snoqualmie, and its links to other waterways of the drainage and watershed, in turn linking everyone to resident immortals and to more remote peoples and places through marriage, ritual, and trade.

Rank

Within any community, families were ranked as high born, freeborn commoner, or slave. Everyone was respected, though authority was qualified by rank, by age, and by gender. The different strengths and advantages of a family derived from various partnerships set up within this triple system of two freeborn social classes (upper and lower) and an underclass of slaves. These three classes were recognized by all North Pacific Coast tribes (Donald 1997). Wealthy families, with strong, ancient bonds, had an "endowment with family – with knowledgeable and resourceful relatives, rather than with wealth alone" (Bierwert 1996: 103).

Leadership derived from support of close kin and affines, both women and men. Indeed, leadership was and is a corporate and not a personal responsibility. Rank, family pedigree, diligence, resourcefulness, and resilience remained highly valued, yet each person had to be firmly linked to an immortal and be able to convey access to all-pervading power. Such access was manifested in leadership positions (Suttles and Lane 1990; Boxberger and Miller 1997; Miller 1992d; Miller and Boxberger 1994, Tollefson 1916).

High born individuals had to be active and constantly diligent, every moment of their time used efficiently and wisely. They were the managers of resources and social interaction, constantly alert to needs and abuses that impacted on the wellbeing of all forms of life. Prominent families indicated their profitable bonds by sponsoring religious events such as initiations and displays for the singing of power songs, and by providing shelter and food for visitors at these gatherings. In this manner, they spread their reputation for sharing far and wide. Sometimes, such families went deliberately outside their home territory to gather or purchase delicacies from other areas, fostering intertribal networks based on visiting, trading, and ritual which often led to intermarriage, adoption, and even closer cooperation. Their primary relaxation seems to have been traveling to other regions where they were guests instead of hosts.

High status was validated by continuing personal successes among many family members across generations, bolstering a sense of confidence, competence, and authority for the kindred.

Culture

The high born led by arranging successful group hunts, winter ceremonials, giveaways, elaborate cures, and the building of houses, canoes, and fish weirs (Collins 1974: 113). Generosity, reliable support, kindness, and good advice were attributes of these good families.

Ordinary people, without a venerable pedigree or specialty career, made up the commoners. Freeborn commoners had access to whatever a birth place could bestow, although that access was somewhat constrained by the rights of the high born. They labored hard during fish runs, participated in various harvesting activities, and enjoyed leisure in between.

Slaves were tainted by capture, purchase, or birth. Most slaves could only benefit through their masters. In his fieldnotes, Haeberlin (1917 Notebook 39: 33) was told that war captives taken into slavery went to the afterworld of their original tribe after death, but those born into slavery went to the afterworld of their masters where they remained slaves forever. This fate suggests the strength of the bond between a human, a spirit, a community, and a locale. Clearly, the strongest bond was that created by birth at a specific place, the abode of a particular immortal.

All successful effort had to be sanctioned by a blessing from an immortal. While any of the spirits could provide a career, only the most powerful, for good or bad, conveyed the ability to cure or to kill as native doctors ~ shamans. Occasional reports indicate that even slaves sometimes entered into a partnership with an immortal, but elders were quick to stress that these were the least powerful sources of power.

Personnel

Any viable community was sustained by its specialized careers, organized by its leaders, performed by age and gender, and both healed and protected by its doctors. From the vast array of careers and specialties, four have survived as traditional roles.

Genders

For Lushootseeds, all "persons" have gender – humans, animals, plants, rivers, mountains, and other inert materials. Sexual equality was and remains strong. With proper supernatural[36] sanction any man or woman could perform any task. However, gender roles did exist in a statistical sense. Men tend to do some things and women to do others. A summary statement by a Suquamish elder distinguishes both appearance and activities of men and women:

Ellen George noted men and women had different ways of dressing and different tasks to do. Women parted their hair in the middle and braided it on both sides. Men had long hair but they didn't braid it so it was allowed to hang around the shoulders. The different jobs included the following:

    drying = women did all berries, meat, and fish
    cooking = women did it all
    weaving = women made blankets of dog wool and mats, cutting cattails for them

---

[36] This remarkable gender equality derives from the greater importance of social rank, which overwhelms gender.

baskets = women made them and got their own material like cedar boughs, bark, grasses, and roots {men made the open work clamming baskets}
canoes = made by men
clams = women dug them and dried them, but men sometimes watched the clams drying over a fire to see they did not burn
berries = picked and dried by women
fishing = men did it
hunting = men
paddling canoes = both men and women

In addition, men put up houses for curing meat and fish, built fire places for cooking, made cradle boards, speared ducks, woodworked planks and carvings, got fire wood, made long wooden needles for mats, and prepared ironwood stakes for cooking salmon and clams (Miller with Snyder 1999: 134).

Since the immortal spirits also had gender, a woman performing usual men's roles was presumed to have a male spirit helper. Anyone undertaking a quest could expect to receive a spirit of either gender since there was no obligation for male spirits to appear only to men or for female immortals to gift only women. For example, Dr Bill, a famous Snoqualmie shaman, had a female Little Earth spirit that enabled him to predict the quality of the berry harvest or cure babies (Miller 1988: 18).

Among the Fraser River Sto:lō to the north, the vital image of Salmon is used explicitly to convey a sense of mutual cooperation such that women are said to be like the backbone, and men like the nose, with the ready understanding of all fishing folk that "the nose is, of course, first, the forward tip of the head which is not followed but propelled by the backbone" (Bierwert 1986: 340). Moreover, gender is defined by actions, not by overt body differences alone.

Since careers assigned to each gender were mutually interdependent, they functioned best in the context of marriage. The complementary contributions of husband and of wife supplied the complete range of needs. Indeed, adults could not properly display a spirit power during its annual winter return without emotional and musical help by a spouse. Stable couples cooperated in endeavors, even as they observed sexual continence required for hunters before a hunt, women before harvesting, shamans before a cure, and warriors before a battle (Amoss 1978: 57). While her husband was in pursuit of food, the wife prayed and sang to assist him, as did his sisters (Smith 1940: 165). Women often would lie inert so that game would be similarly incapacitated.

Men and women expressed a skill in all of its ramifications (Miller 1999: 96). For example, a canoe maker also produced paddles. An expert at drying clams may also make coarsely woven clam baskets. However, most baskets were made by specialists in that craft. Those with sanction from ghosts or the dead served as undertakers, corpse washers, and coffin box makers. Only these specialists could move human bones that had fallen out of their grave container, or rebury a loved one with appropriate ceremony if the resting place had been disturbed by earth or human forces.

Culture

Man

From the time they were toddlers, boys were given toy tools such as bows, arrows, slings, and carving knives to practice at adult careers (Smith 1940: 139, Collins 1974: 75). As they got older, these toys were made larger. Work that was done primarily by men included making open-work clamming baskets, fish and animal traps, nets, weapons, canoes, and houses. Men did all the hunting, fishing, and woodworking. They constructed fire-proof hearths, cradle boards, adzed handles, carvings, multipurpose planks, and smokehouses for curing meat and fish. They got firewood (if no children or slaves were available), whittled long wooden needles for sewing cattail mats, and split the ironwood stakes (fish-sticks) for cooking salmon and clams.

All specializations enhanced family and personal prestige, granted by guardian spirits as religious sanction for success. For men, specialist careers included those of chief, warrior, doctor, and ritualist. A man could excel as canoe maker, hunter, storyteller, gambler, wrestler, eater, and harpooner. While all men hunted, career hunters honed the talents and powers needed to harpoon sea mammals or pursue mountain goats. They wore clothing and carried equipment, such as quivers, made of cougar skins to augment mystically their hunting ability. While every man could work wood, the building of houses and canoes called for experts with appropriate spiritual partners, such as Woodpecker, Adze, or Cedar. Carpenters acquired spiritual techniques along with manual skills. If a leader was not personally handy, a carpenter finished any building needed. After metal tools were adopted, a skilled native carpenter gained entrance into white settler society since he could as easily make a coffinbox, shamanic effigy, rattle, or power boards as construct a table, stairway, or closet. In this way, Puyallup elder Jerry Meeker made window and door sills to earn added income (Meeker 1948: C).

Woman

Girls were given toy needles, awls, and cooking utensils to play at sewing, weaving, and keeping house. In theory, a first complete basket was made during a girl's puberty seclusion. It was given away to a worthy elderly woman in return for her blessings for a long life, healthy family, and bountiful food supply.

Women primarily cared for the house and family. Women and girls prepared meals, tended children, and nursed the sick. Women regularly shredded cedar bark, spun goat and dog wool, prepared skins, and made baskets and weavings. They made clothing and rain gear from softened, shredded cedarbark, which invigorated by lightly chafing the wearer's skin (Miller 1999: 119). They wove goat and dog wool blankets for clothing and cattail mats for bedding and seating. They prepared the necessary cedar boughs, bark, grasses, and roots for making baskets. In upriver and mountainous regions, both men and women wore leather leggings when walking overland as protection from underbrush and donned snowshoes for winter treks. Women made the leather clothes and footwear.

Women cultivated and harvested roots, berries, and fresh shoots. They dried and smoked fish, venison, and shellfish. They carried wood and water if there were no slaves to do these tasks. Women specialists acted as midwives, their abilities proven by their own numerous, healthy children. They also specialized as baby doctors, able to diagnose physical and spiritual illnesses and to return the lost souls of infants. Other special skills were cooking at large gatherings and story telling.

Age

Children were known by kin terms and nicknames. When they were about twelve, they usually received an ancestral family name (Collins 1966). In high rank families, where everything was more structured, a child was named at a very early age, and then acquired a series of names during the course of his or her life. Names could come through the father or the mother, but the father usually suggested the first one. These names specified gender, but could be held by males or females depending on status. Leader names were usually male and often ended in *-qən/-qəd* meaning "head."

Freeborn children had their foreheads compressed by an angled wooden cradleboard to produce a high sloping head shape. The earlobes and nasal septum were pierced to hold dentalia shells and other ornaments. Paint, tattoos, and cosmetics further enhanced appearance among the high born (Haeberlin and Gunther 1930: 37-41).

The adult years of any person's life were filled with economic and social activities, as appropriate to their gender and rank. Adults were responsible for keeping the family and community intact and healthy, both physically and spiritually.

Persons who survived to old age were regarded as elders. They held the history of the family and community and related this history at gatherings. They also were called upon for advice by the younger adults when important decisions needed to be made. Aging elders were usually cared for by children and younger adults, who were expected to learn the teaching imparted to them in the day-to-day process of living.

Chief

The term for leader is sd^{z}ix^{w}qs ~ "one + nose". This can be translated as the "first nose, to point before." A leader's specialty was that he or she was an expert in human emotions, foibles, and concerns. He or she epitomized dignity, open-handedness, restraint, wealth, and knowledge of traditions. Events sponsored by chiefs were expected to be elaborate and guests who attended would be well rewarded. The sponsor of an event was publicly acknowledged by speakers who served as his or her representatives. Although many treaty signers were chiefs, some also were speakers who represented their leaders.

At times, certain names became associated with wealth and position. For example, the foremost Suquamish leader had long been Kitsap. In time this position was assumed by Seattle ~ si'ał, whose name came from his mother, a Duwamish. The name, which originated in the White River area, came to prominence on the Sound because of the effectiveness of Seattle in his role as chief and because he was first treaty signer.

Sometimes a chief would deliberately stigmatize him/herself to have an excuse for a potlatch. In the early 1800s, at Suquamish, šalqəb deliberately went too close to his hearth so his blanket caught on fire, giving him an excuse to host a potlatch to cover his embarrassment and show people he was generous (Miller with Snyder 1999: 157). šalqəb was the second chief after

Kitsap and ahead in rank of the young Seattle. Such staged dramatics were an excuse to display generosity and were an aspect of the chiefly role.

Warrior

A warrior was forceful, aggressive, dominant, imperious, quick-tempered, implacable, and despotic (Amoss 1978: 10). He alone could flaunt a hot temper, stamina, indifference to physical risk, and a willingness to be mean by inflicting pain. His dagger and club were so closely associated with the killing of men that displaying such an unsheathed weapon at a public event was tantamount to a declaration of war.

War was a complex business. Although men were defenders, women were sometimes seen as instigators. Among Mid-Sound neighbors, the war between Lummi and Stockaders (downriver Nooksacks) for the present mainland near the mouth of the Nooksack River started when an insulted wife tangled her fingers in her Lummi husband's hair to hold him until her Stockader brothers could behead him (Miller 1999: 17). Though Lummi took over this mainland, they could not successfully use its resources until they first hired, then intermarried, survivors in order to inherit proper Stockader rituals and prayers to assure river fishing success.

Doctor

Medico-religious specialists, variously called doctors ~ shamans, had both career and curing spirits with great power. The shaman, man or woman, often had a separate house that was used as a clinic. Each shaman provided their family and settlement with security from mystical attack by spirits or hostile or evil shamans. Their duties were to explain the cause of hardships, treat the sick, and counteract malevolent sorcery (Elmendorf 1989). Although shamans were generally treated with deference (sometimes tinged by great fear), a shaman who was a family member was the best of allies. Because of constant and direct access to power, it was possible for the doctor to resort to selfish, criminal, or hostile acts. A doctor who lost a patient often was suspected of sorcery. The doctor might be killed by the next of kin of the deceased unless he or she could escape until the situation quieted.

Prophet

During times of crisis, men and women arose to lead people toward a more satisfying way of life. During the past hundred years, some prophets have been more successful than others. Several of the prophets in the 19th century were leaders who attempted to consolidate different groups in defense of their lands against encroachment by settlers or other native groups. Other prophets worked to adapt spiritual beliefs and practices to altered circumstances. In recent times, none were more significant for the entire region than John and Mary Slocum, who founded the Indian Shaker Church near Olympia in 1882 as a blend of traditional spiritual beliefs and Christian teachings (Amoss 1982, 1990; Barnett 1957; Collins 1950; Jilek 1982; Richen 1974; Tollefson 1989a; Waterman 1924; Wike 1952).

Ceremonial

Usually, a river was the focus for major community rituals. Four primary rituals include thanksgiving for the return of the First Salmon, the special initiation of the Growlers, the *spədak* ceremony, and *Syowin* winter dancing. These major rituals were all described by Warren Snyder, who worked with elders at Suquamish in the 1950s (Miller with Snyder 1999; Williams 1916).

First Salmon

Annually, the First Salmon ceremony welcomes the first run of fish with singing, processions, and feast. Because most communities lived along a river in western Washington, it was easy to observe the first appearance of a fish run. The ceremony culminates in the ritual eating (communion) of the first salmon caught, with salmon bones carefully placed back in the river.

As the Suquamish had no major river, their ceremony differed (Miller with Snyder 1999: 144-156) to honor a dog salmon with a deformed jaw which they cooked and served to children, who were supposed to swim, acting like salmon to attract others. Salmon bones were placed back into the water "to let the salmon know they wanted them to come back again the next year". Wilson George remarked that Suquamish "could always get some salmon in the Sound, so it wasn't like the river people who had to wait for the runs of salmon to arrive".

Growlers

Saltwater communities of Suquamish and Duwamish were distinguished by the privileged membership of certain leading families in a secret intertribal organization, sometimes known as Dog Eaters (Miller 1999: 101), that spread from tribes further north in British Columbia in the mid 1880s. Its name in Puget Salish languages translates as "growl at each other" (Wilson George in Miller with Snyder 1999: 151).

spədak

The *spədak* ceremony was the major public religious expression throughout the region. Each enactment was customized to features of locale, personnel, and the immortal helpers specifically invoked there (Haeberlin 1918; Miller 1988, 1999; Smith 1941; Waterman 1930, 1973). Enactments included the use of a canoe outfit made of boards, poles, and painted or carved figures.

Although *spədak* is known in the academic literature as the spirit canoe or soul saving ceremony, the word represents something much more complex.[37] *spədak* is a world renewing rite of great import.

---

[37] After struggling for years to find a better English term, Miller (1988, 1999) has come to use the term shamanistic odyssey in order to describe this spiritual journey, during which a

Culture

According to Wilson George

They usually started for the spirit land in the morning. The trip took from 6 to 12 hours. If the sick person did not get better, then they made another trip. If the patient then showed signs of getting well, they don't make any more trips. If he didn't show any improvement, there was nothing left to do. It was seldom that even two trips were necessary (Miller with Snyder 1999: 155).

Syowin

Since *Syowin* is a living tradition of great sensitivity for native peoples (Amoss 1974). In private homes and public smokehouses, people gather all winter long to express in sacred song and dance their on-going bonds with spiritual helpers who provide them with power to benefit their families and communities.

Puget Salish societies have great local diversity with respect to the spirit world. Groups living inland, upriver, and along the southern Sound emphasized kin-based society with spirit quests and a lesser emphasis on inherited privileges (Roberts 1975: 32, 35, 77). Those in the north Sound emphasized rank and social class, although not to the extent of the groups yet farther north.

The Mid-Sound people believe that the entire world has passed through several epochs. Efforts by semi-divine Transformer(s) led up to a last universal change, likened to "capsizing". In a moment, almost everything came into its present form in the modern world. Across land- and sea-scapes, beings became immortal. Some were cast in stone; some became human. Each occupied a known or revealed place, where, over generations, its resources were shared with members of the leading human family.

Two examples suggest the importance of spiritual sharing. The first example shows that spiritually significant events can occur during mundane activities. Suquamish leader Jacob *Whahalchu* was hunting ducks off Alki Point as a young man (Miller 1999: 12, 59-60). When he paddled out to retrieve his spent arrows, he looked down and saw a plank house under the water. It was surrounded by abundant animal life, elk herds near the sides and fish above the roof. Such a vision was an indication of the immortal being that provided humans with great wealth. In this situation, spiritual help was needed, the kind that is best provided by a father. Unfortunately, Jacob's father was away at the time and, because he lacked the necessary spiritual help, Jacob missed this chance at great wealth. This example shows that spiritual bonds were fundamental and that they also could be elaborated into considerations of rank.

The second example, also from Suquamish, reveals certain symbols of spiritual activity and shows the importance of community events.

The final drying of dog salmon meant that people had to prepare for the return of their spirit powers and songs. While curing spirits were always present, career powers came for the winter and left in the spring. When each spirit arrived in the

---

variety of symbolic vehicles were used to save a variety of soul and spiritual entities. In this work, the Whulshootseed name of *spədak* is used.

fall, its human partner became "sick to sing" and hosted a gathering to ease his or her condition by singing the song in a group setting. Each return was a time of danger and uncertainty until the song was "brought out" and the spiritual bond affirmed. According to John Adams, the Suquamish did not use the "boom, boom" (drum) like the Yakima do. When they were singing in a house, they would take a long pole and hit it on the roof to keep time with the singing. Anyone could keep time with the pole. This was a long pole about 8 or 10 feet tall. John saw one when he was about 10 years old about 70 years ago. The pole was painted red (Miller with Snyder 1999: 145-151).

Potlatch

At its most lavish expression, drainage solidarity was upheld in the complex ceremony known as the "potlatch," meaning "to give" in Chinuk Jargon, derived from the Nootkan native language of the West Coast of Vancouver Island. In ancient times, a potlatch was an event confirming high status. Today, it has merged with the general give-away held in connection with the Winter dance's final "thank you" hosted by new dancers and their families.

Wilson George reported that, for Suquamish, hosting a potlatch required the building of a special big plank dwelling that was divided into sections for groups coming from different areas.

Wilson went to many potlatches as a boy. The last one he went to was given by John Seattle at Green River. John was not related to the old chief, he just took the name.

When all the people were there, the leader started, singing his power song. Then he spoke to the people, saying "so and so has come in. That is the last of the people I have invited. Then he changed to another tune of his song and kept singing until he got to the end. Then he started to give away what he had collected together, saying "The first person invited was so and so." Then that tribal leader was given presents, and so on until they got to the last one to come in. Then his {spirit} helper started his own song, finished it, and gave out his own gifts in the same order. The giver usually called on his relatives to help him. He gave only to the leading members of other communities.

After the gifts had been given to the chiefs, and the feasting was over, there was a Scramble. Everyone was allowed {but the high class thought it too crass to behave in so undignified a manner}. A platform was made on the roof and blankets were piled on it. Then the people would crowd around below it. A man would throw the blankets down at them, one at a time. Everyone tried to grab one of these. They didn't pull or tear it. The one with the firmest grip would claim it. Then he had to pay the others also hanging on to it for their share. Sometimes an old man would get hold of a blanket and a strong young man would pull it away from the others until he could give it to the old man for his own. {This showed respect and regard for the elders.} Poles were also thrown down and people would try to take hold of them for each represented one canoe. The person left holding the stick had to pay the others for their share.

58

During the first part of a potlatch, when the gifts were given out to the invited leaders, these headmen could either keep all that they received or they could give some of it to members of their group. It was up to them, but a wise leader shared what he had.

The reasons for holding a potlatch included 1) Naming – this was the most important, whether giving a name to a child or changing one later in life; 2) Remove Stigma – for a daughter sent home by her husband, the father would announce what had happened and say he didn't know why his daughter had been sent home, this cleared her name so she could marry honorably again; 3) Status Changes – mark the death of one chief and the elevation of his heir.

John Adams said they would invite people from all over, tribes friendly to them. They wouldn't invite enemies. It was always a chief who gave the potlatch, but he had other men go out and do the inviting.

The guests arrived singing their own songs. Chief Seattle had a potlatch at Old Man House around the 1850s. He went to Victoria {founded 1849} for some blankets. When he left, he told the people, "When I leave Victoria, you will hear Thunder and then you will know I am on my way back." This happened. John Curly was the speaker for Chief Seattle at this potlatch (Miller with Snyder 1999: 156).

The subtle, discerning, and valued appreciation of customs was such that insiders, in contrast to outsiders, understood the complexities of "the feud, the snub, the verbal innuendo" and accordingly "were appropriate guests for a ceremonial feast" (Roberts 1975: 79). The potlatch served to confirm membership within each social and community united into a cultural whole.

Seasonal

The distribution network of locally available foodstuffs was an important aspect of drainage solidarity. Movement of foodstuffs up and down the waterway served to shared periodic abundances. Thus, prepared shellfish and other marine foods moved upriver as dried meat, hides, berries, and roots moved downriver. Generally, these exchanges took place in a ritual or kinship context that set them apart from ordinary trading instances. Trade driven by a profit motive seemed overtly commercial and therefore, somewhat crass. Thus, for the duration of a marriage, in-laws constantly exchanged gifts with each other to indicate their on-going kindness and goodwill. On a wider scale, members of a community always shared what they had, only trading or selling resources to those who could be characterized as outsiders and foreigners. Everything born ~ indigenous along the drainage was shared willingly and generously among all living members, whether human, biotic, or spiritual. This sharing took place primarily during the winter at invitational gatherings commonly called potlatches or *syowin* powwows.

Culture

Subsistence

The cultural landscape can best be understood only in the context of local resource abundance and variability as utilized by families and communities. The discussion of subsistence in the lowlands of the Mid-Sound presented herein focuses on information that has been assembled from less-known primary sources, although more readily available published sources are also noted. It is not meant to be an exhaustive overview of local subsistence data. Although the discussion is focused on the greater Seattle area, reference is made to other locations within the Puget Sound basin in order to provide more complete coverage.

Most of the data for Puget Sound was collected by Arthur Ballard, expanding from Muckleshoot to a variety of elders: Duwamish were Charles Sotaiakum, from the Cedar River and lower White River area; Mary Dominick of Muckleshoot, whose mother was Duwamish and father from a tributary of the Green River; Lucy Williams, whose mother was from the head of Elliot Bay; and Sam Wilson, from Suquamish, who had Duwamish relations (Ballard 1950: 87-90). Ballard (1950: 90-91) also relied on the field notes of Herman Haeberlin and publications by Gibbs (1877, 2017) and Smith (1940).

Encouraged by academic friends, near the end of his life, Ballard published thirty years of research on the Lushootseed calendar, as well as details about a salmon weir on the Green River. His compendium provides the basis for understanding the scheduling of subsistence activities in lieu of time frames.

Descriptive materials for Elliott Bay and adjoining drainages comes from Suquamish elders and the highly detailed but unpublished materials provided by Jerry Meeker in 1948 (Miller 2000). Meeker was a respected and wealthy Puyallup elder interviewed by Alfred John Smith, a grocer and writer gathering materials for a novel, *Old Lukh ~ Leschi in Love*. Economic data appear in Notebooks A and B, herein cited by page number. Condensed, paraphrased notes have been fleshed out, providing whole words and sentences for abbreviations and paraphrases.

Because foods and diets were localized, we begin with variations in the calendar, then describe foods and resources harvested by season within a year.

Calendar

At the base of regional interconnections was respect for nature and its bounty, according to season. The abundance of foods at different locations kept people moving over the landscape. They harvested what the earth provided and gave thanks all along the way. Native understanding of climate, tides, and winds provided a comprehensive calendar, customized for each region.

Moons were correlated with appropriate human activities, but these varied by locality and economics (Ballard 1950: 81-86). Communities along the saltwater might term these lunar periods as "<u>tide</u> of X," where inland communities recognized "<u>time</u> of X' to emphasize their own situation. Ballard (1950: 81-86) placed the X of these moons in a roughly chronological ~ sequential order, with some reference to overlaps with Gregorian calendar months. While Ballard assembled into an overall structure the terms for these moons, he removed them from any sensitive local context likely to be favored by the speakers of a specific place. In general, the terms refer to features of nature, economy, kinship, and religion. A summary listing of

English translation of these names shows seventeen seasonal divisions that begin in late February and crowd the summer.

- frog's face ~ whose appearance and croaking announces the end of winter, thaw (late February) – blowing, budding, pregnant
- flowering, calming
- salt water shining
- clamming
- salmonberries
- red elderberries
- creeping blackberries
- salal berries
- humpy salmon (alternate years)
- jack salmon {young salmon}
- silver salmon
- hops (September)
- fluttering leaves
- singing
- storming, storing paddles, taboo, starving, older sibling (December)
- younger sibling, sticking to (January) (Ballard 1950: 81-85)

Within each year – divided into cold and warm – winter and summer seasons were recognized, with localized attention always given to the arrival of particular foods, such as humpback salmon. Winter was spent in cedar plank longhouses, with most of the time devoted to religious activities. In the spring, families moved out into small groups to begin harvesting the natural bounty for immediate consumption and for preservation for winter use.

Variations were many and locally distinct. For example, salmon and other species have different names in the northern and southern dialects of Lushootseed, so the moon terms vary accordingly. Most of the activities that provide names are ancient, though a more recent addition is the hop picking season in September that was of sufficient economic importance to receive its own term, as it provided funds for family upkeep and school expenses.

Ballard remained skeptical that natives noted the movements of the moon and sun along the horizon during the year, marking the solstice and equinox, though this was specialist duty throughout the region (Miller 1992c). However, Marian Smith, whom Ballard introduced into the area, reported that women used knotted strings to keep track of phases of the moon, tracing their own menstruations and pregnancies (Smith 1940: 135). Meeker also noted that his "Mother judged month from "period" ~ kept a string on her finger for each full moon at the time the moon is full" (Meeker 1948: A57).

Typical designations for local months, known as moons, were recognized by Mid-Sound people, here correlated with Gregorian calendar months, and as spelled in Alfred Smith's notes:

December: *hequskas slugqalab* ~ big winter moon – when moon is full
January: *el soqa stas* ~ little winter moon – younger brother

February: *waqwaqos* ~ frog singing (month) -month of the frog − frogs begin to sing, if it snows it will only melt on the ground.

March: *cpospuqhegad* ~ windy month – strong south wind (tear off roots and all of trees), throwing out of winter. Don't haul on saltwater. They put up canoes and paddles. Don't go far. Only small fishing boats go out. Big canoes put up.

April: *qaqelaB* ~ resting easy, relax – good weather, refurbishing time = get tackle, etc. Relax from the tiring winter.

May: *padhadab* = summer is May, pad = becoming {pəd-}

June {July}: hadab = summer, lumped together because it is always warm

August: *padtulos* Autumn is [blank]

September: [blank] becoming fall weather, grass will grow

October: [blank]

November: [blank] (Meeker 1948: A56-57)

The terms "stowing, laying low, staying off the water, keeping quiet," are common throughout the Sound in referring to the month of December (Ballard 1950: 84). They are applied to late winter/early spring (March) and are tied to the epic story of The Winds.

John Adams at Suquamish said,

> They had names for the different times of the year: ƙaqlab means everything was nice and quiet now, about May; *alska* meant older brother and was December, followed by əłsoqʷa, younger brother; *waq̇aq̇os* was when the frogs started in February or March; *pal'xʷay* was dog salmon time in October; *paƚkoli* was in the fall when they started to dry salmon and pick huckleberries; and *pədhədəb* was the summer months of June, July, and August when they picked berries (Miller with Snyder 1999: 111, Appendix F).

Wilson George, also at Suquamish, said that the coldest part of the year was called xaʔxaʔ, followed by a month named Younger Brother because it wasn't as cold and the weather was milder (Miller with Snyder 1999: 110). Early December was called *šičalwas* – put away, stowing your paddles. This was the time when they stopped hunting and fishing.

Each day was tracked by the progress of shadows, while the year itself was marked by a ten-foot pole set up on Yelm prairie along the Nisqually River (Smith 1940: 135). There four or five stakes set along a circle showed the progress of the sun over a day (and presumably a year). The recently identified sky stone overlooking Alderton also seems to have astronomical alignments (Gerald Hedlund, pc 11 May 2000). Other sky observatories made from carved stump seats are reported for the Northwest Coast (Miller 1992c).

However, in the Northwest, winds and tides generally provide better information than the gray and rainy skies. Indeed, all people in the drainage understood the tides sufficiently so that those upriver arrived on beaches in time to take advantage of winter low tides for clam digging.

Specific accounts of food-gathering activities clearly vary according to the individual, particularly in terms of gender and geographical affiliation. Each moon or month was devoted to a particular activity:

No body ever went hungry. Always can get something fresh. Something to eat any time. Never heard of anybody among Indians starving to death. Lots of all kinds of dry meats, fish, berries, clams. And one could always get something fresh (Meeker 1948: A69).

The following calendar of monthly tasks was provided by Wilson George at Suquamish (Miller with Snyder 1999: 110), beginning with summer when people are camping:

July = spent drying clams, catching early salmon, and picking blackberries, blackcaps, red huckleberries, and red elderberries

August = continuing to dry clams, pick salal berries, eat fresh summer dog and humpy salmon (not good for drying), and hunt for fattened deer

September to October = much activity with the fall salmon runs, the beginning of duck hunting, and picking huckleberries

November = had things winding down except for taking ducks

December = start of sacred season, first games and ceremonies, although they still dug some clams and took bottom fish from canoes heated with banked fires inside

January to February = spent at ceremonies and visiting

March = beginning of salmon returns

May = salmonberries and red elderberries, with some camas dug on Smith Island, steamed or kept dry in a basket

June to July = brought salmon trout, with some dried after it was cooked

A variant yearly cycle at Suquamish (Miller with Snyder 1999: 111-112) is:

June to July = picking and drying blackberries, traveling to the areas where they were found and living in summer camps, little fishing then, women berrying and men hunting. Women dried berries and meat, along with cockles, horse clams, and butter clams

August = picking and drying salal berries, stored in deer intestines. Men went hunting, started getting ducks

September = fall salmon runs, silver and tyee (king), moved to the streams where salmon were going up, to build dams {weirs} across them and spear fish to be sliced and smoke dried. Body was split and held open with cedar sticks. There were no berries now. Women busy drying salmon, also getting and drying clams. Men hunting ducks, eaten fresh not preserved.

October = ate fresh huckleberries, worked hard catching and drying dog salmon. Men started fishing for smelt and continued through early December.

December = There was little doing, cold weather and snow brought the people back to the winter villages for ceremonies

January to February = herring started to run in late January and continued into early March. They were caught and dried, together with spring {King} salmon {differing by dialect as southern Lushootseed ~ Whulshootseed *saċəb*, and northern Lushootseed *yubeč* when fresh and ʼtalu?b when dried

March to April = no particular fishing, mostly hunting. People remain in the permanent winter villages.

May = left winter villages and went to various camping areas. Salmonberries ripe, eaten fresh and not dried. Salmonberry sprouts eaten with dried salmon eggs. Only went for bottom fish (flounder, sole, and skate), available year around. Bad month for doe because fawns were on the way, so only killed bucks

In November, adults devoted time to creek fishing, as children got late huckleberries or cranberries (Meeker 1948: B40-49). Women began making baskets and mats. Once foods were in storage, men of a community might undertake a raid for slaves and booty. By December, everyone was back in their winter homes ready for the ceremonial season and feasting. Winter was occupied with dramatic events that included *spədak* enactments, gambling, dances, and gatherings to cure those who were "sick to sing" their power songs.

Seasons as reported by women contain more detail on the cultivation of plant resources. Berry patches were burned over to encourage fresh growth in the spring and abundant harvests in the fall. Roots were stored in baskets cached in the ground, while baskets full of berries were placed in cold streams (Miller 1999: 85). Hazelnuts were kept loose in big baskets (Meeker 1948: A60).

Julia Jacobs, the mother of Lawrence Webster, said that cattails were gathered in the fall, about September. They were best then because they were strong and stiff. They grew at Jefferson Head, at Indianola just west of Julia's home, at Richmond Beach, at Edmonds, and at the mouth of the Duwamish, where they were best of all before the Army Corps straightened and paved the sides. All of these places were harvested from their canoes.

They were spread and dried in the sun. When dry, they were split into strings. They took a cattail, doubled it, and then rubbed it on the thigh under a hand. This string was tied into the hole in the needle. The other dried cattails were laid side by side on the ground. They used string to tie the ends of the cattails together. When these were secured, they ran a long wooden needle into rows of cattails lying on the ground and pulled the thread through. They used several needles to make holes at even intervals along each cattail. When all of the needles were in place, they turned the mat over and sewed it on the other side. They used the mats for beds, piled several layers thick to be about six inches. They rolled up mats to make pillows (Miller with Snyder 1999: 115).

Throughout Puget Sound, women cultivated root and berry plots in meadows and tended shellfish beds. It appears that some plots were owned, in the sense that the same woman or family members returned to them year after year. This kind of ownership has limited documentation, such as clam beds along Swinomish beaches (Miller 1999: 35) and plots of tiger lily and wild carrots along the Skagit River (Collins 1974: 55-57). However, among most Puget Sound groups, women acknowledge that they inherited knowledge from their mothers and grandmothers about cultivation practices at specific traditionally used locations. Other tended plants included camas, several types of ferns (bracken fern, swordfern, etc), wapato, willow, and lichen (Norton 1980, 1990; Turner 1975).

Harvesting

The waters, meadows, and forests of Puget Sound basin provided natives with an abundance of varied foods. Information about fish, shellfish, game, and berries dominates the ethnographic record, summarized below from the Jerry Meeker (1948) notebooks, for the Mid-Sound area. Harvesting most of these foods took place in the summer and fall months, approximately May to November.

Fish ~ Salmon were the staple throughout the region, with locales and techniques controlled by leading families, along with specialized gear, such as stationary weirs and trolling locations, lines, and hooks. About May, people began trolling from canoes for king salmon, following the runs as they went upstream in July. In June and July natives congregated in Commencement Bay[38] for the start of fish runs.

Large weirs made of poles were set across rivers to trap migrating salmon. Ballard (1957) gives a detailed study of a weir on the Green River, though the same type of weir, with modifications, was present in the major river drainages of southern and eastern Puget Sound. Five major traps were set along the Puyallup River. Nordquist (1963) compiled information, photographs, and drawing of several large weirs in Puget Sound for comparison with an ancient trap buried at the outlet of a small tributary of the Snoqualmie River.

The salmon weir was a partial barrier in the river (Bagley 1929: 744; Ballard 1957: 38), placed to impound migrating salmon in sufficient numbers for processing and storage for the winter months. Never build across the entire channel, a side route allowed salmon escapement for purposes of spawning for succeeding years.

Weir construction began by setting Douglas fir timber tripods into the riverbed (Ballard 1957: 38), with the number and series depending on the width of the stream. This assemblage was often placed at a bend in the river with a high bank at one side and a low bank on the other, with the largest and sturdiest tripod set in the middle of the stream (Bagley 1929: 744).

Horizontal V braces were lashed to each tripod both to give it stability and to serve as the floor of the scaffold platform where a fisherman stood (Ballard 1957: 39-40). Tripod tops extended ten to twelve feet above this brace. Runways of timbers across the stream were lashed against the tripods, served both as further braces and as walkways for fishermen. A series of pointed stakes like fencing rested against this runway, as well as additional suspended timbers that also served as footrests. Timbers set horizontally across the bottom of the weir added strength to it. Webbed sections of wattle screen, later chicken wire, held in place by the current,

---

[38] Named for the start point of Lt Peter Puget's 1792 survey of the Sound for Capt George Vancouver.

rested against this bottom log and suspended timbers. Trash had to be removed from these screens on a regular basis, to allow for free flow of water.

The dip net was the essential fishing implement, made of a vine maple hoop and cordage from pussy willow bark or nettle fiber. Cross-arms holding the net were two straight, lashed together fir poles. The dip net was lowered from the tripod platform to the bottom of the stream, then lifted up when the fisherman felt a salmon enter the net. The fish was pulled up to the floor of the platform, clubbed, and placed into a canoe.

Each weir had a manager, just as the fishery in each river was managed to assure that those furthest upriver and last in line would not be shortchanged. A dozen men qualified as specialists by possessing the skill and spiritual aid vital to build a river weir in a fast, frigid current. Children helped gather the necessary materials, and women assembled the fence and screens on the bank, as these men emplaced the crucial supporting tripods. Every late spring these traps washed away, and then had to be rebuilt after high water peaked.

Although salmon could be caught during daylight if the water was murky, more commonly fishing began mid-afternoon and continued through the night. Also customarily, some fencing was removed during the day to allow more salmon to continue upstream for capture or spawning.

Two to four men could fish with dipnets at one time, and a scaffold floor could hold 20-30 salmon. When the full canoe load was brought to shore, fish were apportioned by the leader's wife among the women of her village to be cleaned and prepared for their families. She gave to all the women of leading house first, then to the poorer peoples, and lastly to outsiders.

Only the rich could own and use dip nets because the hemp cordage used was very scarce and had to be purchased with slaves. Heavily processed, it was red brown in color like cedar bark and had to be dried, cured, and shredded. Net mesh size was carefully calculated depending on the size and motions of the intended fish species.

Commoners traveled to the fishing sites with their leaders as part of their village). They worked steadily, but tried to do extra work for the chief and his family (leader's house group), bringing them extra water and firewood. Women cooked for the leaders and their guests because leaders were busy entertaining and making decisions. Young men volunteered to fish for people who were too old, fearful, or uncoordinated. Commoners helped serve the food to guests. Poor people were told when they could use the fish traps.

The first catch was served as a First Salmon Feast for everybody, including the poor. "One of these big summer salmon could feed 30-35 people – with dry berries." After two weeks, the builders had enough fish, and the weir was left to the poor and outsiders. When saltwater people could not get any more salmon in Puget Sound, they visited upriver traps to get fish by their own efforts. Such visitors stayed a week or ten days, then moved on to berrying or clamming grounds.

If someone's weir was briefly not in use, it was appropriate to lend it to someone in need. When the owner of a dip-net was out of fish, whoever borrowed and used his net would leave enough fish from his own catch for the owner's daily needs. If this were not done, they might be refused further use of the trap and net. Ballard (1967) reported incidents of retaliation against weirs that were misused or greedy.

Poor people who could not afford weirs or trolling gear, but did have the use of woven basketry traps. An average size was 7-12 feet long. A large family or multiple families shared one over 14 feet long, with a 2-foot-wide mouth, while a single family used a 6-feet-long basket trap. The largest trap would be owned by a whole household. After men cut the sticks, women tied and wove the trap together. If terrain were level, people on a stream would make a small dam weir of 34 foot-long slats, as scaled down versions of those that extended across rivers.

Conical traps twisted of cedar boughs by children were placed at the mouths of streams to catch fresh salmon in intertidal waters. Kids splashed upstream to drive fish backwards into the funnel. Older children also sat in the stream with their legs spread apart, catching and throwing fish onto the bank. Sometimes fish could be clubbed in the water. Fishing in the creeks continued into November. Salmon were hooked out with gaff hooks only during daytime.

A fisherman never packed or cleaned his own fish. His wife carried them from the canoe and cleaned them. Each salmon species at each catch location provided different flavors and preservation qualities, whether dried or smoked. King (*tyee* in Chinuk jargon) salmon was summer food and only half-dried and smoked for short term use. Humpy salmon spoiled too quickly and worms got into the fat next to the skin so they had to be eaten right away, roasted before the fire. Silver salmon crumbles if dried so it was eaten fresh like humpies and never preserved for winter. To keep it for a time, it was sometimes half smoked, half dried, then heated and eaten. Jack (young) salmon was sometimes dried and smoked for a few days, then put in baskets to be used as trip food ~ journey snacks.

People wanted the fat dog salmon. Although the dog salmon were never as fat as the summer salmon, they were preferred for preservation. However, dog salmon that had been more than a week or so in fresh water were mushy and not eaten. Males were the best because they were not as thin as the females became after laying eggs.

About November, dog salmon was dried and stored in loosely woven baskets, each about 3 feet long by 2 feet wide. These baskets held 60-80 salmon packed close together in fillets. Dog salmon were the preferred staple winter food. Heads were dried and put in baskets for making soups later.

When smelt, herring, and other small fish spawned near a beach, a coarsely-woven drag of cedar or hazel branches was used to take fish. A herring rake, with pegs set along one long side, was used for smelt and other smaller fish running in schools.

When fat summer salmon or porpoise were cooked before a fire, dripping oil was collected into clam shells, stored in deer bladders hung up away from the fire, and later used as a dip for dried salmon.

In the fall, people took ling cod, sole, flounder, and skate, as well as marine mammals such as porpoise and seal. Some bottom fish were taken at night. Flounder beds were privately known and fished. Teenage boys went with men to help paddle and steer the canoe while an adult man speared the flounder.

Whenever people gathered and worked hard, as they did during fishing, the off hours were devoted to lively diversions like gambling and visiting. Children played games of all kinds. Usually, only people related would come together. Visiting outsiders would be welcomed, so long as they knew them or knew about them. They would let strangers stay overnight if it got dark, provided they asked permission to stay, but then they had to move on.

Shellfish ~ In April, May, June, July, women dug and dried butter and horse clams. They dug using an ironwood dibble ~ digging stick sharpened at either end so it could be reversed.

The number of basket-loads filled depended on family size and degree of generosity expected of it within the community. Drying clams was a big job. Women did the digging and smoking, though the men got wood to feed the drying fires.

A drift log served as a heat reflector behind a fire that was 30-40 feet long, helping to cook clams inserted onto sticks and set vertically beside the fire. Each stick was about two feet long, holding 20 butter clams or 10 horse clams. When fully smoked, these clams were strung onto strands of cedar inner bark, each one holding the contents of two sticks. These strings were then spread over a cribwork roof of crossed-sticks, and left for another week ~ 10 days of further smoke flavoring. The clams were then layered between fern branches in a basket. Usually, a woman stored between 15 and 20 baskets in one season.

During the lowest tides, four times a year "lots June, second in July" people dug geoduck clams. Most were eaten fresh, though some were dried as food snacks for traveling. Other foods included China slippers, devil fish (octopus), and mussels. Oysters were eaten fresh, not dried.

Game ~ Men hunted whenever meat was scarce, but large hunts were held in the fall and winter. Deer was hunted most commonly, whereas elk was not regular fare.[39] Most deer and elk were taken in snares, set along a runway ~ game trail, made of looped hazel branches. Sometimes a sapling was bent over the trail with a slip knot at the end. A series of deep pits were also dug into a path and concealed. Such traps also served for bears, taken for food, grease, and hide. Other game that was trapped included the land otter, mink, beaver, cougar, wolf, coyote, and raccoon – taken mostly for their pelts. Smaller animals like squirrel and beaver were shot with bow and arrows, sometimes clubbed.

Hunters working together dispersed, some to wait along a runway trail, while others scared up game, and yet others made an animal bolt in a particular direction. In April, fawns were killed for their tender meat, fed to toothless elders, and soft skins. A hunter lured the fawn by blowing across a grass leaf held tightly between thumbs pressed against adjacent index fingers.

If hunters got lots of game, they had slaves and others to help pack the quartered meat out. If hunters had time, they carried some fresh meat home, but usually they got someone to go after it. Young men were eager to go so as to appear as successful hunters. For winter, a family tried to put up almost as much meat as dry salmon. In November, a group of hunters might camp out for two weeks to jerky enough meat. Everything was saved and used, even the blood. A camp was always near a stream to make the rinsing of butchering easier and the camp cleaner.

Venison was cut thin and dried in the hunting camp, then carried into the winter house in bundles tied at the ends with cedar boughs. Elk, deer, and bear meat was best if jerked – dried and smoked enough to prevent spoilage, sliced thin, and then dry cached. Deer tallow was kept in a bladder and used by women for dressing their faces, sometimes mixed with red paint as a cosmetic. Tanned elk and deer hides served for moccasins, clothing, and bed covers (Meeker 1948: A64). Bearskin was favored for hats.

---

[39] Of note, although the historical ethnography indicates that elk was not regular fare, elk bones are found in archaeological sites with such frequency that they must have been hunted at a time when they yarded in the lowlands during winters.

Ducks were snared in an aerial reef net 14 feet long by 5 feet wide that was looped onto twelve-feet tall stakes in such a manner that allowed it to rise and fall with each tide change. As the ducks floated out with the tide, they would dive under the net but the narrow mesh acted like a gill net to restrain their heads and drown them. Other nets were stretched in the air at flyways, to snare ducks when they were flying low at dawn or dusk.

Bows and arrows were also used to hunt birds, which were also taken with spears during night hunts when a pitchwood fire burned upon a layer of soil set on the bottom of a canoe. This fire both attracted and blinded the waterfowl. Historically, the spear was 6 feet long with a head of ironwood, secured with hemp cord, and covered with boiled fir pitch. Bone points of deer or elk had been used for spearheads, attached by string to the shaft.

Natives recognized six duck species known as black ~ rubber back, orange nose, mallard, butterball, widgeon, and brown head. Sometimes, ducks were clubbed with a paddle. Three types of geese – white ~ snow, Canadian, and brant – were trapped by net or loop snare.

Blue and ruffled grouse, locally called "pheasants," were hunted and eaten in the early fall. When "housed-up" hidden into trees during winter, they could be taken in large numbers with bow and arrows. Birds generally were not jerked or smoked, but eaten fresh.

Berries ~ Berry harvests in the Puget Lowland began in late June and July, often associated with fishing, hunting, and clam harvesting. Fall berrying was more intensive, accompanied by mushroom gathering. While women and children picked berries, men were fishing and hunting. Boys and girls had to be at least 14-16 years old to pick berries any distance away from adult activities. Younger children picked close to camp.

Women worked in groups to pick berries and dry them in the sun, putting up mat roofs if it rained. A fire set under the drying rack also smoke flavored berries. When partly dried, berries were compacted into large watertight baskets woven of cedar roots and bark, each holding about 20 gallons. A smooth rock, shaped like a dumbbell with a thin grip, was used to mash the berries, pressing out juice.

Blackberry pulp was made into dried cakes, usually six inches round, sometimes an 8-inch oval, about 1-inch thick. The cakes were further dried inside on a rack, sometimes also smoked, before being stored in medium-sized openwork baskets, 3-feet wide and long by 2-feet high. These were soft baskets, but water tight, with loopholes along the top to hold the string securing a tied down lid. A woman tried to have 2 to 3 baskets full of blackberry cakes. For six people, half of one blackberry cakes was mashed in water, sometimes mixed half and half with salal berries, and served as a sweet.

Salal berries were picked, smoked, and dried in August to be stored in small watertight baskets for use as "Indian sugar."

Blue huckleberries were picked October to November, smoked, dried, and stored in the same manner as salal berries. Red huckleberries ripened in August were eaten fresh, but never dried since then they had a dull taste.

Wild cranberries were harvested from local bogs in late fall, with women and children doing most of the work.

6 ~ KINSCAPE

Kinship binds communities, enabling reliable survivance in good and bad times. Kin groupings (corporate ~ bilateral ~ cognatic) among Coast Salish have benefited from studies of kinship in Southeast Asia as well as the central Northwest Coast, exploring increasingly more inclusive (and diffuse) family-based groupings. Traced through both father and mother are **kindreds**, variously either **nodal** for lower ranks or **stem** for their high social class. These further diffuse into a **sept**, traced bilaterally over a wide region for at least four generations, regardless of where members were living. These kinspeople interacted with members of nearby comparable units – in rituals, games, feasts, and marriages – to form "overlapping intervillage social units, which Wayne Suttles,[40] with some misgivings, called kithreds, referring to kith of country or neighborhood. Herein they are called **intersepts**. Residence relies on claims to these various memberships, which are not themselves localized since claims to places are based in hereditary names verging on titles that originate at a specific place and time.

Salish kinship (Appendix G) is proposed to be prototype for all Native America because its "distinctive ... bilateral organization" and "variability in regard to rules of residence," made it "more widely distributed in North America than any other type of social organization," suggesting it was "the original type from which most other North American systems have arisen"[41] as defined by gender, age, and decedence = whether a linking relative was dead or alive (see next chapter).

Various geographical, linguistic, and residential considerations formed what has been called the "tribe," though this term has become discredited among academics, even as it has become enshrined in federal Indian Law.[42] Instead, each watershed ~ basin ~ drainage embraced cultural overlaps that were tribally and linguistically distinct. Elite intermarriages and social interactions, especially name conferrals, further confounded notions of firm tribal boundaries.

Hereditary names, especially renowned ones, serve as the labels for these groupings, though some moderating consideration is always given to the moral qualities of inherited traits, such as "good or bad" blood (*stulig^wəd*)[43] and family resemblances traced as body peculiarities, abilities, and personalities. Jerry Meeker's own *lehaldx^w* name is a good example, because its preceding holders had lived on both sides of the Cascade Mountains and spoke languages of very different stocks, but, as Jerry noted, hearing that name immediately identified its original locale and sept as anchored at a specific Nisqually town.

Kinship links – traced through both father and mother – aligned Lushootseeds into discrete *kindreds* – bilateral = kinship traced through both sides of a family located within

---

[40] Wayne Suttles, *Coast Salish Essays* 1987: 221, note 5.

[41] George Peter Murdock, Algonkian Social Organization, *Context and Meaning in Cultural Anthropology* 1965: 31.

[42] A tribe is now regarded by many academics as an unstable transitional stage, caused by colonialism, after the breakdown of a chiefdom, between a band and a chiefdom, but it remains the preferred native term based on common homeland, language, and social patterns. Lawyers and judges continue to insist on its use in courts because its political meanings are embedded in federal law.

[43] Its derivation seems to be *tul-* = flow *-ig^wəd* = inside body, *LD*: 115, 230.

households. In most cases, each formed a "nodal kindred," where the node was a bond of parent and children or, after those antecedent's death, that of siblings, often brothers who jointly owned a winter house. For most families, a kindred had cohesion only as long as it had a dominant node, sometimes expressed as attenuated family prestige derived from previously hosted events.

Of particular note, however, was the permanent node based in an elite name, the basis for a *stem kindred* which continued over time because succeeding holders of that name stemmed across generations. Since the system was and is bilateral, the actual inheritance of that name was optional, to some extent – passed to the kinsperson with the best success in upholding overall kindred honor, prestige, reputation, and generosity. All those publicly aligned with and accepted by the "stem name" comprised the diffuse *sept*.

Tracing kinship bilaterally makes for large numbers of relatives. Siblingship, however, counted foremost, so that the birth order of ancestors continued to apply down the generations. The child of an older brother was always senior to the child of a younger one. Kin were regarded as either close or near, literally as q̓ʷu'šəd 'feet together' and iišəd 'feet near'.[44]

Important families asked their leader's opinion before sending out messages of intent for a betrothal or marriage. They consulted with the rest of the family, for all to agree. By receiving approval from leaders, this marriage was protected from the bickering that often damaged hasty arrangements, and could escalate into violence.[45] Gifts were given to parents, who gave something of value, often a new canoe, in return to the new couple. Especially prestigious gifts were blankets woven of mountain goat wool (*gʷasdolitsa*). Fur from a special breed of woolly dog also produced valuable robes. George Gibbs, while living at Fort Steilacoom and assembling his Nisqually dictionary, had a pet woolly dog named Mutton, whose hide has been at the Smithsonian for over a century. A medium-size dog, this pelt serves to correct the prior misunderstanding that woolly dogs were small.

Twin Kindreds

To rephrase with more precision, in addition to considerations of personal identity as free or slave, Lushootseeds traced kinship through the "bloodlines" of both parents.[46] The immediate family grouping (derived from four grandparents) is technically called a *kindred*, while the huge

---

[44] *LD*: 197.

[45] Brothers were obligated to protect their sisters and avenge reports, even rumors, of wife abuse. Rank, honor, industry, and respect were important considerations. Two contrasting examples are the attack at Fort Nisqually by Patkanim, Snoqualmie leader, and his many brothers in response to the rumored domestic distress of their sister. A local white, Leander Wallace, was killed by accident, leading to the imposition of US justice and the hanging of two brothers. By contrast, during her brief first marriage to an Upper Skagit, Angeline, Chief Seattle's famous daughter, raised pampered, was publicly denounced as lazy by her husband and immediately returned home.

[46] June Collins, Multilineal Descent: A Coast Salish Strategy 1979: 243-254. Twana, compact along Hood Canal, named these kinship units, as kindred (*sčəla'*), blood relations, and inlaws (affines), William Elmendorf, *The Structure of Twana Culture* 1960: 327, 348.

extended family, which was and is transnational ~ intertribal (through eight great grandparents), is herein called an *intersept*.

Among ordinary kinspeople, a *nodal kindred* formed around its senior member, often the grandparents as a long-married couple. After the death of the last surviving spouse, the kindred regrouped around their children, siblings led by the eldest, if fit and able, and so on through a generation or two. Leading families, however, formed a *stem kindred*, which continued across generations because the stem consisted of the line of holders of its famous name, conferring control of locations and resources that made up the "estate" of these nobles. Influence from Wakashans of Vancouver Island may have fostered occasional *ramages*, descent based on birth order, especially a seriated line of eldest sons or eldest daughters who were expected to intermarry with first-borns to maintain the *ramage* rank.

Traced through all of the bloodlines of great grandparents, a *sept* had its own network that even now extends beyond space and time, as a "nondiscrete, nonlocalized, property-holding group",[47] existing wherever and whenever its members lived and including ancestors from the past and children yet unborn. It had no fixed size nor place, except in family lore explaining the origin locale of its famous names. It was managed by the oldest able elder (male or female), who provided guidance about the proper use and conservation of resources, as well as the transmission of names, positions, *dicta*, heirlooms, and artifacts within the kindred.

If it contained a famous name, stories about past holders of that name and their fea(s)ts served to specify places where the kindred indeed had a birthright through past actions, particularly on-going partnerships between the spirits of these places and family members. The most powerful spirits dwell in most remote locations, either high up in mountains or deep in water, either ocean or river. Its most prized possession is 'wisdom' ($x^w dik^w$, also advice, teachings, know-how, lore), which included special formulae (*dicta*) to control activities for good or ill, genealogical details, and epics from the beginning of time and at crucial junctures.[48]

Household

Spaces along the four walls of a house were usually assigned by rank. The high born were in the sheltered back, nobles in the corners, ordinary commoners along the sides, and slaves exposed in the doorway, though they could never really claim any place as their own. Ranks were also assigned to separate houses in a town. "Poor" houses included a few nobles as leaders, but were tainted by this mixing of classes.

Senior siblings, as nominal owners of a house, lauded themselves by carving and painting evocations of their spirits on the houseposts located in the center or corners of the house. Painted houseposts were the rule; carved ones were the exception. In addition, a strong leader might arrange for the building of an especially large house, called a "potlatch house" in English, where s/he and kindred hosted public events and out-of-town guests were billeted. It was just this ability to accommodate large influxes of invited people that defined a central native town (a hub) and great leader. Only the prime house of a town would invite in outsiders, while "poor" houses invited only other locals. Some towns also included special buildings, such as the Minter

---

[47] Wayne Suttles, *Coast Salish Essays* 1987: 210.
[48] That Salish Feeling … , Vi taq^{w}šəblu Hilbert and Jay Miller 2004.

"schoolhouse" that was over 100 feet long, where training, eating contests and winter dances were held, attended by large crowds until these were devastated by epidemics and slaving raids.

Successful efforts had to be sanctioned by an immortal's blessing, for either career or curing abilities. While any of these "spirits" could provide a career, only the most powerful, for good or bad, gave doctors the ability to cure or to kill. Any large community was sustained by many career specialists, organized by its leaders, and both healed and protected by its doctors. Among Twana eat-all visitors was a man with Lizard power that enabled him to return the wandering spirit of a Minter woman from Mt Rainier. In thanks, Damasq, herself town leader and wife of the acting headman, passed out valued dentalia shells to these visitors.

Overall, therefore, while Lushootseed people have adopted more goods, clothes, boats, and housing of mainstream society, their most creative survivance response to Euro-American society has been in terms of religion, beliefs about their place in the universe, epitomized by the joint efforts of John and Mary Slocum to found the Shaker Church after 1882.

Indeed, Sound natives coped well with the pivotal economic presence during the first half of the 1800s of the British-ruled Hudson Bay Company, trading for furs and labor at Fort Nisqually, built in 1833 in the heart of Whulshootseed territory. Problems increased, however, when American squatters, settlers, and would-be homesteaders, encouraged and bankrolled by commercial lumber and mining operations shipping to California (especially San Francisco), took over their lands by fair means and foul under the color~cover of title and "protection" of Anglo law. Co-resident in an area, these settlers knew only too well when villagers would move away during seasonal rounds to garner foods elsewhere, leaving their homes unprotected and ready for arson by white neighbors intent on homesteading an already developed location.

Intersept (~ Kithred)

Living along waterways facilitated frequent interactions, except where hostile intent or enforced tariffs set up native obstructions ("tollgates"). Throughout the entire Northwest Coast, its commonalities were never homogeneous, but rather the result of a complex series of overlappings with neighboring communities of diverse ancestral languages. Suttles,[49] with misgivings, called them "kithreds," derived from Old English "couth" for familiar country and neighbors, though "intersept" (punning on "intersect, intercept") seems more apt. Renowned hereditary names come to the fore in these networks since prestige relies heavily on standing in allied communities, in turn, reinforcing status and rank at home. Underpinning such prestige was a valued currency of wealth that included slaves, canoes, goat ~ dog wool blankets, fur robes, pelts (especially of sea otter), clubs, dentalia, and, after European traders, guns, factory blankets, and silver dollars.[50]

Elmendorf insightfully highlighted five overlapping population networks, from Chinook to Klallam, for Twanas, living in their more discrete territory, and his findings apply equally well throughout the coastline. These *intersepts*, moving outward throughout the southern Salish Sea, were concerned with local eating contests, disk gambling games, elite intermarriages, secret society ~ guild initiations, or warfare at more remote locales. In corroboration, Suttles plotted

---

[49] Wayne Suttles, *Coast Salish Essays* 1987: 221, note 5.
[50] William Elmendorf, *The Structure of Twana Culture* 1960: 331.

genealogies centered from Musqueam to show overlapping intersepts among neighboring Coast Salish, as Dorothy Kennedy[51] has done from a Squamish standpoint further to the north.

Maps and charts in the *Sto:lō Atlas* also add a totemic dimension since certain families in various communities trace their ancestry to a sky being or a transformed primordial Animal, as either progenitor or patron.[52] Leading families across *intersepts*, sharing the same totem, regardless of language or locale, use its image as their identifier, often bolstered by an epic account of their common origins. At Gig Harbor, beyond Tacoma Narrows, residents traced descent from transformed Killerwhales, marked by two rocks, a big one representing the mother Orca and a flat one as a platter where food offerings were daily left for her and her family. Puget Sound tribes ~ drainages also had their own totems, such as Beaver at Sauk, Thunderbird at Puyallup, Cetacean at Snohomish, and Bear at Skykomish.

Families forged links by seasons. During summer economic efforts, families moved widely, camping with chosen kin for companionship in the work of harvesting from nature. During winter, families hosted key members of their networks at public events, where they were housed, fed, and gifted. Leading families with renowned names, like the wealthy everywhere, had more than one cedar plank home[53] to strategically take advantage of local natural resources as well as travel routes. Their hospitality to guests and visitors bolstered their reputations.

In-laws were particularly important both for extending far-flung, radiating connections and for their role in transforming food into wealth. Blood relatives had to be fed and supported without reserve or question, while in-laws stood at a remove such that a return gift was expected when they were given food. In consequence, in-laws served to turn perishable foods into more permanent wealth goods able to sustain family prestige and rank over time.

The extent of the later 1800s Minter network is shown by its range of marriage ties as well as the final dispersal of community members among neighbors. Meekers settled at Puyallup, where Jerry advanced church, school, carpentry, and sales into his own prosperity. Tyee George, though Suquamish, also moved to the Puyallup Valley, and his granddaughter married among the Klallam. Speym went to North Bay on the other side of the Key Peninsula at the head of Case Inlet, then later took land on the Squaxin Island Reservation. Hawk, Damasq's grandson, settled at Skokomish on Hood Canal.[54] Hummelgood married into Duwamish and had kin at Muckleshoot, though he stayed at Joe's Bay (~ Lake Bay) and joined Mary Sloane and family when they dried fish at Glencove, and sometimes back at Minter, which continued to feed its residents even after they could not live there all winter. Jimmy Cross's family dispersed. He had married Betsy, a Nisqually woman, and moved to the Puyallup Valley. His one grandchild at Muckleshoot, George Cross, had children there, while his brother Silas Cross and family lived in the Puyallup valley. Descendants also moved over the globe during the past century. Jerry's grandsons fought in Asia and Italy during WW II, and one married an Italian Catholic bride.

---

[51] Dorothy Kennedy, Looking for the Tribe in the Wrong Places: An Examination of the Central Coast Salish Social Network, 1993; Threads to the Past: The Construction and Transformation of Kinship in the Coast Salish Social Network 2000.

[52] Keith Thor Carlson, *A Sto:lō and Coast Salish Historical Atlas* 2001: 25.

[53] William Elmendorf, *The Structure of Twana Culture* 1960: 271.

[54] Hawk's wedding to Emily Hines and move to Skokomish is mentioned by Edwin Chalcraft, *Assimilation's Agent* 2004: 110.

Kin

Comparisons

Canadian Coast Salish recognized both owned property and "commons," which applied to "hunting territories, clam beaches, fishing grounds, camas and wapato areas, berry patches, and weir sites".[55] Corporate-owned properties include "sturgeon and salmon fishing sites, clam beds, cranberry bogs, wapato ponds, Indian carrot plots, camas grounds, egg-gathering sites, waterfowl refuges, bear-hunting areas, sea mammal hunting sites, and mountainous areas where mountain goats were hunted".[56] On Vancouver Island and the mainland, "the types of descent group-owned marine, intertidal and riverine resource areas include clam gathering areas, raised duck-net sites, bird-nesting areas, islets for sea-mammal hunting, reef-net fishing sites, fishing rocks in the Fraser Canyon, fish weir sites on the Cowichan River, sturgeon trap sites, and some of the small fishing streams and bays."[57] Pentlatch at Comox Harbor owned a burial grove, where coffins were set by heights in accord with rank.[58] Claims to clam gardens were asserted by rock walls built along the sideshore.[59] Within prairies, burnt-over regularly, women of a matriline, regardless of where they were married or living, inherited rights to tended plant gardens.[60] Overlap was expected; elders and lawyers have recently argued that firm boundaries are a colonialist tactic to disadvantage First Nations.[61]

The key role of the *House* is much debated by academics, with Kennedy[62] denying it any validity. Physically, this building served as "food processing and storage, workshop, recreation center, temple, theatre, and fortress".[63] Among the matrilineal northern tribes, the house is the pervasive unit, and its influence was felt to the south, where some communities strove to assert claims to a similar but unique house as an aspiration rather than an ingrained routine. Thus, standout examples include the Whale House (*saɬultxʷ*) comprised of five high ranking Comox communities near Cape Mudge,[64] and, especially, the famous Demarked House of the Snoqualmies east of Seattle.[65]

---

[55] Kennedy, Threads to the Past: The Construction and Transformation of Kinship in the Coast Salish Social Network 2000: 323.

[56] Kennedy, Threads to the Past: The Construction and Transformation of Kinship in the Coast Salish Social Network 2000: 204.

[57] Brian Thom, Coast Salish Senses of Place: Dwelling, Meaning, Power, Property and Territory in the Coast Salish World 2005: 308. These data are used despite potential native displeasure because of his tainted near-slave status among Sto:lō.

[58] Kennedy, Threads to the Past: The Construction and Transformation of Kinship in the Coast Salish Social Network 2000: 60.

[59] Judith Williams, Clam Gardens, Aboriginal Mariculture on Canada's West Coast 2006.

[60] Kennedy, Threads to the Past 2000: 215.

[61] Thom, Coast Salish Senses of Place 2005: 390.

[62] Kennedy, Threads to the Past 2000: 329.

[63] Wayne Suttles, The Shed-Roof House, *A Time of Gathering*, 212-222, 1991: 214; Kennedy, Threads to the Past 2000: 76.

[64] Kennedy, Threads to the Past 2000: 52, based on Barnett 1955: 25.

[65] Vi Hilbert, Jay Miller, and Zalmai Zahir, *Puget Sound Geography* 2001: 178 #9.

Salish houses, repeatedly, have been called "similar in many ways to a 'House' in the sense of European nobility {holding} property, tangible and intangible, names of heaven-born First Ancestors, confidential knowledge (*sniw'*), ritual property (*ts'uxwten*), legends, songs, dances, secret words, medicinal remedies, and ceremonial prerogatives".[66] All of these are place-based, as inalienable patrimony, such that "senses of place focus attention on the connections and interrelations between myth, legend, ancestor, spirit, song, identity, language, property, territory, boundary and title".[67]

In his unpublished notes, Diamond Jenness, closely attending to his own elder interviews, carefully distinguishes between corporate ownership and the commons.

> The real political unit was therefore not the village, but the big house occupied by a number of kinsfolk – an enlarged or genealogical 'family' to which the Saanich applied the term *hunit's'lakum*, and we in speaking of the similar European nobility use the term House. Each Saanich House, as we many call it then, possessed its own long shed-roofed dwelling,[1] its own camas beds on Galiano and neighboring islands, its own set of ancestral names or titles, and its own stock of legends, songs, and medicinal remedies.[68]

The accompanying footnote expands on such privileged property:

> #1. Almost any departure from established custom might become the privilege of a House, heritable by later generations, and by them alone, provided the public had ratified it; and the public ratified it when during some potlatch it heard the statement of claim without demur and accepted the gift that followed the statement. All such privileges or rights, however, hinged upon proof of lineal descent, and the most obvious indication of such descent was the possession of an ancestral title.[69]

At Duncan, Cowichan Houses owned nearby weir sites along the river, but

> On the other hand, the sea near the villages, the hunting grounds and berry patches round about, were common property; any villager, whatever his station in life, might fish and hunt wherever he wished within the village territory.[70]

Elite families owned property that included several houses, as noted, occupied over a year at seasonal resource sites, famous art works, and claims to epics, songs, displays, and rituals. Senior members, both men and women, of elite families doubled as religious and political leaders, depending on the season. Summer was devoted to economy, and winter to

---

[66] Homer Barnett, *The Coast Salish of British Columbia* 1955: 141, 191; Jenness, Saanich fieldnotes, 1935: 52; Thom, Coast Salish Senses of Place 2005: 85.

[67] Thom, Coast Salish Senses of Place 2005: 409.

[68] Diamond Jenness, Saanich fieldnotes 1935: 29.

[69] Jenness, Saanich fieldnotes 1935: 29.

[70] Jenness, Saanich fieldnotes 1935: 29.

religion.[71] The lowest class was largely immobile, confined to a small area from birth to death, and marked by a strict provincialism.[72]

An apt comparison to Nuchahnulth ~ Nootkan kinship and noble descent indicates "The situation among the people of the West Coast is not unlike that of medieval Europe (a comparison suggested to me {a Welsh national} by a Toquaht chief) where the descent principle was fully utilized only by the elite of society and where the common people neglected to trace their genealogies the further they were removed from aristocratic rank.... In addition, both principles need not be of equal importance for all members of the group".[73]

Salish kinship interwove several factors, with age and birth order highly significant. "Relatedness to members of the society can include companionship, affinity, friendship and adoption, as well as biological ties."[74] Marriage and coordinate rank networks rely on propinquity and residency. "Effective affiliation with the elite owners of such sites required not just kin ties, but also residence, the investment of labour, and, in former times, the acquisition of an ancestral name belonging to the group represented by the elite residents ... an individual could, at any time, withdraw his allegiance by moving to another village. Similarly, an in-marrying woman attained a form of membership for the duration of her marriage. Her offspring's membership to the natal village began at birth, although a child's status required formal socialization through the bestowal of an ancestral name, usually occurring around puberty, which marked the individual as a fully-socialized adult, now capable of receiving and distributing goods."[75]

Among Central Coast Salish, the *kindred* is generally known as "one family".[76] The overall unit has been called a *sept*, but this generally means an endogamous group like a parish, though, over time, with the incest taboo, a *sept* tends to become exogamous, like the Salish *intersept* (extended kindred). In practical terms, the functional category, aptly noted for its flow, is the "bloodline."

Tribal names, illustrated by a standard Lushootseed area map of the Sound,[77] show that downriver ones usually end in *–bsh*, while those for upriver end in *–bix^w*. Of particular note, the origins of the latter suffix, which implies something basic, link it to bloodlines since "**-mix^w* = life force, "mana," person(s), animals, world, land, river; woman's breast, milk".[78] Kennedy[79]

---

[71] Kennedy, Threads to the Past: The Construction and Transformation of Kinship in the Coast Salish Social Network 2000: 7, 160, 326.

[72] Kennedy, Threads to the Past 2000: 125, from Smith, *The Puyallup-Nisqually* 1940a: 410.

[73] Susan Kenyon, The Kyuquot Way: A Study of a West Coast (Nootkan) Community 1980: 85-86.

[74] Kennedy, Threads to the Past 2000: 73.

[75] Kennedy, Threads to the Past 2000: 321-22.

[76] Called xʷənc'aləwəm in Halkomelem, xʷənc'ɛləwəng in Saanich, nch'ay'u'am in Squamish, Kennedy, Threads to the Past 2000: 163.

[77] Jay Miller, *Lushootseed Culture and the Shamanic Odyssey: An Anchored Radiance* 1999: 16.

[78] Aert Kuipers, *Salish Etymological Dictionary* 2002: 205-6, with a whole page of examples for this Proto-Salish suffix.

[79] Kennedy, Threads to the Past 2000: 50.

misconstrued this as an argument for place instead of geo-political namings, and cited two counter examples that instead, on close inspection, support the more general argument. The upriver Puyallup site[80] ending in "bsh" was located in a huge prairie that "had strong contacts with the Nisqually villages to the south of them" on saltwater. The Suquamish shoreline site[81] ending in –bix^w is associated with a place name making reference to "diarrhea," and thus with both blood and less cohesive fluids.

In all, the pursuit of ancestral land claims in British Columbia has refined our understanding of Salish kinship, property, and ecology. *Kindreds*, especially stem kindreds, retain their important role in these societies, as do larger intertribal events for confirming the prestige and pedigree of names and possessions of the septs and tribes.

Components

Salish kinship has long been remarkably flexible and versatile. Its kin ties flow from blood and sharing, while intersept ~ kithship follows from marriage and includes in-laws. Traced through both mother and father (bilaterally), kinship follows "bloodlines" that are free flowing from past to present. Its full compliment of components have yet to be fully examined, so an attempt is made here to delineate them. They include at least six features involving both nurture and nature, as well an organizational gradations from core to fringe.

DESCENT carefully traced from both parents, especially in terms of pedigree, with recognition of close kinship bonds that embrace the four 4 grandparents and eight 8 great grandparents; more distant generations might be traced through the inheritance of ancestral names within a stem kindred.

RESIDENCE at familiar resource locales associated with family members, foods, and materials. Wealthy families had more than one house, shifting with seasons, harvests, and events among their dwellings, as well as making prolonged visits to distant kin and friends. Patrilocality was preferred, with other options fully acceptable depending on various contingencies of the couple.

INCORPORATION ~ INGESTION of foods grown at particular locales and events, provided commensal (co-eating) groupings made up of the same nutrients fortifying all their bodies. Adoptees gained full membership via this process of eating locally.

LABOR contributed to the food supply by hunting and harvesting, to the construction of houses and weirs, and to hosting ceremonial events sponsored by the household, family, kindred, or sept.

CLASS ~ RANK defined by "good blood" and "unblemished" pedigree distinguished noble ranks from generic commoners, with slaves a stigmatized group not fully human. Leaders of

---

[80] Marian Smith, The Puyallup of Washington 1940b: 20 #9.

[81] Warren Snyder, *Southern Puget Sound Salish: Texts, Place Names, and Dictionary* 1968: 133 # 44.

unquestioned rank sometimes flaunted rules with impunity, proving their special status. By the same token, chiefly families provided social welfare, feeding the needy and taking in orphans or forsaken children to offer safety and security.

TOTEM as emblem, logo, and ancestor (progenitor or patron) linked a kindred to a venerable species and habitat, as well as providing vague behavioral characteristics, such a bird-like swiftness or bear-like grumbling.

INITIATION into the Growlers, *Syowin*, or certain churches confer family ties upon members, who celebrate the date of their induction as another birthday and regard their age mates as siblings (sibcuz) and treat their inductors as parents. Today, a dozen song types serve to group *Syowin* initiates according to the sharing of the same spirit with its own distinctive drumming rhythms. Formerly, all Growlers collectively shared the same patron spirit.

CORE / FRINGE gradations further define these memberships such that pivotal kin units, especially siblings, provide the nexus at the core of these groupings, with a blurring fringe along the outer limits of kin.

In all, Salish kinship interwove several factors of land and quasi-lineage, with age and birth order highly significant. Kin drew on biological ties and benefited from companionship, affinity, friendship and adoption. Intermarriage and ranked networks grew from propinquity, residence, labor, and family treasures, especially honored and ancestral names held up by the elite. One's natal village became a life-long focal point, aided by training and travel. Property and food circulated throughout the system of overlapping networks, including those of species and spirits specified in stories.

In all, survivance balanced dualities: exchanges of Uppers with Lowers, camas with salmon, old Slahal family with new chiefdom, stem with nodal kindreds; and all swirling around the lethal Falls where ancestors emerged and kinship blossomed, foiling the death of parents with decedence kin term shifts. More recently, whims of USA, BIA, and BAR, delisting the tribe in 1953, were trumped by restoration in 1999, though continuing petitions to postpone a final membership roll combine with a casino providing millions of dollars to keep them in a triumphant limbo frustrating detractors.

7 ~ DECEDENCE

A key feature of Lushootseed survivance was a special moving closer of parental bonds. Indeed, the distinctive features of Salish kinship were that it was descriptive, bilateral, and relied on factors of generation, gender, age, and **decedence** =~ whether a linking relative was dead or alive (Collins 1974: 86). While the other criteria were fairly common, decedence, a change of kin terms precipitated at the death of a linking relative, is rare. The term (as a substitute for "condition of life," the last of 8 principles listed by Kroeber in 1909) was introduced by Murdock (1949: 101) as a possible feature of classificatory kinship systems = generation, sex, affinity, collaterality, bifurcation, polarity, relative age, speaker's sex, and decedence: "the last and least important of the nine, based on the biological fact of death" (1949: 106). Because biology is basis for so much of kinship, in terms of gender and age, recognition of kin's death adds yet another dimension.

In most societies, death called for circumlocutions and polite forms, rather than the use of separate kin terms. Often, these consisted of adding lexicals *tu-* meaning "the late" to circumvent references to the deceased or the introduction of actual necronyms for defining classes of people who are mourning specific types of relatives (cf Buchler and Selby 1968: 170). In most cases where decedence occurred, it was a reflex of the marital alliances between families, moving a former affine into the category of "potential spouse" anticipating levirate or sororate inlaw remarriages.

Among the Salish, however, decedence was a prominent and wide-ranging feature, applied to both affinals and collaterals. Yet it was the application of the terms to collaterals that appeared problematic because it involved surviving siblings (aunts and uncles) and their niblings (nieces and nephews), the children of the deceased. Few explanations have been proposed for decedence, such as concern with entitlements, with responsibilities, or with custodianship of family resources. In general, Goodenough (1970: 90-93), who found decedence "of considerable interest," suggested that it represented how the "entitlements" of kin relationship were transferred at death.

More specifically, Galloway (1977: 530), working among Fraser River Sto:lō (Upriver Halkomelem Salish), suggested that their decedence terms show a shifting of "responsibilities" to survivors. Among his examples were two terms which mean deceased person (other than a parent) responsible for Ego, such as uncle, aunt, and grandmother. He concluded, "The Sto:lō way of viewing ... these terms is that you are related to a person who dies or you are related to a person through another person who dies. These terms are looked at as a process."

Thus, for much of your life you were supposed to be the responsibility of your parents, and, secondarily, of other adult members of your family. With the death of your parents, however, you became the responsibility of other surviving adults. Modern Lushootseed elders explain that decedence terms were adopted "for the sake of the children," but not necessarily orphans. Among the Sto:lō, for example, the term for orphan (*weləm*) was indeed included within a term for "the orphan child of a deceased sibling."

The full explanation, however, involved more general considerations. Indeed, decedence was invoked for the sake of the "family," the broad kindred holding corporate rights to traditions and resources, but most particularly, the inherited ancestral wisdom called "advice." Moreover, since children were the epitome of family; its hope and pride for the future, special care had to be taken to give them easy access to family traditions, which were put at risk by the death of a parent.

Decedence

Throughout the world, while the welfare of children was a central concern of kin term usages, corporate "ancestral house" of the Northwest was lacking. Elsewhere in North America where decedence also occurred, such as native California, it relied on other factors (Drucker 1937).

In aboriginal California, decedence was so common in the northern and southern regions (Gifford 1922: 257) that the Huchinom felt put upon to explain why they did not use it. Everywhere else, "The continued use of the terms {for parent and collaterals} is said to be 'on account of the ch{ildren}'" (1922: 119). After a mother died, her children were "fed" by her parents and brothers, along with their father. By implication, then, families kept in contact for the benefit of children.

Yet, of the nineteen Californian "tribes" listed,[82] almost all of the decedence terms involved only affines. For example, among the Karuk, "For all terms of affinity following the death of the connecting relative the term _gardim_ is used" (1922: 33). Only the Tolowa (1922: 17) specified terms for parental siblings: _trixne_ for deceased parent's sister and _trine_ for deceased parent' brother, both of which were related to _trixne_ meaning "ghost ~ spirit". In addition, they applied _tamage_ to all affines after the death of the linking relative. Such data confirm the link between decedence and on-going marital alliances through sororate and levirate.

Unlike other areas of Native North America where "The terminologies for American Indian cultures are rarely complete with respect to the relationships brought about by death of a relative or by death and remarriage" (Edmonson 1958: 13), Salish and Lushootseed terminology is well reported, although given little if any cultural context.

Among the Lushootseed, four terms reflected decedence. These are /yəlab/, /sqəla(y)jut/, /sbalutsid/, and */cəɬbaskayu/. These terms were first discussed by Ballard (1935: 111, Appendix G), who learned Lushootseed as a child.

Noteworthy is the change in nomenclature employed in certain cases upon the death of the intervening relative. Thus upon the death of one's spouse the term _sbalucid_ is substituted for $k^{w}ətiw$, in so far as any relationship is presumed to continue. Incidentally, it seems to have been obligatory for brother, or sister as the case may be, to marry the surviving spouse of the deceased. Upon the death of one's parent the surviving brother, sister or cousin of the deceased is called _yəlab_. Upon the death of _yəlab_ he or she is again called 'qəsi or əpus. Reciprocal to _yəlab_ is sqəla(y)jut{aɬ}, substituted for the term _stalət_. Accordingly the expressions _yəlab_ and sqəla(y)jut{aɬ} are used between elderly persons and young persons distantly related.

According to the first Lushootseed dictionary (Hess 1976: 631.2), _yəlab_ is "either parent's sibling of either sex when the parent is deceased." The term _yəl-_ means 'both, pair' (1976: 631.1) and _-ab_ is a suffix that extends a meaning. Thus, the designation seems to mean 'embracing both sides'. Of related interest is the use of the term /yəlyəlab/ to mean 'ancestors' (1976: 631.3). Skagit speakers explicitly recognized such collateral ties when speaking English, remarking that their genealogies traced the "fathers of our uncles."

---

[82] Tolowa, Yurok, Karok, Shasta, Hupa, Yahi, Sinkyone, Lutuami, Kawaiisu, Tubatulabal, Serrano, Luiseño, Mohave, Cocopa, Diegeño (N&S), Yokuts, Tachi, Wappo (1922: 17, 33, 36, 56, 60, 68, 70, 71, 77, 115)

Decedence

The term *sqəla(y)jut* has been translated as "nephew~niece when sibling link is deceased, reciprocal of *yəlab*" (1976: 375.2). It is based on the term *qəl* meaning 'bad' and may mean 'badly off, unfortunate.' Also, there is some dialectical variation in the suffixes applied to it. Ballard (above) used {-*əł*}, while the term in Suquamish as spoken by Lawrence Webster has {-*ut*}.

The third term (*sbalucid*) has been translated as "in-law when link is deceased" (1976: 18.3), although the verbal form means "court a girl, be going after someone" (1976: 18.3). Related words include *balbal* 'confused, mistaken' (1976: 17.3) and -*ucid* "lexical suffix 'gap, opening' and 'mouth, language, door, river'" (1976: 541.5). It seems to mean 'to cover a mistake (or embarrassment),' giving added credence to the observation by Ruth Underhill (1965: 69) that in the Northwest "Death was an insult that had to wiped out, not by avoidance of the dead but by glorifying them." As applied to actual situations, the term connotes "intended spouse", much as English refers to betrothed individuals as 'intended' for each other.

As diagramed by Hess (1976: 383), during the lifetime of a parent, a *yəlab* was known as either aunt (*'əpus*) or uncle (*'qəsi*), and the nibling was called *staləł*. In the southern dialects, pus was the term for aunt, as recorded by Ballard. Their vital link with living traditions is shown by the fact that, after their own deaths, parents' siblings are again called 'aunt' and 'uncle,' fitting back into their former genealogical role within the family. The terms *yəlab* and *sqəlayjut* remain in effect while the uncle or aunt and the nephew or niece still live. When they die, they are again called *qəsi*, *'əpus*, or *staləł*.

The last term – *tciłəbskayu'* "related through the dead," previously related by marriage (1935:116) – included reference to the dead: /*skayu*/ 'corpse, ghost' (1976: 232.1), and used the productive prefix of *cəł-* 'make, build' (1976: 95), which indicated step-relationships when applied to kin terms. Thus, the term for a step-father meant 'made a father'. The term under consideration seems to mean 'created by death'. Other dialects used other prefixes. At least some of the southern dialects used {*cił*} (cf Ballard (1935) and Hess (1976: 52.2)).

Different from some Salish languages such as Squamish, Puget expresses step-kin by compound words rather than with prefixes. In Snohomish the expression for a step-relative is compounded of {-*əł*} "order ~ law" plus the regular consanguine term. In Skagit it is {*cəł*} 'make' and the consanguine term (Hess 1971: 69, note 12; Hess 1976: 458.3 where -*əł* is corrected to 'make').

The medial -*b*- may refer to repetition and thus mean "made again by death", but it may also derive from –*ab*– 'belonging to'. It applied to in-laws, especially parents-in-law who were called /*sk̓ʷəlwas*/ during life (1976: 254.6). The term *k̓ʷəłiw* (1976: 261.1, cf Ballard above) now means to change residence at marriage, to go to the home of in-laws.

While the other three terms are known and used by present speakers, this fourth term is not, although its meaning makes transparent reference to the dead. Present confusion about this term may be due to the fact that it severed a relationship rather than created a new one. As Ballard (1935: 112-113) wrote

82

Decedence

Any relationship formerly existing between them {the blood relatives of the surviving spouse} and the blood kindred group of the deceased is regarded as severed. They are called *tsiɫəbskayu*, 'related through the dead.'

This suggests that it might actually be more in the nature of an anti-kinship term, as with the English prefix "ex-" for relationships which have been denied or legally severed.

According to native speaker responses, modern Lushootseed are particularly insightful with regard to the collateral terms, but less clear on the affinal ones. For *yəlab*, people said that it signified that "someone became like a mother or a father;" while a *sqəla(y)jut* "became like a son or daughter." The implication was that the shift to these terms moved the kinspeople closer together. Similarly, *sbalucid* was said to indicate "the person you're going to marry," or "the person you're next in line to marry." Of course, given the levirate and sororate, when a sibling died, their surviving spouse became "intended" for a surviving sibling.

In her rigorous treatment of Skagit (Northern Lushootseed) terminology, June Collins (1974) gave careful attention to important features of this system. What she said about this specific instance has direct bearing on more general conclusions.

Collins confirmed the fundamental bond of siblingship for understanding the system, as "the most tightly knit, firmest bond in the society" (1974: 91). When siblings died, their children became the concern of surviving brothers and sisters (1974: 94), who argued for levirate or sororate marriages out of "fear of unkind treatment by unrelated stepparents" (1974: 102).

Among the Skagit and other Lushootseed, divorce was infrequent among good families, particularly because "both parents had to give up the children because of the fear already discussed of allowing the children to live with "wicked" stepparents. Parents could not dispose of a child as they wished ... Both families had to agree to the child's residence" (1974: 105).

Other reasons against divorce included an unwillingness to return any of the gifts and property exchanged, and the dangers that might befall a lone woman making the journey back to her parents (1974: 105). The only acceptable grounds for divorce were a barren wife, adultery, or excessive cruelty. Even after marriages were ended by the death of a spouse, where children were involved, everyone in the immediate blood line had a say in the care of any underage children.

In all, then, the feature of decedence among the Skagit and other Lushootseed revolved around a concern for children, not for general family alliances, as was the case when decedence applied to affinal terms. The effect of the terminological changes was "a closing of ranks" to look after the welfare of younger heirs. This tightening was also consistent with the manner in which kinship was traced by the Salish.

By a process of overlapping, people will adopt a kin claim to someone on the basis of a relationship that has already been acknowledged by a linking relative. Thus, people will often say, "I call that person 'nephew' because he calls my close-cousin 'aunt'." Obversely, someone who lays claim to a relationship might find their statement rejected or acted upon coolly because that person and family was not highly regarded. The rebuff often took the form, "s/he's the only one I ever heard about that connection from."

Other societies acknowledge such kin realignments in other ways, so the explanation for the Lushootseed system must be found internally. The tight bond among siblings and kindreds among the Salish rests firmly upon a belief in what Wayne Suttles has called "advice." Among the Lushootseed this might better be called "wisdom, teachings, knowledge" since these words were closer to the meaning of the native terms, which include /$x^w dik^w$/, /$x^w dig^w id$/, /$g^w \ni zada'$/, and /$'ug^w usa\l$/, the last specifically meaning 'teachings' (Hess 1976: 681). People who consistently transmit and practice these teachings became appropriate members of the upper class. People who did not were either low class or slaves.

These teachings included the full range of the traditional heritage and family treasures, including stories, dances, songs, and artistic traditions, all linked to a stock of immortal names. These teachings encoded proper, elite etiquette through hereditary names, moralistic narratives, and information about the effective use of prime resource areas. It was the importance of these inherited teachings that gave the Northwest much of its distinctiveness, providing the basis for distinguishing a variety of corporate groups localized within households.

In the north, these corporations were characterized by matrilineal sentiments, establishing clear channels of responsibility within matrilines (Durlach 1928), regarded as impervious to death because the immortal names were inherited through and across generations.

Among the Salish and others of the central coast, these kindreds were ambilateral and localized in households. While the system itself recognized open bilateral components, actual choices were limited to the households of acknowledged grand- and great-grand-parents. In practice, households included three generations of actual residents, along with, at least, a fourth generation recalled through hereditary names (Amoss 1981: 237).

Among the Lushootseed, every individual represents the conjunction of several of these "families" ~ kindreds. In addition to the term for ancestors based on the collateral term, Lushootseed also uses /$s.\ni lw\ni\-\ni d$/ meaning "root (especially cedar root), ancestors (figurative)" (Hess 1976: 531.3). Cedar roots were widely used for basketry and bindings, so they were much in evidence. Also, they grow in every direction away from the tree, sending tendrils through the landscape. Like a network of roots, Lushootseed recognized that an individual represented a 'coming together and stretching out' of links from many different places. As a tree fed from diverse roots, so the person came from many sources.

Of these, those of the father and the mother were most important. They were each terminologically distinguished (contra Spier 1925: 74) by terms translating as 'on the entire side of the father' and 'on the entire side of the mother'. (See Miller 1985 for the actual terms and their possible relationship with the term for 'born' (*gwac*). Even the word for the House ($g^w\ni zaltx^w$ ~ ancestral House) derived from the same lexical.)

For ranking families, an argument can be made that the transmission process involved replacement rather than succession. Names and possessions were defined in terms of the timeless age of epics. Since the universal change that coincided with the arrival of human beings, people have been trying to recreate these immortal conditions by "giving people to the names".

Reviewing the four Lushootseed terms in the light of wider distributions, two emerge as having the greatest significance for understanding decedence. The term referring to the dead can be removed from consideration because it has gone out of use. Of the three remaining, that for intended spouse has a broad distribution, presumably reflecting the importance, noted above, of continuing marital alliances to safeguard children. As Sapir (1916: 329) observed "the levirate itself is known to have been in force among most or all of the tribes of Washington and Oregon."

Most distinctive of the system, therefore, were the two terms for parental siblings and for niblings, which occurred only among the Salish and neighboring Southern Nootkans. The neighboring Sahaptians did not have such terms probably because of different strategies used by the Salishan and the Sahaptians to encourage intertribal contact.

The Salishans used intertribal gatherings (to dance, visit, gamble, and trade) over many days, which also fostered intermarriages, while the Sahaptians sponsored day-long feasts. Because the Salishans, especially of important families, expected to marry among diverse groups, the death of a parent would be more disruptive to the transmission of teachings because of the greater distances and differences involved. As a hedge against this, collaterals changed terms to assume greater closeness, at least when speaking Lushootseed.

Among the Salish, this close/remote relationship pervaded the entire cultural system. In Lushootseed, the term used for close(ness) is $\dot{q}^w u$ 'gather, collect' (Hess 1976: 432.2), with a range that included "assembly, council, and gathering".[83] Ballard (1935: 112) reported it signified "join, unite, assemble." Appropriately, at large gatherings, individuals still donate money to someone through a speaker, who announced that the offering was intended to show that the donor was "claiming X (that specific someone) as a relative." Given the extensive network of kindreds in a bilateral system, such periodic reclaiming of some weakening links served to strengthen the relational ties among elite families, functioning in the present as a reflection of its greater importance in the past.

Similarly, Thompson Salish have two terms for affines after the death of the linking relative: one for a decendence affine of a close relationship and one for that of a distant relationship (cf Miller 1985). It was, therefore, logically appropriate and internally consistent for Salishans to invoke this symbolic distinction to 'close ranks' and bring kinspeople nearer together after the death of a linking relative.

While this solution was distinctly Salishan, its practice was much more widespread. Fred Eggan (1955: 94) noted the importance given to "brotherhood" in Plains and other Native American kinship systems. Among the Numic-speaking Comanche and H3kandika,

> The institution of formal friendship among men also entails the use of the brother terminology. The friend ... takes the status of his brother in the relationship system of his comrade's family, thereby taking over all the privileges and restrictions which go with the new status (Hoebel 1939: 448).

By invoking kin terms and behaviors, friends become kin, intent becomes kinship. The next step in this process was shown by Nez Perce usage.

> *yelept* = friend. One fights in war side by side with his *yelept*. When he dies, his son becomes the survivor's nephew, the survivor becomes the orphan's paternal uncle (Aoki 1966: 360).

The Nez Perce also had a term for friend (*lawtiwa*) that did not invoke quasi-siblingship. What was notable about <u>*yelept*</u>, of course, was that it moved a quasi-siblinghood into a stronger relationship after the death of the linking person. In motivation and intent it was a weaker form of

---

[83] Same root as in crucial place name #40 səḏ̣^{w}uʔq^{w}uʔ ~ 'by means of gathering' near the Falls.

decendence, closing ranks and strengthening voluntary bonds between participants. Among the Salish, however, the vital store of teachings, class rankings, and family pedigrees were not left to emotional chance. Hence, the significant role given to decedence in their terminology reflects the greater corporate structuring of their society.

While the Salish are fairly well known ethnographically and very well known linguistically, there has been scant analysis of their cultural ramifications so pivotal for understanding Native North America. Spier (1925: 74) first considered Salish terminology in its own right, and Elmendorf (1961) studied it in greater detail, tracing its diversification into lineal Coastal and bifurcate collateral Interior forms. While Murdock derived Salishan structures from the Hawaiian type (1949: 350), he later characterized the Salish system, because it combined bilaterality with alternative residence options (1965: 31), as the fundamental kinship system of North America.

	dPSb	dSbC	dSbSp	dSpSb	dCSp	dSpP	other
Lushootseed	X	X					
Twana	X						
Chehalis	X	dSbS				dHM=I	
Klallam	X	X	dSbR	Rdl			
Samish	X	X	X				
Nitinat	X	X	I				
Saanich	X	X			X		PSbdC=PdCl
Sechelt		X	dZH				dSbl
Squamish	X	X		X(I?)	X =	X	
Chilliwack	X	X		dSpR	dR		dC(S,D)
Thompson	XdMZ						dRl
Columbian	X,sS	X,sD	X =	X	X =	X	
Ahousat			I=dBW				
Hesquiat			I=mZl				
Kootenay			X =	X	X =	X	
Klickitat	dMF			dSpSb			
Nez Perce							
Proto-Sahaptian				dSpSb			

Abbreviations Used:

A)unt, B)rother, C)hild(ren), Cz~cousin, D)aughter, d)eceased, F)ather, f)emale('s), H)usband, I)ntended, l~affine (in-law), M)other, m)ale('s), N)ibling, Nc~neice, Np~nephew, P)arent, R)elative, S)on, s)tep-relative, Sb~sibling, Sp~spouse, U)ncle, W)ife, X~term attested, Z~sister, = term overlap.

8 ~ SURVIVANCE

The 1953 delisting of Sdok^w^albix^w^ ~ Snoqualmie came to greater Seattle's attention during their struggle to protect the religious significance of Snoqualmie Falls, site of a power plant for a century and a restaurant for several decades (now, ironically, owned by rival Muckleshoot). With the support of the Church Council of Greater Seattle, making good on their official apology for past wrongs, Snoqualmie Falls was long the only TCP in the state until Cowlitz had Mt St Helens listed in 2015. State officials continue to slow any others, making this Falls TCP all the more remarkable. Sdok^w^albix^w^ belief that the rising mist from the Falls carries prayers to heaven is particularly vivid in public understanding.

Sdoq^w^albix^w^ also involved themselves in major public projects, such as the excavation of the Tolt site prior to the building of the Brightwater sewage treatment plant serving north Seattle. The tribal chair briefly resigned to act as worker and liaison during this work. Later he also worked on the Sound Transit project. During work for the 520 pontoon bridge replacement, Sdok^w^albix^w^ council passed a unanimous resolution asking for the protection of Foster Island, a former native cemetery in those trees.

Indeed, historic Sdok^w^albix^w^ leaders received prominent burial. Patkanim is in the chief's row at Tulalip, Martin Saduwa is beside Highway 2 in Cashmere with prominent Plateau people, and more recent Lakes leaders are at Sammamish. Head of a chiefdom created by his immigrant family, *Patkadəb* died a US supporter and faithful Catholic who played the system of bounties on heads to his advantage during the Treaty War. Saduwa kept in motion, with a much wider region of expertise and contacts, especially through the Slahal family network. Along with the Lakes, they built strong ties with the Denny, Yesler, and other key pioneer Seattle families.

Located near Seattle on a major highway, Sdok^w^albix^w^ have been graced by a host of scholars helping and documenting their traditions, including George Gibbs, TT Waterman, Arthur C Ballard, Erna Gunther, Ken Tollefson, Doug Penoyer, Harriet Turner, Nels Bruseth, Astrida Onat, Sally Snyder, June Collins, Bruce Miller, Vi Hilbert, and Ed Davis.

Well informed elders once exerted moral force for calm and order, especially respected Ed Davis long resident at Lake Sammamish, Inglewood, and Monohan where Sdok^w^albix^w^ settled after being harassed out of Seattle. Ed was one of the four men in the famous photos taken by Douglas Leechman for TT Waterman enacting the Spədak Redeeming rite with the 2/3rd size boards Jerry Kanim made and sold to the Heye Foundation, and now in DC.

Seeking academic help for their relisting petition, Sdok^w^albix^w^ reached out to Ken Tollefson, anthropologist at Seattle Pacific University and ordained minister. After writing a dissertation about Tlingits at Angoon, he worked with colleagues on the federal recognition petition for Snoqualmie and then, by himself, for Duwamish. Working with the Sdok^w^albix^w^'s lawyer, incongruously specializing in criminal not civil law, they responded to hostile filings from Tulalip, whose lawyers opposed this petition. With restoration in 1999, this lawyer repeatedly filed to postpone the submission of last of the seven criteria: the official membership roll. Nine rolls spanning a century had been included in the petition, but a final integrated resolution of current members, constitution, and Roblin roll remained in limbo when the elder, who was probably never eligible, died while compiling this ultimate roll. This postponement continues, with the dubious council well aware that enrollment records are tainted or bogus and many voters are entirely unqualified. In recent years, Tollefson has repeatedly said in public "They lied to me!" Even the purported leader Jerry Kanim turns out to have been enrolled at Muckleshoot and had only the most tenuous if any claim to the Kanim name. Devout and helpful, Tollefson became increasingly disturbed by the growing graft and corruption among Sdok^{w}albix^w, fueled by huge revenues from their successful casino. He submitted an affidavit to the BIA citing three quasi-sisters with key roles in Snoqualmie government, while lacking any valid claims to membership under the constitution.

Yet this same constitution has a banishment clause, used repeatedly to expel families from membership, only to have them restored by legal action in US courts. In many cases, these families included a prior chair whose acquired power and funds were thereby clipped. Of note, expected concerns with "due process" and "conflicts of interest" did not apply in Indien country until the passage of the Indien Civil Rights Act of 1968.[84]

Sdoq^{w}albix^w had long benefited with monetary stability. Lakes found employment in sawmills and yards, Lowers logged and fished, and Uppers had the enormous hop yards. They also employed survivance strategies. During the Treaty War in the mid 1850s, Patkanim supported Washington Territory with his own troops, while playing the system to claim bounty on many more chief's heads than commoners. Still, he drowned alone.

Saduwa chose mobility ~ crisscrossing the Cascades, strengthening the Slahal family, and keeping to the highlands. Luckily, in the late 1800s, following the lead of Ezra Meeker, the upper prairie became huge hop yards, where natives were hired to tend and harvest these clusters, able to live in their homeland. Tourists would take a train from Seattle and stay at a large hotel to watch them work. After hop lice aphids infected the coast crop, fortunes were lost and Meadowbrook and Tollgate Farms were sold off by 1908. Agent Charles Buchanan at Tulalip encouraged many Sdok^{w}albix^w to enroll at Muckleshoot, where there were mill jobs. Some, like the Moses family on Indian Hill, stayed on their own homesteads. Others gathered at Tolt, eventually renamed Carnation after that dairy company took over the town. Because they could hold out above the Falls and support themselves, these Sdok^{w}albix^w kept a prime claim for recognition, based on active interchanges with the BIA until 1953 and reinstatement in 1999. The roll unofficially in use for the bogus elections – votes virtually accepted by BIA as evidence of government continuity – was done in 2004 without noting blood quantum. Then came the lucrative casino in 2007, after a balloon price for the lands then placed in trust.

Because members were low key and scattered, often enrolled elsewhere, the Saduwa line was virtually ignored in the petition. Only years later, during the intratribal conflicts, did it reassert itself with the intention of providing a focus for stability and honesty by "taking back the tribe." One heir was officially vetted and certified as a valid Sdok^{w}albix^w according to the constitution, making him the only actual member by law and BIA. Thus an ancient hereditary line strong in tradition arose in opposition to that of intergenerational appointed chiefs of dubious ancestry which is still being played out with suspicious deaths, slashed tires, failed brakes, and mortal threats. Lawyers near and far have volunteered to aid various factions, in hopes of winning their client access to tribal funds and receiving retainers.

The Saduwa line has also been advancing the cause of the Slahal family of ancient peace makers, gathering in "cousins" across the state and nation. Sdok^{w}albix^w casino funds paid for the

---

[84]

day-long 2012 meeting at Seattle Pacific University ~ SPU, providing lunches and gifts of cedar boxes containing an empty bottle with the story of Moon (Appendix A) etched into its side. Telling Slahal epic of Humans against Animals to set their future diets highlighted the afternoon.

A genealogist hired by Tulalip to help with their interactive wall display of tribal genealogies at their Hibulb Museum was then hired by the Sdok^{w}albix^w council to produce a roll with blood quantum, but it ended in limbo. Overall, it lacked a clear methodology and accountability, and was unfamiliar with native pedigrees, biased toward Christians, too trusting of documents, and unaware that the final product would be reviewed and audited by scholars. Elders of the true Kanim family offered DNA samples to "test" the kinship claims of others.

Contracts signed on 27 June 2012 by a lawyer, myself, and the council secretary to do a census review toward an official tribal roll resulted in her being fired from the council, cut off from funds, and smug ignorings of it all. Another flurry involved letters sent out by the FBI promising protection for individuals during an investigation of RICO ~ racketeering and organized crime at the casino. Yet calls to a listed FBI phone number went unanswered.

In consequence, there has been a decades-long "constitutional crisis by a rogue state along I-90." Their 1999 restitution as SIN ~ Snoqualmie Indien Nation led to a lucrative casino built along this main east-west highway, as well as chances for personal greed. For uneducated poor, fate provided a crap shoot, a way to play the odds and to grasp funds after lifetimes of hard labor, desperation, tragedy, and hardships. Some later leaders began as caretakers, holding elders hostage, and parlaying their mere presence into outright membership, despite obvious disqualifications according to the approved, but never implemented, constitution, much as slave Mamlukes became rulers of Egypt. Once in public office, they banish challengers, subvert laws, stash money, and threaten denial of medical services or physical harm to critics.

Implicated lawyers, who bill for these confusions, benefit from financial main chance, cash cow, messy affairs, and outlets as predator ~ parasite. Utterly wily, their names are left out of all public and private records, keeping their every presence unproven. Only their periodic firings by SIN council, as 17 January 2013, provides negative evidence of their strong presence.

Seattle Times (Mapes 27 May 2012) summarize the still on-going situation:

The terms of office have expired for most members of the Snoqualmie Tribal Council, and an enrollment audit … has revealed the chairman … and two members of its council aren't qualified under the tribe's constitution to hold office or vote.

Neither is the tribal member on the board of a new gambling venture in Fiji, in which the tribe has already invested $1.5 million {and more}.

The tribe hasn't had an election in two years, because of members' inability to agree who is qualified to vote or hold office, due to an ongoing tribal-membership dispute.

Stan Speaks, Northwest regional director for the federal Bureau of Indian Affairs, said the tribe is perilously close to a takeover by his agency if it can't muster the ability to hold an election.

"If they can't do that, they are hardly really a tribe," Speaks said. He said his agency is loathe to step in ... the official offering memorandum issued to potential buyers of $330 million in bonds the tribe sold to pay for its casino in North Bend requires the casino to be overseen by a tribal Authority Board, the members of which are the same as the 11-member tribal council.

Rating agencies recently raised the casino's bond rating, based on improved revenues. The tribe also has caught up on financial audits that had been in arrears, and it received a clean bill of health for compliance with regulations by the National Indian Gambling {Gaming} Commission....

Speaks, of the BIA, traces the trouble back to the time of the tribe's battle for {re-} recognition by the federal government.

Once the federal government recognizes a tribe, it is up to the tribe itself to decide who is a member, using factors from degree of Indian blood to decendancy from treaty signers or a combination of characteristics. Tribes may also change those requirements when and however they like....

"They have not addressed one major issue, and that is their membership, from day one," Speaks said. "The recognition group evidently did not look very carefully at their membership and the criteria for membership. That has carried over to where they are today. That has really been their downfall. They can blame anyone they want, but internally, that was their responsibility. They just didn't take care of it."

At Snoqualmie, the present constitution requires that anyone who runs for office or votes must possess at least one-eighth degree of Snoqualmie blood. A person may still be a Snoqualmie tribal member with less blood degree ... Some say everyone on the base roll is at least one-eighth Snoqualmie. Others want confirmation, by independent genealogical research, and even DNA testing.

The enrollment issue came to a head in 2007 once the tribe moved to open its casino in North Bend, taking on $330 million in debt ... The fight burst into the open when Jerry Enick overturned a 2007 election, igniting a dispute that culminated in a 2008 federal-court case over the banishment of nine Snoqualmie tribal council members, including the tribal chairman....

The BIA's Speaks said he had never seen such a breakdown of a tribe in all of the Pacific Northwest.

A general council meeting held at Monroe, chaired by an outside official, ended suddenly when a huge wind gust cut off electric power. A candidate forum before an election was abruptly cancelled, and a hired lawyer, who had to pay a fee to appear in tribal court, filed a TRO ~ temporary restraining order and OSC ~ order to show cause to postpone the election, but it went ahead under hired police guard using a version of the 2004 roll. Native hiring preference has silenced much intratribal opposition as critics have been given higher paying and less laborious jobs.

In all, survivance balances dualities: exchanges of Uppers with Lowers, camas for salmon, old Slahal family with new chiefdom, stem and nodal kindreds; all swirling around the lethal Falls where ancestors emerged and kinship blossomed, foiling the death of parents with decedence kin term shifts. More recently, whims of USA, BIA, and BAR, delisting the tribe in 1953, were trumped by restoration in 1999, though continuing petitions to postpone a final membership roll combined with a casino providing millions of dollars keep them in a triumphant limbo frustrating detractors.

In all, unresolution has its own viability, cleverness thrives and money drives survivance.

APPENDICES

92

A Star Child and Diaper Boy + Star

99

B ~ Snoqualmie 20 April 1856 Census ~   Nathan Hill Holmes Harbor

101

C ~ James Teit 1910 Letter to Franz Boas

104

D ~ *Tacoma Sunday News Ledger* 24 December 1916: page 6 ~ Duwamish Indians name
   Agent Roblin ~ "Qua-Whad" After Title of Old Wise Man ~ Roblin Background & Work

113

E 1933 Land Claims Snuqualmi Testimonies

115

F Lushootseed ~ dxʷləšucid ~ (t)xʷəlšucid 118 Chinuk

119

G Kin Terms by AC Ballard & Zalmai Zahir

125

H BAR 7 Criteria

127 – 150

Bibliography

151
Thanks

152-56 Index

Appendix A

Star Child and Diaper Boy

Two sisters of high rank were camping on a prairie, digging fern roots. The world was new, with very few males, so, one night, each girl fantasized marrying either a white or a red Star. The next morning they awoke in the sky beside their husbands. The older sister was married to an old man with white matter in his eyes, the younger sister was married to a handsome red-blooded man. They continued to dig fern roots in their new home, but their husbands warned them not to dig any root that went straight down into the ground.

The older sister was soon pregnant by her wiser, older, kinder husband, but, unhappy, she sought escape. Digging deeply, she broke through the sky to see her home below, so she convinced her sister to dig twice as many roots so she could make a cedar bough rope to lower herself down without alerting their husbands. Her sister stayed in the sky when she escaped.

Once on earth, a voice advised her to change a log into a grandmother to baby-sit newborn Star Child, to build a house, and to make a fish weir.[85] Dull witted and confused, the grandmother kept singing lullabies for a boy instead of a girl, as the mother demanded.

Meanwhile near the Chehalis River, a lone Changer made another weir and began carving a canoe, but as he could not be at both places, he left his anus (or feces) at the trap.[86] As dull as the log grandmother, the anus confused debris until an actual salmon was finally caught and eaten by Changer. Denied any food, the anus puckered up, as they remain now.

The salmon's milt (or eggs) was warmed, prayed over, and, days later, became two girls. Though Changer began by calling them his 'daughters,' once together in his canoe, he called them his 'wives.' Alarmed, these girls fled by land until they heard the grandmother swinging Star Child to a blatantly male lullaby, stole him, and went upriver to the east. When grown, both married him; one sister birthing all trees and shrubs, the other all fishes.

Sensing something wrong and rushing home, the mother kicked the grandmother back into a log.[87] Devastated, she took a soiled diaper and fiercely washed it in the river. Blinded by tears and grief, she wrung it until startled to hear a baby cry and discovered Diaper Boy in her hands: cross-eyed, bald, and twisted in her agony.

Unprotected, Raven enslaved the defenseless mother and babe, treating them very badly.[88] Though Diaper Boy was warned never to go east, as his wives warned Star Child never to west; these brothers eventually met, the younger was cured, and together they planned revenge on Raven. Star Child arrive at the town with an elk in his canoe, announcing that the girl who

---

[85] These four support posts were living trees, supporting an animate equation among all such limbs when images of house and body overlap.

[86] These "missing" sections of Star Child appear in Thelma Adamson (1934: 379-384), called to my attention by Dale Kinkade. The mother is variously Earthquake or Pheasant, both associated with rumbling or "drumming," while the grandmother is variously Hell Diver, Inch Worm, Marsh to fold up the earth to shorten distances.

[87] Though unstated, she probably became the first nurse log, a fallen tree trunk nourishing seedlings. In 1975, Dora Solomon insisted that by kicking the grandmother back into a log, the older sister thereby kept everyone from reaching ripe old age. Because of her angry act, therefore, some people now die before their time.

[88] This enslavement was punishment for abandoning her husband in the sky.

lifted it out would become his wife. Several women tried until Dainty Green Frog won and everyone feasted, setting a trap for Raven, who gorged on their feces, rich in elk fat, and transformed {burst} into the bird of today.

At the wedding, the brothers decided to prepare the modern world. They threw everything that they could find – tools, clothes, baskets, bowls, pelts, and house planks – into a huge fire that burned for many days. Later the cooled ashes were placed in a pouch and scattered over the earth so that humans would ever after be able to find most of what they needed wherever they settled. Thus, the brothers made the world ready for today's humans, towns, and tribes. Trees and stones were now available at most locations to allow humans to make a variety of necessary tools, clothes, buildings, and traps.

In addition, during this scattering, the brothers confirmed the sacred qualities of the world and acknowledged the supreme importance of immortal spirit beings for achieving success. As they re-created the world, the brothers named all of its aspects with special words (instituting the "*dicta*"), which were only learned by the most important chiefly families.

These words controlled the world because they linked together minds by the sheer force of disciplined will power to accomplish a variety of personal ends.[89] Animals were summoned for easy killing, people's moods shifted, and catastrophes averted by this power. Sometimes, by its harmful application, people were made to do things against their will.

When the brothers finished, an old woman asked about light and they decided that the earth itself needed a soul so they prepared for Sun and Moon. Star Child attempted to be the Sun, but as he rose into the sky, the earth became very hot and people jumped into the water to cool off. When he returned, Star Child was told that he would not do. Instead, Diaper Boy became the Sun and Star Child became the Moon, going into the sky with his wife, who became the Frog on the face of the moon. She became involved in every woman's monthly discharge of blood and also kept track of the months until a baby was born.

Things continued for some time until Mink claimed to be a son of Moon and went along through the sky. Moon always took along a cane to vault over the river in the sky, which was the Milky Way. A few days later, Mink decided to go alone as the Moon, but he forgot the cane. When he came to the river, he tried to jump over, but missed, fell into the Milky Way, and drowned, causing the first eclipse.

The brothers met and decided that they needed to move away from the earth so they would have no more unwelcome visits from people like Mink. Besides, the world was now ready for humans. They gave names to every bay, nook, cranny, bend, confluence, and prominence, along with every lake, hill, mountain, and spring, allowing some duplicates. They named the tribes who would live in each place, taking the name from the eco-characteristics and spirit of that location.

The rope still hung in the air, used as a swing until Rat, denied its use too many times, chewed through it so it fell to the ground to become a rocky hill (#37). Another swing came down in the Skagit, where it became *yədwastə* ~ the heart of the land.

---

[89] Known as *xachədəd*, this mind control concentrated all intelligence. Its strongest form was called *siyu'id*, derived from the high god, and very exclusive. Some epics have two versions, either an innocuous story or an esoteric formula with symbolic force. In a familiar story of Coyote trapped inside a cave, he takes himself apart and reassembles his body outside. In the esoteric version, he names his pieces with special *dicta* which enables each piece to remain alive. Tibetan monks have similar practices for confronting mortality.

Diffuse Light itself was brought to the world by Changer, sometimes in the guise of Raven, and the contest between Bear and Ant set its phasing as a 24 hour day. Ant won because of her greater self-sacrifice by painfully ever tightening the belt that left her with a tiny waist, in lieu of the year-long day wanted by Bear for a longer hibernation.

STAR[90]

"It has been a hard day and I am very sleepy," one sister said to the other. They were camping away from home, up in the hills, so they could gather berries for the winter.

"It is a warm night," the elder sister said. "Let's sleep outside under the sky. I'll move our mats out of the tent and you bring the robes because it might get cold before morning."

"Good idea," agreed the younger one. "If we sleep over there in the hollow, we will also be protected if the breeze turns into a wind."

Soon their beds were made and they were nodding off. Just as the older was falling asleep she yawned and said, "Look up, sister. See those two big stars. One is bright red and the other is dull white. Don't you wish that we were married to them. Then we would have help with the heavy work, lots of meat, and warm beds."

"Oh, you silly woman," mumbled the younger sister, "If we were married to those stars, we would have even more work to do. We would have to keep house better than we do. We would have husbands to feed, and we would have children to care for all of the time. Remember what our mother always said, "Be careful what you wish for, otherwise you might get it and rue the day of your presumption. Take care and don't be silly. Go to sleep. Now."

But the Stars had heard and they too wanted wives. So, while the sisters slept, they floated up into the sky and each came to rest in the bed of one of these two men.

With the dawn, the sisters awoke. "My wish came true," exclaimed the older woman. "Here is a fine handsome man to be my husband." Then she looked across the way and saw the man married to her sister and moaned, "Oh, no."

The other sister was awaken by the familiar voice and rolled over to look at her husband. She began to cry. "Woe Misery Here is a very old man with drippy eyes. It looks like puss."

Angry, she looked at her sister and cried, "This is all your fault. You wished for this and now see what happened to me."

"No, this is all your fault, younger sister. You did not wish for the best. You got what you deserve."

At the sound of angry words, both men awoke. The young man said, "We are both fine husbands. Give us a chance. The old man may not look handsome, but he has many skills and talents and will keep all of us well fed. Trust him."

"Oh, but he is ugly," cried his wife. "I want a handsome husband like you. Can we exchange or can you marry me, too?"

"No, that can not be," explained the young man. "In the sky there are so many stars than we can only have one spouse each. Otherwise there would not be enough husbands or wives to go around. The old man has already been married, and happily, too, but his wife became a

---

[90.] Marriage to a Star is pan-American, cf Ojibwa & Arapaho (Thompson 1929: 126, 128).

shooting star and so has left us. I was waiting for a wife and now one has come. Dry your eyes and make the best of things. It will not be as bad as you think."

"Yes, do that sister," coaxed his wife. "We will now live in the sky and do what we must as married people."

Still, the younger sister cried and they left her alone. The men took the older woman on a tour of her new homeland. By the time they returned, the other sister was resolved to make the best of things.

"Good, my wife," said the old man. "I am not mean or hurtful. I will be a good husband. I only ask that you help out here with the food and house. I will do the rest. Here in the sky, women dig roots for our food and grind them up to make biscuits. I only ask that you not dig roots that go straight down or that grow deeply into the soil. Those are not very tasty and should be avoided."

"I am used to helping out. I will do as you say," his wife responded. "I only ask that you sleep apart from me. I do not want to get near to you and your dripping eyes."

"I will do as you ask. It will not hurt me," the old man said. "We have already spent a night together and you will have my child. I am pleased."

Again the younger woman began to sob. "I am not ready to be a mother. I do not want a child. How can this be? Take it away."

"No That can not be," the young man challenged. "Children are needed in any world. It will be healthy and strong. You will bear it and we will raise it. We are a family."

Turning to the older sister, his wife, the man said, "I think your sister is spoiled and irresponsible. Shall we send her back?"

"No Please do not do that," pleaded the older sister. "She was raised by a loving family and was always the youngest. She was indulged, but she was not spoiled. She knows that her place is to help and to share, and she will do so. Won't you, sister?"

Taken aback by this frank discussion, she could only nod in agreement. "I am ashamed," she muttered, but, even so, she made mental plans to escape.

"Come, sister," said the elder one, "Let us dig roots for our supper." The sisters went off.

When they were far away on the plain, the younger sister spoke earnestly. "I truly do not like it here. Why can't I go home? Why can't you help me?"

"It is not a good idea," the other explained. "I will be lonely without you and it would not be safe for the baby. Please consider your responsibilities here. We are married now and have to act mature."

"I will try, but I do not think it will work. I am unhappy and homesick. Life below was better than this."

Still, the sisters took up the task of digging roots for their meal. The bulbs were large and fresh, much better than those on earth. The sisters wandered apart as they dug more and more roots. When both baskets were filled, they went home.

Their husbands had been out hunting, also returning with food for the meal. The sisters butchered the game and hung some meat slices up to dry. A few steaks they put on to cook, along with a kettle of roots and spices. They did not grind the roots to make biscuits that night.

Supper was quiet, with little discussion. Afterward, the men smoked while the women cleaned up the dishes. Then, when it became dark, the couples went to bed, only the old man and his wife slept separately.

At first light, the women were up, feeding the fire and getting ready for the day. They went to the stream to bathe. Then the men got up and bathed separately. After only a cold snack, everyone went out to get food. They did this for a week.

One morning, the younger sister said, "You realize, sister, that we now have to travel further and further from our camp in order to get enough roots. Soon we will have to move camp to a new location. How do we know what other people are here? We see only our husbands. Are there enemies? friends? monsters? Who can say? Surely you must realize that our husbands are hiding something. Don't you want to leave? I still do."

"Stay calm," said the older. "You make too much of things. We are living and eating well. All is pleasant. Why can't you be content?" "This is not our home," the younger sister stated. "It is now," replied the elder.

The sisters continued to dig and talk because the plants were close together in that section. Suddenly, the younger dropped to her knees and said, "Oh look, here is a root that grows straight down. I am following it, the soil is very loose and keeps slipping away. Where does it go, I wonder?" "Don't do that. We were forbidden to dig roots like that. They are not good to eat. We were warned. Stop," shouted the older sister.

"You are too late. Now I know why we were warned," gasped the younger. "The root made a hole in the sky and I can see the earth. I am looking down at our village. I can not make out the people, but I can see tiny ant-like figures walking on two legs. I can study the village and I know where our house is. I can almost see our family. Oh, sister, I truly want to go home. There are lots of people there and I will not feel so lonely."

"Move over," said the older. "I want to see. Indeed, that is our home. That is where we came from. It looks so nice and pretty. I can see our house, our home. You are right. That is where we belong. Maybe our husbands will join us, going home as married people."

"But that can not be," explained the younger sister. "Those men are stars. If they come to earth, they will die. Remember that the wife before me became a shooting star and was lost to them. Only we can go back, with my child. He or she will only half belong to the sky. We can not tell our husbands. We must work in secret. Be careful. I will cover up this hole so that no one will know we know about this possibility. Meanwhile we will plan our escape."

"What can we do?" pleaded the older. "I have a plan. If you will dig more roots everyday to fill both baskets, I will braid fine tree roots into a rope that will reach down to the ground. It will take time, but we'll be able to climb down then."

After digging a few more hours, the sisters went back home to prepare supper. Over the meal, the old man said suspiciously, "You women must know that it is very still here. We are above the clouds so our weather is always the same. Yet this afternoon, there was a breeze. That is very unusual here. Do you know anything about it? Have you been careless with nature?"

"But we felt no breeze," replied the sisters. "We were out on the plain for hours and the weather was always the same. We noticed no change." "Well," hinted the man, "Be careful. Things in the sky have a certain way about them. They can not be upset."

"But we do not really know the way of the sky," defended the older sister. "You say there are many stars, but all we have seen are you two. Where are the others? Are they friend or foe?"

"Oh," said the old man. "You must understand that with so many stars we like to live far apart. If we lived close together, our light would not be clear and precise. We would look hazy or like a blob. We would not make up many fine dots in the sky. We neither like nor dislike each other. Sometimes we visit, but we do not stay long. When the child is born, he will live with us, but when grown, he will have to go far away to a place of his own."

"But that is cruel," cried the younger sister. "On earth, our children stay with us and take care of us as we grow older. That is what makes us a family." "But that is not the way of the sky. Our son will leave in time." Disheartened, the younger woman was mute, as was her sister. After cleaning up, everyone went to bed, but the older sister slept apart from her husband for the first time.

In the morning, at the digging ground, the older sister said, "Now I know that you were right, sister. Things are too strange here for us to stay. We will follow your plan. I will dig extra roots to fill both baskets, and you will make cord to get us home."

And for weeks that is what they did. As more and more rope was made, they had to disguise it as a hill, covering the surface of the heap with loose soil and a few well placed plants.

"My stomach continues to grow," said the younger. "It is well that I get to sit here making rope otherwise I would soon become exhausted from the labor of bending over and reaching down. I can barely see my feet."

"I wish it were the same for me," moaned the older one. "I get lots of exercise, but doing double the work means I am twice as exhausted at night. Still, it is for a good cause. Soon we will escape. It will have to be during the day. Probably at noon because then the stars are away or hidden and we will not be seen."

"I agree," echoed the pregnant one. "I only ask to go first because I so want to go home."

"You will get your wish soon enough," said the elder. "Just keep braiding and twisting, while I keep digging."

Finally, their pile had gotten quite high and they thought there was enough rope to reach the earth. On the day they set to leave, they did everything as usual in the morning. They fed the fire, bathed, and fed a cold snack to the men. They wandered out onto the plain, and began to move as though digging roots. They kept near the hill until noon.

"Now," whispered the younger, and the older sister agreed. They rushed to the hill and brushed off the dirt. One end of the rope was tied around a huge tree and the other was taken to where the covered hole was.

"Quickly, uncover the hole," the younger urged. "Place the end of the rope into it and shove the rest down as fast as you can. When most of it is through, I will grasp the rest and start down." And that is what she did.

Meanwhile, the old man tensed in the forest where he was. He called to the younger husband, "Come quickly. The breeze is back and I fear the worst. The women are trying to escape and will kill themselves. We must save them and drag them back. We need my son if our own plans are to be successful."

Together the men rushed into the breeze and soon came to the hole, only to find a rope sticking out and tied to a tree. "Now they have done it," screeched the old man. "Let me see how far they got. They can not have reached the lower earth, yet." The younger man leaned over the hole, while the old man looked down. Far below they saw the older sister. And far below her was the younger one."

"Let us teach them a lesson," snarled the younger husband as he reached for the rope. They had no knives and could not untie it, so they began to shake it. As the tugs began to move down the rope, it began to sway back and forth more and more rapidly.

"They are after us," cried the older sister. "They want to throw us off. They want to kill us. Hang on. Hang on tightly for dear life." "I hear you, sister, but I am almost there. It is you who must be careful. Don't look down and be sure to hang on tightly. I can see some of our relatives rushing to the end of the rope. They can not reach it. It is not long enough. Our father is coming with a hide and he will have everyone hold it so that we can jump and be saved. Just come down closer, sister."

As she spoke, the wave action of the rope reached her. She was ready and hung on tightly. Soon her feet were at the end of the rope and she looked down. "Jump, daughter, Jump," shouted her father. We have a skin stretched tightly and it will break your fall." And it did. In a short time, the older sister did the same.

From the ground, everyone looked up into the sky to see two tiny faces scowling at them. Then they disappeared. Ever cautious, the father warned everyone, "Go back home. Quickly. Those men have gone to get knives and they will cut the rope. When it falls it will kill whatever it falls on. Go home and hide."

Everyone did just that. When the rope fell, it made a tremendous noise and created a mountain where none had been. The dirt that had covered the rope in the sky world turned to stone in this one, but many rats soon came to live there because they discovered that if they burrowed into the mountain there was lots of rope to chew up.

The sisters soon married human husbands, but when the boy was born and grew up, he was always looking at the sky. In time, he became the astronomer of the tribe and he helped advise the chief and predict the winds, tides, and seasons.

Appendix B

~ Snoqualmie 20 April 1856 Census ~
Nathan Hill Holmes Harbor

Name	age	hgt	wives	kids	M	F	Remarks
1 Pat Kanam	38	5-4	4	6	2	2	Head Chief
2 SiHowie~Jim Kanam	32	5-7	3	1	1		brother to Pat paper
3 John Kanam	28	5-3	2	1			brother to Pat paper
4 Cush cush am	45	5-6	3	1	1	2	Second Chief
5 Hutty-a-Kanam	48	5-6	2	7	3	2	Sub Chief
6 Klemish-Kanam	34	5-9	3	5			Sub Chief
7 Yel-a-koose	18	5-7	0	0			son {inserted into list}
8 Nuque-a-Salt	26	5-7	1	1		3	Sub Chief "John"
9 Sah dah wah	43	5-8	2	6	1	2	Sub Chief
10 Wha ack	42	5-6	3	5			Sub Chief
11 Zul qua Kanum	26	5-8	1	1			Sub Chief "John"
12 Tah none a muck	38	5-6	2	2			Sub Chief, taken prisoner by Pat Kanam
13 William	18	5-3	0	0			son or ward Cush cush am, "Yay-a-letv
14 William	16	5-3	0	0			son of Hutty-a-Kanam
15 "Tom"	17	5-5	0	0			ward of Sah-da-wah ♂
16 "John"	18	5-4	0	0			son of Sah-da-wah ♂
17 Ayetsaka	33	5-5	1	1			Sub Chief, "Samuel"
18 Tow-ε-Pass	44	5-5	1	3			
19 Qua-lash-con	25	5-8	1	0			son in law Hutty-a-Kanam
20 Ash-hah-na-pow	44	5-5	1	2			taken prisoner by Pat – now ran off
21 O-hal-a-eck	?	?	1	4			taken prisoner by Pat – now ran off
22 Squi-que	45		1	0			taken prisoner by Pat – sent to see Owhi
23 Shmal-lo-wee	60		0	0		2	taken prisoner by Pat – sent to see Owhi
24 Kilose ~ "Tom"	24	5-5	1	0	0	0	I believe half slave to Pat
25 Quee lege	25	5-8	2	3		2	
26 Dui a oo Ko	19	5-4	1	1	1		"Charlie"
27 Cush sit	50	5-5	2	1			
28 Wah-wahs-at	25	5-7	1	1			son in law to Senocton
29 Sεnecton	46	5-6	0	2			
30 Cau sulk	16	5-3	0	0			son of Senocton
31 Swoot-Kanum	50	5-9	1	0		1	children all grown, Doctor ~ Tamanowas man
32 Sto-dock	24	5-7	1	0			half slave {word means 'slave'}
33 Tzalk-la-yuw	26	5-6	1	0			~~son of above doctor~~ half slave 1/2
34 Stick Kanem	45	5-9	1	0			relative of " "
35 Way tr cone	28	5-6	1	3	2	2	
36 She col ton	26						
37 Yep-pau-saa	28	5-8	1	2	2		
38 Mucklee	26	5-7	1	1			"John"
39 Twow-hock-sha	56	5-8	0	4			
40 Asi-how-et	?	2	2				son of above
41 Swud-shka	18	5-5	0	0			son of above
42 Sonuck-lu-ya	26	5-8	1	2			

Name	age	hgt	wives	kids	M	F	Remarks
43 Tosh-kate	44	5-8	1	2			
44 Swee-Rau	60	5-8	1	1			
45 Sill-a-qua	26	5-7	0	0			
46 Col-ta-gut	28	5-6	1	1	1	2	
47 Ka-pap-pa	18	5-6	0	0			"Charley"
48 Ass-how-oose	36	5-8	2	1	1	2	
49 Sos-hoi	18	5-5	0	0			Son of above
50 Whod-skate	18	5-4	0	0			all same as son
51 Ho-a-bill	22	5-4	1	2			
52 Sa-ba-hult	32	5-5	1	4			
53 Be-ya-Kanem	28	5-5	1	3			
54 La-ho-bit			1	2			"John" killed by Collins
55 Sa-whul-at	50		1	5			
56 Take-let	26	5-6	1	0			"George" used to live at Seattle
57 Zqua-but	24	5-4	1	0			"Tommy" used to live at Seattle
58 Tha-quilsh	35	5-8	1	3	1	1	dead killed by Collins
59 O-Ooh	22	5-6	0	0			"Dick" dead killed by Collins
60 Tgat-lop	56	5-5	0				
61 La ha buitch	30	5-6	1	1			son of Zat lop {~Tgat-lop}
62 Quait-la-huk	50	5-5	1	0			{shift to thin ink}
63 Sta-ba-luke	22	5-6	1	1			son of Cush cush am
64 So-ooke	24	5-9	1	1			relative of Cush cush am
65 Ska-op-ka	28	5-9	1	2	1		
66 Za-za-kuse	24	5-6	1	0			
67 Statch-lut	41	5-5	2	9			
68 Ya-ack-quilt	28	5-6	1	1			
69 Wah-chios	24	5-10	0	0			
70 Yo-ɛt-tun	50	5-5	1				
71 Why a Kanum	28	5-5	1	1			
72 Milleck-Kanum	50	5-6	1	0			
73 Hote lum cult	28	5-8	1	0			
74 Ka dah	33	5-6	1	11	2		"No Face"
75 Tug as Kanum	35	5-8	2	7			"sick"
76 Ky zon some	44	5-8	1	1	2		
77 Tzu zat lum cult	52	5-9					
78 Slock-kate	48	5-7	1	3			
79 Sde wah hud	18	5-5	0	0			
80 Whul-te-lat		25	5-6	2	1		
81 Stah te qualt	40	5-7	1	2	1		
82 Clud Kanum	36	5-7	1	3	1		
83 Ya-ha-bult	54	5-8	0	0			
84 Elsh kate	34	5-7	0	1			
85 Elos Kanum	32	5-5	1	2			
86 Tgud-ɛ-w-kte	28	5-5	2	2			
87 Quot-cum	28	5-6	0	0			

p2/3

Name	age	hgt	wives	kids	M	F	Remarks
88 Zat-lum-kin	33	5-5	1	3			"Chu Charco"
89 Qua-luck-bit	22	5-8	1	0			
90 Qui-ole-gult	40	5-9	1	4			
91 Ass-how-εεs	33	5-6	1	2	4		
92 Ka showl gult	26	5-6	0				
93 Kae a ka zuse	16	5-4	0				
94 Ho-qua-salt	40	5-6	1	0	5		
95 Say-zuse	36	5-8	1	2			
96 Ya-huck	42	5-7	1	3			
97 Hus-sate	38	5-9	1	2			Left arm broken by a bear
98 Sla-hote	32	5-6	1	0			
99 Skla-use	33	5-9	3	2			"Daniel"
100 Klat-soot	28	5-8	1	2			
101 Pap-pa-shu	18	5-6	0	0	1		"Charley"
102 W-sunk	44	5-6	1	3			
103 Who-lat-at	26	5-8	1	1			
104 Stad da holt	26	5-8	1	3			
105 Ah-whel-use	17	5-5	0	0	3		
106 Tzop-Kanum	40	5-6	1	5			
107 La-ha-zuse	38	5-8	2	3	2		
108 Ad-ha-em	45	5-7	1	4			
109 Gu-si-zuse	25	5-10	0	0			"John"
110 Say-use-kum	33	5-7	1	1			"John" p3/4
111 Squal-at-come	38	5-9	1	2			
112 Dε-da-da-use	18	5-6	0				son of the above
113 Hkah-be-a-cult	46	5-8	1	3			
114 Stick a may zuse	24	5-6	1	1			
115 Yo whay zuse	44	5-8	3	6			
116 La-wa-hut	24	5-6	1	1			
117 Chi-ya-use	30	5-8	1	1			
118 Ka-ba-oose	16	5-4	0	0			
119 Ny-es-Kanum	48	5-8	1	0			

Columns are:
 age, hgt = height, wives, children = kids, wards or slaves, male = M, female = F
Held in Hill Family papers box {MSS 12}, Jefferson County Historical Society, Port Townsend

Appendix C

27 June 1910 Kenneth Hotel Seattle

To: Franz Boas

Before the Flood all the people spoke one language. I got a migration tradition from the Snohomish as follows. "a large band of Indians (men women & children) came from east of the Cascade mountains and took up their abode {see Chapter 1 #40 səq̓ʷuʔqʷuʔ} in the Snoqualmie country on a prairie about one mile north of Snoqualmie Falls. Here they made their head quarters for a long time and in the winter time lived in underground [5] houses (from description *kekule* - houses like those of Interior Thompson. J.A.T.) The remains of nearly 100 of which may be seen there yet. These people hunted a great deal. Before coming there they had had a war with some other people east of the mountains & had as a result left their country.

Just five generation ago (the present old people yet living make the fifth generation in descent) the chief of these people gave his daughter in marriage to the son of the Snohomish chief who had gone to visit them. After this seven men of these people with their wives and children left there, and settled among the Snohomish (The names of all seven men are remembered and I got them. They are Interior Salish personal names, and might either be Columbia or Thompson &c J.A.T.). One old man years afterwards and his son went back again and eventually settled among the Wenatchie, the rest of them remained & they have descendants among the Snohomish.

These people intermarried a lot with the Snoqualmie with whom many of them [6] eventually settled, and eventually they disappeared as a distinct people. Some of their descendants among the Snoqualmie could still speak their language about 50 years ago. Among the Snohomish it died out three generations ago. No one now living knows a word of it. These people had not been very long at the Falls (perhaps one generation) when the seven families left & settled among the Snohomish.

It is said the Klickitat (Sahaptin) did not come through the Natches Pass very long ago, they think long ago only Wenatchee speaking people came. The Snohomish have a tradition there was formerly a severe war between etakEmut {itakʷbixʷ = Suquamish} and the Chimakum, and the former occupied Port Madison country which they think was Chimakum before. The etakEmut spoke the Nisqually language and were closely related to the Dwamish. The Snohomish like almost all the other tribes used underground fortresses, but no *kekule* house proper.

… The Snohomish like almost all the other tribes used underground fortresses, but no *kekule* house proper. The Nootsak used the latter with entrance from the top. It was never however the common house of the tribe.

… First horses in West Wash. came (by way of Natches Pass) from the Wenatchee to the Snoqualmie. Snohomish & Skagit got first horses from latter. Also the Nisqually, Up Chehalis, & Cowlitz got horses from there. Later all the latter tribes got horses from the Klickitat & Taitnapam, and became well mounted. Horses were known to the Cowlitz & Upper Chehalis, if not owned by them, before the Klickitat brought horses. As evidenced by the Nisqually name for horse being adopted by all the tribes. Nootsak and Lummi heard of first horses from the Skagit & think got first ones from them.

… Indians used to use all horse mea, left nothing, dressed skins for shoes, and in the hair for robes, also much used for parfleches.

James Teit

Teit published these eight names, not the seven he reported in his letter, in The Middle Columbia Salish, *University of Washington Publications in Anthropology* 2 (4): 83-128, 1928, in both their original and Thompson versions.

1 TExaidek ~ TExai'nek (chief)   Toxei'.nEk
2 TsElExkai'nEm   TsElē.xkai'nEm
3 CElEkai'n   SEleqai'n
4 Yo'xolEk   Zu'sEmkEn
5 Yā'xolEk   Zā'xElEk[41]
6 SiānEmkEn   .siā'nEmkEn Zanemqain
7 MexkEnitsa the youngest   Mex.kainītsa[42]
8 WEtskEla'tce   ??

  #6 SiānEmkEn = returned east when an old man, and settled at Wenatchee
  #8 WEtskEla'tce = son of #6, returned east of the mountains

[41] y & z interchange in different dialects
[42] There is a man of this #7 name among the Okanagon. Forms of #2-6 are used by living Thompson men. #8 is unfamiliar, but seems to be Salish. The suffixes -īnEk, -qai'n, -kEn, -itsa are very common in personal names of the interior salish, tox, tsEl, sEl, tsos, are common root-parts of names.

Thompson versions

Toxei'.nEk = hanging down belly ~ hanging down ~ suspended bow, generally considered a woman's name among the Thompson
TsElē.xkai'nEm = standing around the head ~ top
SEleqai'n = spinning around ~ revolving head
Zu'sEmkEn = tied head ~ top Tso'sEmkEn rattling head
Zā'xElEk ~ Za'xiäuk = long tall tree, also nickname for a tall man, like saying "long legs."
.siā'nEmkEn ~ ZanEmqai'n = traveling in a circle head
Mex.kainī'tsa = hair hanging loose over top of robe ~ head of robe hanging loose
WEtskEla'tce ? I don't know of any Thompson equivalent

What is most remarkable among these names is how easily *patkanim* fits among them.

Appendix D

Duwamish Indians name Agent Roblin
"Qua-Whad," After Title of Old Wise Man
Honor Man Sent to Do Enrolling Work
History of Tribe Is Fascinating
Scattered Stock Comes from Salishans,
Whose Chief Was Tecumsia

Tacoma Sunday News Ledger 24 December 1916: page 6

Special Indian Agent Charles E Roblin, sent by the government to enroll 3,000 Indian{s} of the state, looking toward a final settlement with them by the government, has completed his work with the Duwamish tribe, and in honor of his care and labor has had bestowed upon him by these Indian the name of "Qua-What," meaning "Clear Water." This was the name conferred upon a wise Indian who lived near Mount "Tacobet" by a lake known to the Indians for its purity, as its waters came from the grounds of an untrodden snowfield. As this wise Indian used none other than this pure water, and the mountain itself was God's mountain, this man himself was recognized to be pure and clean. He was often sent for by the Indians, who would abide by his decision on questions involving disputes between tribal groups.

The history of the Duwamish tribe and some of its members, as told by President Thomas Bishop of the Northwest Federation of American Indians, is a fascinating one.

History of the Duwamish

During the first half of the 18th century, the chief of the Duwamish tribe was Tecumsia, the recognized great chief of the Salishan stock, or Indians comprising those of the linguistic tongue living on the western division of the Cascade mountains. This tribe at that time (Salishan) occupied that part of the country known as the western, or south and western part of Montana, extending through Idaho and Washington and up thru a great part of western British Columbia, with the exception of a small tract along the southern part of this state olng {along} the Columbia river district and a small tract along the Pacific coast south of the Makah reservation, and a small tract on the shores of Puget Sound – from the district of Dungeness to the mouth of Hood Canal – then occupied by the Chimakum Indians, and a portion occupied by the Shahartian {Sahaptian} Indians then occupying that portion along the Columbia river district about 40 or 50 miles north of the Columbia to the line of the state of Idaho. The Salishans also occupied a small strip along the northern and eastern shore of the island of Vancouver, up to and a part of the Queen Charlotte sound.

Chief Tecumsia was the head chief of what was then known as the "fish-eating Indians," or those of the fishing tribes, and Chief Moses was then the head of the "Prairie Indians."

The aged chief of today, Charles Satiacum, is the now recognized chief of the remnants of this once powerful branch of the old Salishan Indians, with Chief William Rogers as the first subchief. Chiefs Satiacum and Rogers are the direct descendants of the great Chief Seattle.

Charles Satiacum lives on his home allotted to him many years ago by the government, with his wife. The aged chief is more than 100 years old and is in good health. He has no living children, tho {sic} he has one grandson, Louis Satiacum, living at Browns Point, and has several great grandchildren, the children of Louis.

Chief Rogers lives on his allotment at Suquamish, or what is known as the Port Madison reservation. He and his wife are in splendid health. They have several children and grand children living at Suquamish.

Agreement With Stevens

In support of a verbal agreement with and also a party {partly} fulfilled portion made with Chief Satiacum during 1855-1856, by Governor Isaac I Stevens, while on their way to the famous Point Elliott treaty, it was understood that Satiacum and his people were to have set out for the Duwamish Indians a tract of land about the mouth of Lake Washington and along the Duwamish river at what is now Renton. The claim of Satiacum is that, owing to the removal of Governor Stevens before the fulfillment by the government of the treaty, the citizens slowly took from them these lands until several years ago they were "pushed off" entirely, and after the discovery of coal at Renton the white people told the chief and his people that this coal land was too valuable for allotments to them and that the government would provide them with other lands, but to this day no{t} a foot of land has been provided for his people.

In support of his claims, Satiacum has given several affidavits from a mind clear and keen. During the enrollment, which took four days, many names and references for the full Indian names were referred to the aged chief, and at every name asked he would at once give the name as if but yesterday he saw it. These names were of the grandfather or mother of the applicants – many of whom he knew when a young man.

The Duwamish tribe is now disbanded as the members scattered to the "four winds" owing to their reservation being taken from them, yet Satiacum is their chief, and is well loved by his people for his fidelity to their cause. He lives quit simply but with a clean example for this "children" to be honest to man and God.

Special Agent Roblin in his enrollment takes great care in tracing the family history of every applicant. Much amusement was had by the Indians during the enrollment at his quick grasping of the pronounciation {sic} of some of these long unwritten, almost unpronounceable names. Mr. Roblin having had a great deal of experience during his last few years of this kind of work, listens with a smile on his face when the names are being jocularly spoken to him yet not more than one-third of the names have been asked for the second time without his having grasped the full name.

Mr Roblin expects to open headquarters in Tacoma. He is now in the southern part of the state and will return about Friday next when he expects to have instructions from the Indian office at Washington regarding the opening of a local office or headquarters here.

On Tuesday he will go to Tolt and enroll the Snoqualmie Indians; he then goes to Marysville. These two places will take about 10 days' time.

The picture shows only a small number of the Duwamish Indians who gathered in answer to Chief Satiacum's summons. Chief Charlie Sotiacum {sic} is seen in the center of the picture, sitting in the rocking chair on the right, a battered hat covering his flowing white locks. Sitting at his left is Chief William Rogers of the Suquamish Indians. To the left of Chief Rogers is John Seattle, great-grandson of the famous Chief Seattle. Agent Roblin is standing in the center of the picture with his hands resting on the chairs of the two chiefs. On his right is Thomas Bishop, and on his left, Willie Wilton, treasurer of the Northwest Federation.

Background

Charles Roblin investigated landless tribes at the instigation of Thomas Bishop and his Northwest Federation of American Indians, founded at Tacoma in 1916. Roblin took over from McClusky, who died at the start of this enrollment, which itself had some bizarre legal aspects.

Roblin had investigated conditions on the Suiattle River in 1916 and done a census of these Sauks. Like those at Lake Sammamish, many families had taken out Indian homesteads but because farming was a requirement for continued ownership and these lands were in national forests, where logging was a ready source of money, many of these homesteads were rejected for failure to comply with federal regulations. Forest rangers were especially cruel, destroying stored shingles and lumber waiting in family yards for sale. After Dr McChesney, long at Lummi agency, died suddenly at the start of the 1918 enrollment efforts, Roblin was called back to finish these tribal registers for the 1919 roll.

Thomas Bishop was an early activist for treaty and Native rights in Washington State. While he talked for forming native "unions," his federation organized communities as tribes since that it how treaty signatories were legally based. Members would collect bits of money to pay his expenses back to Washington, DC to lobby the Bureau of Indian Affairs (BIA) and US officials. He was always resourceful, for himself and others, as need be. Once, when he ran out of money, he worked as a butcher to earn his return fare. Since his role in these exciting times after World War I is not well known, a wider context is herein provided for understanding these early political activities, often taking on the local BIA.

At Tulalip, during US Grant's Peace Policy (1872-1887), BIA Indian agents had to be recommended by the Catholic Bishop of the Diocese (Seattle), as this reservation was one of the few that was assigned to Catholic missions because US policy was predominately Protestant. Then, between 1886-1893, political appointees served as agents. Thereafter they were drawn from the newly-formed Civil Service and their title was changed to "school superintendent."

The first school superintendent at Tulalip was the former agency MD, Charles Buchanan, who served from 1 July 1901 until his death 18 January 1920. During his tenure, Buchanan collected Puget Sound ethnographic and linguistic materials, and wrote for scholarly journals. He generally supported Native rights, as well as the formation by Thomas Bishop and others of the Northwest(ern) Federation of American Indians, which lobbied for the work eventually done by BIA Special Agent Charles Roblin. Bishop was also a notary public who preferred green ink, and many of the applications include a power of attorney form with blanks filled in with that telltale green.

The Bishop family was Snohomish, originally from Tulalip, who moved into the depopulated Chimakum area near Port Townsend and prospered. His brother William was elected to the state legislature and ran a successful ranch. Thomas espoused native causes, including the native right to vote, passed in 1924 in response to native contributions during World War I. In 1915, he published "An Appeal to the Government to Fulfill Sacred Promises Made 61 Years Ago" to call attention to ignored or mangled treaty provisions from the 1850s. With the help of key Natives, such as Martin Sampson, a Swinomish working at the Puyallup federal school in Tacoma, Ed Davis in Fall City, Jerry Kanim at Tolt, Lawrence Webster at Suquamish, and others, he mobilized landless natives by tribe to pursue treaty claims, once the BIA had completed a tally of those who were landless and unenrolled.

In his cover letter of 31 January 1919, Charles Roblin summarized his efforts for this enumeration, remarkably unbiased and undertaken in the interests of general welfare and kind intent. Under threat of losing "excess" lands after these allotments, Quinault, as it is now spelled, hurriedly added and allotted members to save as much reserved land as possible. The tribal council, as Roblin wrote, meeting 4-6 April 1912, got "carried away with the spirit of generosity and 'adopted' whole families, in some cases containing scores of members, without properly considering the merits of the claims advanced" for over 500 applicants. After Roblin finished his study, the council again reviewed all these files on 18-20 December 1918, acting to limit membership (M1344).

The passage of the Act of Congress of March 4, 1911, authorizing the allotment of land on the Quinaielt {Quinault} Indian Reservation, Washington, to the members of the Hoh, Quileyute, Ozette, and other tribes of Indians who are affiliated with the Quinaielt and Quileyute Indians in the treaty of 1855 and 1856, crystallized this movement into one for the allotment of all persons of Indian blood, hitherto unalloted, on the Quinaielt Reservation. . . . This movement ripened in the organization of the Northwestern Federation of American Indians. The leading spirit of this organization is Mr Thomas Bishop, its president. . . . Mr Bishop and his colleagues immediately took the position that all unallotted Indians living west of the Cascade Mountains in western Washington could be allotted on the Quinaielt Reservation; and they spread this word broadcast. This, too, was the position taken by Mr HH Johnson, Superintendent then in charge of the Quinaielt Indian Reservation; and it thus obtained official backing, which lent it impetus.

Mr Bishop organized the Northwestern Federation of American Indians and sought membership applications, and dollars, from all Indians of western Washington who had not had their "rights." Meetings were held in many places in the State, extravagant promises were made, unwarranted hopes were raised, and the organization prospered. Hundreds of mixed-blood Indians, who had not thought, theretofore, of making any claim against the United States Government for land or money, now put in claims; family trees were studied and great expectations were raised.

Some one seems to have estimated the value of an allotment on the Quinaielt Indian Reservation at six thousand dollars {$6000}; and, as many claimants did not want land on that reservation, because they had been raised and lived in the more pleasant climate of the Puget Sound country or southwestern Washington, it was stated that demand would be made for an allotment of land or its equivalent in cash. So, today, many of these people are looking for a cash payment from the Government of six thousand dollars to each person of Indian blood who is not allotted. It is surprising how general this understanding is. I found it prevalent in every part of western Washington. . . .

The full-blood Indians, and those mixed-bloods who are living under true Indians conditions, seem to have been very well taken care of, with very few exceptions.   {Nooksack, Skagit, Snoqualmie, Cowlitz, Clallam, Chinooks ~ Shoalwater Bay ~ and associated bands, Mitchell Bay}

There are many members of other tribes, in the Puget Sound country especially, who are not allotted; and some few who are not enrolled. I have prepared schedules of those I found who are not enrolled, but have excluded from the schedules those who are now enrolled, even though not allotted.

In a letter to Tulalip Agency of 10 May 1926, Roblin provided background:

I was to investigate and report on unenrolled Indians of Western Washington. This matter arose as follows: For many years Thomas G Bishop, and the "Northwestern Federation of American Indians" had made claim that there were many thousand Indians in western Washington who had never shared in any of the benefits derived from any of the treaties of early days and who were entitled to *some* recognition by the Government and some remuneration for lands taken from them, either in the shape of an allotment on the Quinaielt Reservation, or by the payment of the cash equivalent of such an allotment. These were supposed to be "Indians" who were not enrolled at any agency on the coast. Mr Bishop made several trips to Washington on behalf of these homeless Indians, and was advised by the Office that there were no records in the Office showing who these Indians were and that there was no foundation for a request to Congress for relief for them. In 1916, Mr Bishop urged the Office to have an enrollment made of these Indians, so as to get such information in the record. The Office agreed to have such an enrollment made, with the distinct understanding that such an enrollment would not be a recognition of any claims made by the Indians; but an endeavor to have the record show what their claims were. Dr McChesney was first detailed to this work, but he died in Portland soon after taking it up; and I was detailed to it {by telegram of 16 August 1916 to Elbowoods, ND, arriving in Seattle 2 September}.

The Office, in instructions to me, dated 17 November 1916, combined the two tasks; and the first five pages of their letter deals with the matter of Quinaielt adoptions. Then the Office continues:

As the recent decision of the Department restricts the enrollment and allotment with the Quinaielts to the *fish-eating tribes* of the immediate coast, and the other bands and tribes mentioned in the said Treaty of 1855-1856, the Executive Order of 4 Nov 1873, and the Act of 4 March 1911, many of the applicants whose cases are submitted by Mr Bishop for enrollment and allotment at Quinaielt will, of course, have to be excluded. However, the Office desires that a separate enrollment be made of all applicants who, under the decision mentioned, cannot be enrolled and allotted at Quinaielt, to the end that should Congress so request, a full report might be made as to such unattached and homeless Indians who have not heretofore received benefits from the Government. (emphasis added)

To further seek their goal in the Court of Claims, Duwamish et alia (F-275) was instituted by jurisdictional act of 12 February 1925 (43 Stat 886) to allow suit by Washington State Indians and Tribes living west of the Cascade Mountains, an estimated population of 4597 in 1940. The nature of the claims was one of general accounting for funds ($71,496.45) allegedly still due under treaty stipulations, compensations for lands taken, and hunting and fishing rights. The report of 933 pages was forwarded to the Department of Justice on 17 November 1931; the court on 4 June 1934 (79 C Cls 530) dismissed this claim, arguing that it was eliminated by financial and service offsets provided to the plaintiffs. Appeal was denied 27 May 1935 (81 C Cls 976, 295 US 755).

This was a suit by 19 Indian tribes or bands, or remnants of tribes or bands, residing in the state of Washington, to recover a vast sum of money upon 103 separate causes of action. The total amount sought to be recovered as set forth in the petition was $73,365,416. In the plaintiffs' request for findings this amount was reduced to $69,703,466.69 (E Smith 1947).

Stated briefly, the claims of each of the 11 tribes parties to the Point Elliott Treaty (Duwamish, Lummi, Whidby Island Skagit, Upper Skagit, Swinomish, Kikiallus, Snohomish, Snoqualmie, Stillaquamish, Suquamish, Samish) dated 22 January 1855, 12 Stat. 927, were that no considerable portion of the amount of $150,000 as provided by Article VI of said treaty had ever been paid to or expended for its benefit; and that merchandize furnished was charged at grossly excessive prices; that the United States failed to reserve for the Indians, all of the lands specified by Article II and III thereof; that the United States failed to expend any portion of the sum of $15,000 for the purpose of clearing, fencing, and breaking up lands on the reservation created by the treaty; that the United States failed to establish and maintain a school with instructors, to establish a central agency, to provide a blacksmith and carpenter shops and furnish them with tools, and to employ a blacksmith, carpenter, farmers, and physicians; that the United States failed to appraise and pay for improvements as provided by Article VII of said treaty; that the United States failed to set aside a general reservation for the Indians, parties to the treaty; and that the United States encouraged white settlers to take up and live on plaintiff's lands; that said settlers depleted plaintiff's forests of game and their streams of fish.

The claims of the two tribes of Indians, parties to the treaty of Medicine Creek (Puyallup and Squaxin) dated 16 December 1854, 10 Stat 1132, were substantially the same as the claims advanced by the Indian tribes who were parties to the Point Elliott Treaty.

The claims of the Skokomish tribe of Indians, party to the treaty of Point-No-Point, dated 16 January 1855, 12 Stat. 933, were substantially the same as the claims advanced by the Indian tribes who were parties to the Point Elliott and Medicine Creek treaties.

The claims of the five tribes listed as nontreaty claimants (Upper Chehalis, Muckleshoot, Nooksack, Chinook, San Juan Islands Indians) are that white people, encouraged so to do by grants of valuable lands from the United States, destroyed the wild game and fur-bearing animals, depleted the rivers and streams of fish, destroyed their buildings and excluded them from their homes and cultivated lands; and that no payment had ever been made for said lands.

The court held that the plaintiffs were entitled to a judgment under Findings XI, XVI, and XXI, in the amount of $71,496.45 as follows:

Finding XI: The following tribes and bands abandoned the number of houses herein set forth of the value of $259.00 each, when they removed to their respective reservations set apart under the treaties, and have received from the United States no payment therefor{e}, viz:

1	Skokomish, 15 houses	$ 3,750.00
2	Squaxin, 6 houses	$ 1,500.00
3	Puyallup, 45 houses	$11,250.00
4	Suquamish, 28 houses	$ 7,000.00
5	Duwamish, 56 houses	$14,000.00
6	Snohomish, 12 houses	$ 3,000.00
7	Snoqualmie, 11 houses	$ 2,750.00
8	Stillaquamish, 12 houses	$ 3,000.00
9	Kikiallus, 8 houses	$ 2,000.00
10	Whidby Island Skagit & Upper Skagit, 26 houses	$ 6,500.00
11	Swinomish, 6 houses	$ 1,500.00
12	Samish, 14 houses	$ 3,500.00
13	Lummi, 19 houses	$ 4,750.00
	sum	$64,500.00

Finding XVI: There is due the Indians under the treaty $1,535.04 (Treaty of Point Elliott).

Finding XXI: When the Puyallup School was discontinued certain equipment formerly used therein was sold to the Salem and Tulalip Indian schools. To the Salem school the authorities sold equipment of the value of $27,250.13, and to Tulalip school equipment of the value of $6,096.50, making a total sum of $33,346.63. The plaintiffs are entitled to 10.16% of said total sum, i.e., $6,389.21, less $927.80 heretofore paid them, and a judgment will be awarded for the difference, $5,461.41.

The court further held that, although the plaintiffs were entitled to a judgment of $71,496.45, the defendant on its counterclaim, was entitled to an amount in excess of this sum, and therefore, that the petition should be dismissed (Smith 1947).

Outraged by such duplicitous findings, the newly-formed National Congress of American Indians urged Congress to set up a separate Indian Claims Commission, which heard cases from 1946 to 1978, when those lingering cases were transferred back to the US Court of Claims. Northwest tribes received cash settlements for these cases in the 1970s, though some are still pending.

Under the US Constitution no state or federal court had jurisdiction over Indian land claims. Each individual case had to be authorized by a specific act of Congress and then brought to the US Court of Claims. The average case took 15 years to wend its way through the system.... During the existence of the commission from 1946 to 1978, over 852 claims were filed. (The commission's life was extended four times.) ... Over 800 million dollars was awarded.... Although ... the express purpose {was} of providing Indians with the opportunity to obtain redress for the loss of tribal land, the tribes could only receive money, not actual land, based on the value of the land at the time it was taken (Nies 1996: 347–349).

Records of the Indian Claims Commission
(Record Group 279) 1946-1983 [109970 ICC]

Docket 25	Box Snoqualmie
Docket 92	Boxes 187-191 Skagit
Docket 93	Box Snoqualmie
Docket 97	Box 193 Sauk Suiattle
Docket 98	Boxes 194-196 Muckleshoot
Docket 109	Boxes 206-7 Duwamish
Docket 110	Box Lummi
Docket 125	Box 229 Snohomish
Docket 132	Box Suquamish
Docket 155	Boxes 1531-38, 303 Quileute
Docket 161, 159	Box Samish
Docket 203	Box 346 Puyallup
Docket 207	Box Stillguamish
Docket 117	Box Duwamish
Docket 218	Box Cowlitz
Docket 234	Box 383 Chinook
Docket 237	Boxes 2193-97 Upper Chehalis
Docket 242	Box 2208 Quinault Queets
Docket 262	Box Tulalip
Docket 263	Box Kikiallus 1
Docket 292	Box Skagit
Docket 293	Box 2632 Swinomish
Docket 294	Box 464 Lower Skagit
Docket 456	Box Kikiallus 2
Docket 475	Box Upper Skagit
Docket 658	Box Muckleshoot

Lastly, because his personnel file is missing from federal employee records at Saint Louis, something must be said about Charles Roblin himself, based on US census records. That he was a Northwesterner, based in Salem, adds to our understanding of the conscientious job that he did on the roll.

Charles Edward Roblin (1870–1953) was a naturalized US citizen who immigrated from English Canada in 1888 and settled at Salem, Oregon. The local Methodist Willamette College, now University, was his alma mater. In 1891, he was agent for Elwood Steamship on the wharf.

In the 1910 federal census, Charles E, 40, is allotting Agent on the Blackfoot Reservation in Montana, having been naturalized in 1888 at the age of 18. In the 1930 federal census, Charles E, 60, and Ollie M, 47, have a son, Charles D, 13, daughter, Ruth E, 19, and a lodger Robert Henry, 31, born in Virginia of a father from Scotland and a mother from Ireland and working as an automobile salesman. Charles E was born in English Canada, Ollie in Ohio of Ohio parents, Ruth in Arizona, and Charles D in Ohio. Charles is listed as a special allotting agent for the US government. Their home was worth $5000.

In the 1940 federal census, Charles E, 70, born in English Canada, is living in Salem and still listed as working as a supervisor for the Government Indian Bureau at a salary of $2700. His wife Ollie, 57, was born in Indiana {not Ohio}, and son Charles D, 23, was born in Ohio and a cannery worker at $575. In the column for education, Charles has C-4 and the others H-4, presumably four years of college or high school. Their housekeeper is Mabel Robson, 32, born in Washington. Their home was worth $7000.

Charles died 6 September 1953, aged 83; his son Charles Dana and daughter Ruth, then married to Carl Shantz and living in Milwaukee, Oregon, fought each other in court over his will. His most valued possessions were his home place, an arrowhead collection, and an elk's head he bequeathed to the Salem Elk's Club.[1]

In sum, Roblin was a career civil servant who married late, had an over-indulged son and stolid daughter, and exemplified unusually high job dedication. It is ironic that the man who knew most about the landless tribes died in the same year several of them were delisted by someone in the BIA in anticipation of federal termination. Yet his 1919 roll remains the basis of membership and "blood quantum" for several tribal constitutions. Long available only in microfilm black and white, it has now been digitized in color, well illustrating the rainbow of comments by Roblin, Bishop, and others in the pursuit of a useful census, without, however, any lasting consensus.

---

[1] http://or.findacase.com/research/wfrmDocViewer.aspx/xq/fac.19570515_0040106.OR.htm/qx

Appendix E

1933 Land Claims Testimonies by Snuqualmi

For the 1933 Court of Claim F-275
Testifying for Snoqualmies were
25 February 1927 @ Carnation, probably arranged by Jerry Kanim

Watson Martin 83 @ Snoqualmie Falls 10 villages 58 houses
> Pat Kanim chief from Tolt R down, Sanawa (MF) from Tolt up
> 179   Above Tolt: Skashia [5 houses], Toquiki [8], Yetsk [c18] (@ Falls City), Yahakabulch [9], Schwalp [4], Toquill [7], Skwut [3] (Falls), Bokwab [8] (prairie), Tswodum [5], Sotsoks [5 + removable homes]

Corrolated these are Skashia #17 <Sxa'siyats> shrub growing at Griffin Creek, Toquiki #18 <T'qwai'qwai> Patterson Creek, Yetsk #21   <YeLh^w> Raging river, Yahakabulch #26 <Yi'hi^{3}L^{xw}> Little Raging river (See # 21), Schwalp ??, Toquill #28 dəx^{w}q̓al ~ 'place of soaking' <TqEl> "place for soaking things" Tokul Creek, Skwut #30 sq^{w}əd "Falls," Bokwab #36 baq^{w}ab ~ 'prairie', Tswodum #41 <Tutsuwa'dEb> between south and middle forks, Sotsoks #40 səq̓^{w}uʔq^{w}uʔ ~ 'by means of gathering' <Saq^{3}oqo>.   NB Watson did not name #9 xalalʔtx^w ~ 'demarked house' of the Kanims.

Jerry Dominick boy at Treaty, @ Muckleshoot, farmer
> A My father died, and I had no more home after he died, and I had to go to Muckleshoot.
> Q Did you go to the Muckleshoots to get an allotment; was that the reason?
> A No; he says, I went to the Muckleshoots not intending to be allotted, but I chanced to get allotment there.

William Kanim 87 @ Tulalip,
> Raised at Squi-Aulka = forks of Skykomish & Snoqualmie potlatch house + 8 average size houses

Laura Smith 92 @ Sultan, housekeeper

Wilfred Steve 33 @ Marysville, laborer
> Q Do you know of other members of the tribe who have not enrolled?
> A Yes, sir.

Jerry Kanim c50, @ Carnation, trapper "being a full blooded Snoqualmie"
> 193 Pat Kanim his uncle {??}

William Bagley 64 @ Tulalip, working around his house, former logger
> 189 And Pat Kanim spoke as follows: "I want all the game, such as elk and deer, ducks, clams, fish, berries; until you agree to grant us all these I have just named where we make our livelihood, then I will answer to your proposition of buying our

land. I want the dry cedar which I could use to make canoes and to make lumber; I want the dry fir for its bark. I am telling you what I want and then I will answer what you want. Then Governor Stevens answered that it would be all right, that he could have all he wanted to reserve. Then he wanted this place Halalt {Demarked House} reserved, as that is the place where we catch fish to dry.

Edward Percival 54 @ Tulalip, farmer

John Sam 69 @ Tulalip, logger GS of John Taylor, translator at Treaty, buried him

Susie Kanim unknown age, @ Tulalip, no occupation, D of Patkanim

Jerry Kanim says

> 193 Q Have you been recognized by the President as the chief of the tribe, Mr Kanim?
> A Yes.

> 195 Q As chief, have you any authority over the other members of your tribe?
> A Yes.
> Q Isn't it a fact that the title of chief is more or less honorary now than actual?
> A The former chiefs were the had of the tribe, and of course at the present it is a little different than it used to be in the early days.
> Q In what manner did you receive recognition from the President of the United States as chief?
> A He says the certificate that I received from the President I was recognized as a member of this tribe, and the tribe suggest that I should have the right to hold that certificate that was issued of greeting from the President.

> 196 Wilfred Steve is one of the vice presidents of this council of this tribe; Jack Anderson, secretary; Johnny Johnson, treasurer; Bill Bagley is one of the committee; Ed Percival, committee; Joseph Charles, committee. That is all I can remember – Aleck Young, committee.

> 196 I had a number of friends and we used to take a contract {for} clearing lands. I am speaking about not the light timber but the between, where we would have three of us, probably we would get that contract and we will cut it. We have the saw, we have the axe, we have the wedge, and clear it and pile it and burn it, and then sometimes we come to a place where there is wet timber, it takes a long time, it takes about two months to clear that land and put it into cultivation so that it could be plowed. That is 1 acre.

Appendix F

Lushootseed ~ dx^{w}ləšucid ~ (t)x^{w}əlšucid

The Indian people of the Mid-Sound area spoke one or more languages that belong to the Salish language family. Salish is a clustering of languages specific to the Northwest, with no obvious links with the ten or so major linguistic stocks across the continent (e.g., Algonquian, Siouan, Hokan). This regional family once included two dozen separate languages, spoken "from the Pacific to western Montana and from central British Columbia into Oregon" (Hess 1976: xi). Though rapidly dwindling in the US, Salish is still spoken in British Columbia, Canada.

The languages of the Puget Lowland were originally referred to as Puget Salish (Gibbs 1877, Tweddell 1950, Suttles and Elmendorf 1963, Snyder 1968, Hess 1976). However, in many recent publications, Lushootseed has become the preferred term (Bates, Hess, and Hilbert 1994; Bierwert 1996; Miller and Hilbert 1993). Lushootseed Salish is one of the languages within the Central division of the Coast Salish branch which includes 16 languages. Another seven languages belong to the Interior Salish branch to the east.

The change in language name was made in the late 1970s, after Hess (1976) published his first dictionary and Collins (1974) her Skagit work. The International Salish Conference endorsed the use of Lushootseed in place of Puget Sound Salishan in the mid-1970s. The main proponents of this name change have been elder Vi taq^{w}šəblu Hilbert and linguist Thom Hess. Hilbert has used the name Lushootseed Research and Press for her non-profit work that has been conducted to provide tape and CD recordings, bilingual books, and teaching materials about the language. For decades, students in her class and those at her lectures have learned this as the correct ethnonym. The ethnonym has been used in several important publications such as the Smithsonian Northwest Coast Handbook (Suttles and Lane 1990), a second dictionary by Bates, Hess, and Hilbert (1994), texts by Bierwert (1996), and several publications by J Miller.

Lushootseed has two dialects that diverge just north of Seattle (Hess 1976: xii-xiii). The northern dialect is written as dx^{w}ləšucid; while the southern one is (t)x^{w}əlšucid. The names for salmon, pattern number, and other culturally significant features, differ between the two dialects. As Christians expect things in threes, northern Lushootseed (dx^{w}ləšucid) used four and southern Lushootseed or (t)x^{w}ləšucid) prefers five (Miller 1999: 14).

Lushootseed is the Anglicization of the native name used to refer to the language of the greater Puget Lowland area. The anglicized form of (t)x^{w}ləšucid ~ Whulshootseed is preferred by Puyallup, Nisqually, Squaxin, Muckleshoot and other southern speakers. Using Lushootseed (pronounced loo-shoot-seed), greatly enhances any understanding of native regard for the Seattle area. Lushootseed is and should always be written in a customized adaptation of the IPA (Bates, Hess, Hilbert. 1994; Hess 1976; Pullum and Ladusaw 1996). Whenever possible, older terms have been updated and sometimes also translated into English.

Lushootseed Alphabet

English has a written alphabet of 26 letters, though it actually uses more sounds, particularly vowels. Whulshootseed, as written in the customized adaptation of the IPA, has single distinct letters for each of its 46 sounds. Whulshootseed functions with many more consonants and fewer vowels than does English because many of the sounds that are produced at the back or sides of the mouth continue to carry air and so can take the burden of the more open, free-flowing sounds known as vowels. In this manner, basic sounds can have as many as four different pronunciations.

Whulshootseed routinely uses many sounds modified by the back of the throat and with the lips, as with the sounds k, q, or x, like the German word *ich*. Often a sound occurs in four way sets such that it is plain, said much like ordinary English; *glottalized*, said with a raspy pop of air released from the voice box (the glottis) in the throat; and *labialized*, said through rounded or pursed lips. Additionally, these articulated pronunciations can be compounded so that a sound can be both *glottalized and labialized.*

As distinct soundings, each pronunciation is written with an ordinary letter, a letter under an apostrophe (glottal), a ^{w} letter beside a raised (labial), or by both the raised and an apostrophe. For example, k is said unadorned like kin; ǩ is "harsh, explosive" sounding like geek; k^w is said with rounded lips at the front of the mouth, like Queen; and k^w combines the last two.

Other fronted sounds, like the raised ^{w}, include ł (known as a barred L) and ƛ̓ (a glottalized barred lambda). The ł sound is common to Welsh and Polish and is said by blowing air around the tip of the tongue while it is pressed against the roof of the mouth. The sound ƛ̓ is made with a click at the back of the throat while tapping the tip of the tongue against the back of the front upper teeth. It sounds something like the middle sound in Ca<u>th</u>olic or a<u>thl</u>ete.

The following are the 46 distinct sounds of the Whulshootseed language.

a b c č d dᶻ ə g h i ǰ k í ł p q s š t u w x/x̌ y	plain
b̓ c̓ č̓ ǩ ỉ ƛ̓ p̓ q̓ t̓ w̓ y̓ ?	glottalized
g^w k^w q^w	labialized
ǩ̓ q̓̊	both
m̓ n	nasal
m̓ ň	glottalized nasal

These underlined pronunciations are for Lushootseed sounds close to English ones:

a = f<u>a</u>ther
c = ts, ca<u>ts</u>
č = ch, <u>ch</u>ur<u>ch</u>
dᶻ = ro<u>ds</u>
ə = <u>u</u>p, b<u>u</u>t, sof<u>a</u>
ǰ = like dj
ł = lth, ca<u>th</u>olic, nigh<u>t-l</u>ight, a<u>thl</u>ete
λ̓ = lth, said forcefully in throat and roof of the mouth
q = said in back of throat
š = sh, <u>sh</u>ip
x/x̌ = both the same sound, said in the throat
xʷ = said in throat through rounded lips
'/ʔ = lull in uh-oh, a catch in the throat

m m̓ n n̓ b̓ are rare sounds, usually in words spoken by or for children
      or by myth characters like Raven.

     Lushootseed names are used wherever possible in identifying specific places. Additional Whulshootseed vocabulary is used to identify certain important cultural concepts and constructs. Numerous different letters and symbols are used in other orthographies, as different language recorders struggled with Lushootseed words (for example, TT Waterman's s³a'iyexEb). Because several documented sources used different versions or approximations of the IPA, or used the English alphabet to approximate Whulshootseed sounds, several versions of each place name are possible. Also included are anglicized versions of the Chinuk Jargon.

Chinuk Jargon Wawa

Well-born people were expected to fluently speak several of the great variety of languages in the region. They conducted their trading and exchanges in these local languages. However, wider trading interactions and interaction with visitors from beyond the drainages was conducted in a trade language known as Chinuk Jargon (Gibbs 1970; Gill 1909). Commoners and slaves who lacked the advantages and contacts of the well-born relied on this trade language to be understood. With its simple sounds and basic concepts, set in a rudimentary grammar, it facilitated contacts among the peoples of the Northwest and beyond.

When Europeans began trading in the Northwest from ships then forts, Chinuk Jargon expanded from the Northwest into Alaska, California, and even to Hawaii, adding terms derived from English and French (Thompson and Kinkade 1990: 41). In the 1855 treaty negotiations between the US Government and tribes, the jargon was used, although it was not truly adequate to this task (US Court of Claims 1927).

Comparison with neighboring languages shows that the earliest words in Chinuk Jargon are drawn from the Nootkan languages of the West Coast of Vancouver Island and from Lower Chinook, spoken near the mouth of the Columbia River (Thompson and Kinkade 1990: 41). Both regions also used the same type of sea-going canoe, which enabled trade and other exchange. Later words were added from Chehalis, and then European languages, especially French and Spanish.

By the mid-1900s, Chinuk Jargon was rarely spoken anywhere. However, several dictionaries or vocabularies of the Jargon have been published (Thompson and Kinkade 1990: 41). Chinuk Jargon contributed words common to modern American English in the Puget Sound region such as *potlatch* (to give away), *tyee* (senior, chief), *tillikum* (friend), and some food and clothing terms (Thompson and Kinkade 1990: 50).

Appendix G

SOUTHERN PUGET SOUND SALISH KINSHIP TERMS
by Arthur C Ballard

Additional comments by
Zalmai (ʔəswəli) Zahir
within square-brackets [ ]

KINSHIP BY BLOOD

A. Simple terms		
xʷəlšucid	**Plural**	**pastəducid**
1. bad		father
2. sk̓ʷuy		mother
3. qəsiʔ	qəsqəsiʔ	brother or male cousin of speaker's father or mother
4. pus[92]	pupus	sister or female cousin of speaker's father or mother
5. scapaʔ	scapcapaʔ	grandfather, brother or cousin of speaker's grandparent
6. kayəʔ[93]	kaykayəʔ	grandmother, sister or cousin of speaker's grandparent
7. sčabiqʷ	sčabčabiqʷ	great grandfather, great grandmother, etc.; reciprocally great grandchild, etc.
8. kʷəliyiqʷ[94]		great great grandfather, etc.
9. hikʷyiqʷ[95]		great great great grandfather, etc.
10. bədəʔ[96,97]	bədbədəʔ	son, daughter: sex indicated by preceding demonstrative
10a. bibdəʔ[98]	bibdəbədəʔ	diminutive of preceding

---

[92] [ʔəpus (NL)} NB Codes are at the end.

[93] [kiaʔ (NL)}

[94] The term kʷəliliqʷ [ʔək̓ʷyiqʷ (TH)} is said to mean "beyond", hikʷyiqʷ [čəṗyiqʷ - TH} is said to be derived from hikʷ *"great"* and another word meaning "beyond."

[95] [čəṗyiqʷ (TH)}

[96] [bədaʔ (NL)}

[97] [ʔubədab *someone had a child*}

[98] [bibdaʔ (NL)}

11. staləł	staltaləł	nephew, niece, son or daughter of speaker's cousin
12. ʔibac	ʔibibac	grandchild
13. sqa	txʷsqatəd	elder brother-sister, elder cousin
14. suq̓ʷaʔ	suq̓ʷsuq̓ʷaʔ	younger brother-sister, younger cousin
14a. suʔsuq̓ʷaʔ	suʔsəsuq̓ʷaʔ	diminutive of preceding
15. ʔaʔšəd	ʔihišəd[99]	sibling, friend, sister brother: spoken by person of same sex
16. ʔalš	ʔalalš	sibling, friend, siste,r brother: spoken by person of opposite sex
17. qaqʷ[100]		elder brother or sister: term of address
18. yəlab	yəỷyəlab	brother, sister or cousin of deceased parent of speaker
19. sqəlaǰutał[101]	sqəlqəlaǰutał	son or daughter of deceased brother, sister or cousin of speaker: reciprocal to preceding term
20. syayəʔ	syayayəʔ	kinsman, kinswoman; general term, not clear whether restricted to kinship blood [relative, friend]

B. Derivative Terms	
xʷəlšucid	pastəducid
21. badaligʷəd	related on the father's side
22. sk̓ʷuyaligʷəd	related on the mother's side
23. čəx̌sq̓ʷuʔab[102]	having the same father and mother: "joined" ["split (two halves) are joined"]
23a. ciłəbsq̓ʷuʔabitagʷil[103,104]	preceding term amplified: precise meaning obscure, perhaps collective [half related to each other through parents]

---

[99] [relatives, friends, one's own people (TH); person or people with whom there is a close relationship}

[100] [George Gibbs gives qaqʷ *older sibling* used by men, while sqaqaqʷ *older sibling* is used by women}

[101] [sqəlaǰut (TH)}

[102] [prefix: čəx̌- *split;* root: q̓ʷuʔ *gather, unite, collect*}

24. ciɫəbsbad	having the same father: "related through the father" [half related brother or sister]
24a. ciɫəbsbadbitagʷil	preceding term amplified [related to one another, as brother or sister, through father only]
25. ciɫəbsk̉ʷuy	having the same mother: "related through the mother" [half related brother or sister]
25a. ciɫəbsk̉ʷuybitagʷil	preceding term amplified [related to one another, as brother or sister, through mother only]
26. ciɫəbsqəsiʔ	"related through the uncle"
26a. ciɫəbsqəsiʔbitagʷil	preceding term amplified [related to one another through an uncle]
27. ciɫəbspus	"related through the aunt"
27a. ciɫəbspusbitagʷil	preceding term amplified [related to one another through an aunt]
28. ciɫəbscapaʔ	"related through the grandfather"
28a. ciɫəbscapaʔbitagʷil	preceding term amplified [related to one another through a grandfather]
29. ciɫəbskayəʔ	"related through the grandmother"
29a. ciɫəbskayəʔbitagʷil	preceding term amplified [related to one another through grandmother]
30. sqabitagʷil	elder brother, term amplified, perhaps collective [elder sibling, including cousins, to each other]
31. təlix̌ʷ[105] sqa	elder brother, perhaps as distinguished from cousin [older sibling or cousin to whom there is a close affinity and is a relation by blood]
31a. təlix̌ʷ sqabitagʷil	combination of preceding terms [older siblings or cousins to each other. There exists a close affinity and is a relation by blood.]
32. suq̉ʷaʔbitagʷil	younger brother: term amplified, perhaps collective [younger siblings or cousins to each other]
33. təlix̌ʷ suq̉ʷaʔ	younger brother, perhaps as distinguished from cousin [younger sibling or cousin to

---

[103] [ciɫ- *half-sibling* (TH), əbs- (derivative of abs-) *to have,* The ciɫəbs- *to have a relation via someone,* prefix is rendered as ciɫbəs- in Lushootseed Dictionary, bəs- *inherent right of ownership.*}

[104] [=bitagʷil *to one another*}

[105] [təlix̌ʷ *to be related by kinship* (WAS/EB), təlix̌ʷ *full-blooded brothers who are emotionally close to each other* (ML)}

	whom there is a close affinity and is a relation by blood]
33a. təlix̌ʷ suq̓ʷaʔbitagʷil	combination of preceding terms [younger siblings or cousins, to each other. There exists a close affinity between them and is a relation by blood.]
34. ʔaʔšədbitagʷil	sibling or friend of same sex as speaker: term amplified, perhaps collective [sibling, friend, sister or brother to each other. Both are of the same sex.]
35. təlix̌ʷ ʔaʔšəd	sibling or friend of same sex as speaker, probably indicating close relationship [sibling, friend, sister or brother of same sex. There exists a close affinity between them and is a relation by blood.]
35a. təlix̌ʷ ʔaʔšədbitagʷil	combination of preceding terms [sibling, friend, sister or brother to one another. There exists a close affinity between them and is a relation by blood.]
36. ʔalšbitagʷil	sibling or friend of opposite sex to speaker: term amplified, perhaps collective [siblings or cousins to one another of opposite sex.]
37. təlix̌ʷ ʔalš	sibling or friend of opposite sex to speaker, probably indicating close relationship [sibling or cousin of opposite sex. There exists a close affinity between them and is a relation by blood.]
37a. təlix̌ʷ ʔalšbitagʷil	combination of preceding terms [siblings or cousins of opposite sex to one another. There exists a close affinity between them and is a relation by blood.]

KINSHIP BY MARRIAGE

A. Simple terms		
xʷəlšucid	**Plural**	pastəducid
38. sčistxʷ[106]	sčisčistxʷ	husband (Puyallup dialect) husband (Snoqualmie dialect)
sčištxʷ[107]	sčiščištxʷ	
39. čəgʷəš[108,109]	čahagʷəš	wife

---

[106] [ʔučistxʷəb *someone is looking for a husband.*}
[107] [Earnest Barr (Snoqualmie) used sčistxʷ}
[108] [čəgʷas (NL)}

40. sx̌ax̌aʔ	sx̌ax̌ax̌aʔ	son-in-law, daughter-in-law of speaker, speaker's brother or sister [in-law]; reciprocally father-in-law, etc.
41. x̌əłtəd	x̌əłx̌əłtəd	brother-in-law, husband of one's cousin, man speaking [only used by male speaking of brother-in-law or male cousin-in-law]
42. sc̓əbəš[110]	sc̓ahabəš	sister-in-law, brother-in-law, woman speaking; sister-in-law, man speaking [used by female speaking of sister-in-law, brother-in-law or cousin-in-law. Used by male speaking of sister-in-law or female cousin-in-law.]
43. qʷilx̌ʷ	qʷilqʷilx̌ʷ	related by marriage: general term
44. sbalucid[111]	sbalbalucid	surviving marriage relative after death of spouse: reciprocal

B. Derivative Terms	
xʷəlšucid	**pastəducid**
45. ciłəbsc̓istxʷ	co-wife, "related through the husband"
46. čəłbadəb	step-father; husband of speaker's aunt
47. čəłtadəb	step-mother, wife of speaker's uncle
48. čəłbədab	stepson, stepdaughter, son or daughter of husband's [or wife's] brother or sister: reciprocal to the two preceding terms]
49. čəłscapaʔəb	step-grandfather, husband of grandparent's sister
50. čəłkayəʔəb[112]	step-grandmother, wife of grand-parent's brother
51. čəłʔibacəb	step-grandchild, grandchild of speaker's wife's (or speaker's husband's) brother or

---

[109] [ʔučəgʷəšəb (SL), ʔučəgʷasəb (NL) *someone is looking for a wife*}

[110] [c̓əbas (NL) c̓əbəš (SL)}

[111] [ʔubalucidəb čəd *I married my sbalucid*}

[112] [čəłkiaʔəb (NL)}

	sister: reciprocal to the two preceding terms
52. cixʷʔibac[113]	husband or wife of grandchild of speaker or speaker' brother or sister; term possibly reciprocal
53. čə́ɬsx̌ax̌aʔəb	son-in-law or daughter-in-law of speaker's wife's brother or sister, husband of speaker's stepdaughter: reciprocally uncle by marriage or stepfather of speaker's wife, etc.
54. qʷilx̌ʷbitagʷil	kin by marriage; term used in special sense to designate stepbrothers and stepsisters [literally: in-laws to one another]
75. ciɬəbskayuʔ	"related through dead," previously related by marriage
56. sq̓ʷuʔidup	persons whose wives are sisters; whose husbands are brothers; whose respective husband and wife are brother and sister: term derived from root syllable q̓ʷuʔ, "join"
57. ciɬəbstubš	man whose wife is sister to the wife of another (?); "related through the man"
57a. ciɬəbstubšbitagʷil	preceding term amplified [related to one another through a man]
58. ciɬəbsɬadayʔ	woman whose husband is brother to the husband of another (?); "related through the woman"
58a. ciɬəbsɬadayʔbitagʷil	preceding term amplified [related to one another through a woman]
59. təlix̌ʷ sx̌ax̌aʔ	son-in-law related by blood to parent-in-law

APPENDIX TABLES TAKEN FROM
AMERICAN ANTHROPOLOGIST
(N.S., 37, 1935) Volume 37, Issue #1:

---

[113] [cixʷ- *in-law* (TH)}

Appendix H

BAR 7 Criteria
United States Department of the Interior
Office of Federal Acknowledgement SNQ-V001-D004 ~ 408pp

An "unrecognized" tribe seeking federal recognition must present a voluminous petition, meeting seven criteria (below), to the Assistant Secretary of the Interior, Bureau of Indian Affairs, through the Bureau of Acknowledgement and Recognition (BAR), whose employees review the documentary and genealogical evidence presented to prove the following.

(a) petitioner has been identified as an American Indien entity on a substantially continuous basis since 1900

(b) a prominent portion of the petitioning group comprises a distinct community and has existed as a community from historical times to the present

(c) the petitioner has maintained political influence or authority over its members as an autonomous entity from historical times until the present

(d) present government structure and function is documented, including its membership criteria

(e) membership consists of individuals who descend from a historical Indian tribe or from Indian tribes which functioned as a single autonomous political entity

(f) membership is composed principally of persons who are not members of any acknowledged North American tribe, allowing for some exceptions

(g) neither petitioner nor its members are the subject of congressional legislation that has expressly terminated or forbidden the federal relationship

Once approved, the new tribe is eligible for federal services and benefits, along with attendant responsibilities and obligations as well as privileges and immunities due to this government-to-government relationship. All these features, of course, are subject to the appropriation of funds based on official determination of tribal needs.

> 83.7(e)
> A list of all known current members of the group and a copy of each available former list of members based on the tribe's own defined criteria. The membership must consist of individuals who have established, using evidence acceptable to the Secretary, descendancy from a tribe which existed historically or from historical tribes which combined and functioned as a single autonomous entity.

Ninety-six percent of the petitioner's 313 members have established or can be expected to establish descent from the Snoqualmie, a signatory tribe to the 1855 Treaty of Point Elliott. The remaining 4 percent of the membership consists of 11 members who have not satisfactorily established Snoqualmie descent, and 3 members who are non-Indian, but who have been adopted as members. Eighty-five percent of the petitioner's members can trace to ancestors who are identified as Snoqualmie, and either appeared on Roblin's *Schedule of the Unenrolled Indians of Western Washington*, prepared by the Office of Indian Affairs in 1919, or made an application to be listed on the 1919 schedule. Another 11 percent of the membership can trace to ancestors who are identified as Snoqualmie in allotment lists or other Bureau records.

Based upon materials provided by the petitioner, the majority of members (82 percent) possess the one-eighth or more Snoqualmie blood required by the petitioner's membership criteria. Members who possess less than one-eighth Snoqualmie blood but who descend from a Snoqualmie ancestor have been adopted. Twenty percent of the membership are concurrently members of other tribes. Because concurrent membership in more than one tribe or group is prohibited by the petitioner's governing body, these members technically do not meet the petitioner's membership criteria.

Eight former lists of members were either submitted by the petitioner or were already on file with the Bureau. The lists date from 1916 to 1976, and contain substantially the same members. The only noticeable difference in these lists is the gradual dropping off of members who were also members of federally recognized tribes.

Eighty-five percent of the current membership either appears, or has direct ancestors who appear, on one or more of the former lists. Eighty-five percent of the petitioner's members shared in the *1978 judgment distribution awarded to the Snoqualmie and Skykomish Tribes in the Indian Claims commission Docket 93. In order to be eligible to share in the judgment distribution, these members were required to document their descent from the historic Snoqualmie tribe. Descent from the historic tribe can be verified for four members (one percent of the membership) who do not appear on the Docket 93 judgment roll. An additional 10 percent of the current membership are expected to be able to establish their descent from the historic tribe based on their close relationship to members who have already established their descent.

The petitioner has submitted a list of its current members and a copy of each available former list of members based on the petitioner's own defined criteria. Virtually all of the petitioner's members have established or are expected to be able to establish descent from the historic tribe. Therefore, we conclude that the petitioner meets criterion 25 CFR 83.7(e).

The membership of the petitioning group is composed principally of persons who are not members of any other North American tribe 83.7(f).

In the past, the petitioner's membership has included members who were also enrolled in a federally recognized tribe. Some of these former members eventually dropped their membership with the petitioner. In the past ten years, the petitioner has removed approximately 33 individuals (not included as part of the current membership) from its membership list once the petitioner ascertained that the individual was enrolled in a federally recognized tribe.

Twenty percent of the current membership (63 members) can be identified as being enrolled in a federally recognized tribe, leaving a substantial majority (80 percent) of the petitioner's membership who are not enrolled in a federally recognized tribe. The membership of the 20 percent who are enrolled in a federally recognized tribe is dispersed among seven tribes serviced by the Puget Sound Agency, and is based primarily on the member's descent in another line from a non-Snoqualmie Indian ancestor who was affiliated with the tribe.

We conclude that the petitioner's membership is not principally composed of persons who are members of other federally recognized tribes and, therefore, meets criterion 25 CFR 83.7(f).

BIBLIOGRAPHY

Adamson, Thelma
1934 *Folktales of the Coast Salish.* Memoirs of the American Folklore Society 27, American Folklore Society, New York.

Aginsky, Ethel
1934 Field Notes, Puyallup Language. Manuscript on file, Franz Boas Collection, American Philosophical Society, Philadelphia.

American Friends Service Committee
1970 *Uncommon Controversy*: Fishing Rights of the Muckleshoot, Puyallup, and Nisqually Indians. University of Washington Press, Seattle.

Amoss, Pamela Thorsen
1975 Catalogue of the Marian Smith Collection of Fieldnotes, Manuscripts, and Photographs. Manuscript on file, Library of the Royal Anthropological Institute of Great Britain and Ireland, London.
1978 *Coast Salish Spirit Dancing* ~ The Survival of an Ancestral Religion. University of Washington Press, Seattle.
1981 Coast Salish Elders. *Other Ways of Growing Old*: 227-261. Pamela Amoss and Steven Harrell, eds. Stanford University Press.
1982 Resurrection, Healing, and "the Shake": The Story of John and Mary Slocum. Charisma and Sacred Biography. Michael Williams, ed. *Journal of the American Academy of Religion*, Thematic Studies XLVIII, Volume 48 (3-4): 87-109.
1990 The Indian Shaker Church. Handbook of North American Indians, *Northwest Coast*, Volume 7: 633-639. Wayne Suttles, ed. Smithsonian Institution Press, Washington DC.

Anastasio, Angelo
1972 The Southern Plateau ~ An Ecological Analysis of Intergroup Relations. *Northwest Anthropological Research Notes (NARN)* 6 (2): 109-229.

Aoki, Haruo
1966 Nez Perce and Proto-Sahaptian Kinship Terms. *International Journal of American Linguistics* 32 (4): 357-368.

Asher, Brad
1999 *Beyond the Reservation*: Indians, Settlers, and the Law in Washington Territory, 1853-1889. University of Oklahoma Press, Norman.

Bagley, Clarence B
1916 *History of Seattle from the Earliest Settlement to the Present Time.* SJ Clarke Publishing Company, Chicago.
1929 *History of King County, Washington.* SJ Clarke Publishing Company, Chicago.

Ballard, Arthur C
1927 Some Tales of the Southern Puget Sound Salish. *University of Washington Publications in Anthropology* 2 (3): 57-81.
1929 Mythology of Southern Puget Sound. *University of Washington Publications in Anthropology* 3 (2): 31-150.
1935 Southern Puget Sound Salish Kinship Terms. *American Anthropologist* 37 (1): 111-116.
1950 Calendric Terms of the Southern Puget Sound Salish. *Southwestern Journal of Anthropology* 6 (1): 79-99.
1951 Deposition on Oral Examination of Arthur Condict Ballard. November 26, 27, 28. Testimony before the Indian Claims Commission of the United States, Docket 98. Carolyn Taylor, court reporter. Manuscript on file, White River Historical Society, Auburn, Washington.
1957 The Salmon Weir on Green River in Western Washington. *Davidson Journal of Anthropology* 3 (1): 37-53.
1958 Letter to Frank HH Roberts, March 25, 1958. National Anthropological Archives, Washington DC.
1999 *Mythology of Southern Puget Sound.* Kenneth Greg Watson, ed. Snoqualmie Valley Historical Museum, North Bend, Washington. [1929]
1999a Moon ~ The Transformer: 69-80. *Mythology of Southern Puget Sound.* Kenneth Greg Watson, ed. Snoqualmie Valley Historical Museum, North Bend, Washington.

Barnett, Homer Garner
1957 *Indian Shakers* ~ A Messianic Cult of the Pacific Northwest. Southern Illinois University, Carbondale.

Bass, Sophie Frye
1937 *Pig-Tail Days in Old Seattle.* Binfords and Mort, Portland.
1947 *When Seattle Was a Village.* Lowman & Hanford, Seattle.

Bates, Ann M
1987 Affiliation and Differentiation: Intertribal Interactions among the Makah and Ditidaht Indians. PhD Dissertation, Indiana University.

Bates, Dawn, Thom Hess, and Vi Hilbert
1994 *Lushootseed Dictionary.* University of Washington Press, Seattle.

Beavert, Virginia, and Sharon Hargus
2009 *Ichishkiin Sinwit ~ Yakama / Yakima ~ Sahaptin Dictionary.* University of Washington Press, Seattle.

Bennett, Lee A
2003 Historic Archaeological Resources Assessment, Central Link Light Rail Project. BOAS Project Report No. 20005.A2. BOAS, Inc, Seattle. Submitted to Sound Transit, Seattle, Contract No. RTA/LR 69-00.

Bierwert, Crisca
1986   Tracery in the Mistlines: Semeiotic Readings of Sto:lō Culture.   Ph.D. Dissertation, Department of Anthropology, University of Washington, Seattle.

Bierwert, Crisca, ed.
1996   *Lushootseed Texts*: An Introduction to Puget Salish Aesthetics.   Translated by Crisca Bierwert, Vi Hilbert, Thom Hess; annotations by Toby CS Langen.   University of Nebraska Press, Lincoln.

Blukis Onat, Astrida
1995   Culture, Continuity, and the Kitchen Cupboard.   Paper presented at the 1995 Conference of the Archaeological Society of British Columbia and the Wetland Archaeological Research Project, Vancouver, BC.
1999   Tahoma Legends.   Report No. 9300.2b, BOAS, Inc, Seattle.   Submitted to the National Park Service, Pacific Northwest Region, Seattle.
2002   Resource Cultivation in the Northwest Coast of North America.   *Journal of Northwest Anthropology* 36 (2): 125-144.

Blukis Onat, Astrida R, LA Bennett, J Miller, ME Morgenstein, and PD LeTourneau
2003   Archaeological Resources Monitoring and Treatment for the CLLR Route.   Report No. 20005.B2, BOAS, Inc, Seattle.   Submitted to Sound Transit, Seattle, Contract No. RTA/LR 69-00.

Boas, Franz
1919   Kinship Terms of the Kutenai Indians.   *American Anthropologist* 21 (1): 98-101.

Boxberger, Daniel and Bruce Miller
1997   Evolution or History? A Response to Tollefson.   *Ethnohistory* 44 (1): 135-137.

Boyd, Robert, ed.
1999   *Indians, Fire and the Land in the Pacific Northwest.*   Oregon State University Press, Corvallis.

Brunton, Bill
1968   Ceremonial Integration in the Plateau of Northwestern North America   *NARN* 2 (1): 1-28.

Bruseth, Nels
1950   Indian Stories and Legends of the Stillaguamish, Sauks and Allied Tribes.   Arlington (WA) Times Press.

Buchanan, Charles
1916   Rights of the Puget Sound Indians to Game and Fish.   *Washington Historical Quarterly* 6 (2): 109-118.

Buchler, Ira and Henry Selby
  1968 *Kinship And Social Organization ~ An Introduction to Theory and Method.* New York: The MacMillan Co.

Buerge, David
  1980 The Native American Presence in the Rainier Valley Area. Manuscript on file, Rainier Valley Historical Society, Seattle.

Buerge, David, and Junius Rochester
  1988 *Roots and Branches*: The Religious Heritage of Washington State. Church Council of Greater Seattle, Seattle.

Campbell, John
  1950 Report on an Archaeological Survey, Priest Rapids Reservoir. 15 October 1950. Burke Museum Archives, Seattle.

Carlson, Frank
  1903 Chief Sealth. University of Washington Bulletin, series 3 (2): 7-35.

Carlson, Roy
  2015 Interview of 15 January. Coquitlam, BC.

Castile, George P, ed.
  1985 *The Indians of Puget Sound*: The Notebooks of Myron Eells. University of Washington Press for Whitman College, Walla Walla.

Charles H Baker & Co.
  1891 Bird-Eye View of the Puget Sound Country: an accurate perspective projection, showing the topography, resources and development of northwestern Washington and British Columbia. Electronic document http://content.wsulibs.wsu/sid/bin/show.plx?client =maps&image= uw039.sid, accessed February 26, 2003. Charles H Baker & Co, Seattle.

Church Council of Greater Seattle
  1987 A Public Declaration to the Tribal Councils and Traditional Spiritual Leaders of the Indian and Eskimo Peoples of the Pacific Northwest November. Reiterated in 1997.

Collins, June
  1950a The Indian Shaker Church. *Southwestern Journal of Anthropology* 6 (4): 399-411.
  1950b Growth of Class Distinctions and Political Authority Among the Skagit Indians during the Contact Period. *American Anthropologist* 52 (3): 331-342.
  1952 The Mythological Basis for Attitudes toward Animals among Salish-Speaking Indians. *Journal of American Folklore* 65 (258): 353-359.
  1966 Naming, Continuity, and Social Inheritance among the Coast Salish of Western Washington. *Papers of the Michigan Academy of Science, Arts, and Letters* 51: 425-36.
  1974 *Valley of the Spirits* ~ The Upper Skagit Indians of Western Washington. University of Washington Press, Seattle.

Costello, James Allen
1974 *The Siwash* {sic}: Their Life, Legends and Tribes. Reprinted, Paine Field Printers, Everett. Originally published 1895, Calvert Company, Seattle.

Courtois, Shirley, Katheryn Krafft, Catherine Wickwire, James Bard, and Robin McClintock
1999 Final Technical Report [on] Historic and Prehistoric Archaeological Sites, Historic Resources, Native American Traditional Cultural Properties, [and] Paleontological Sites, Final Environmental Impact Statement. Central Link Light Rail Transit Project. Central Puget Sound Regional Transit Authority (Seattle), Seattle.

Cowan, Ian M, and Charles J Guiguet
1978 The Mammals of British Columbia. BC Provincial Museum Handbook Number 11, Victoria, BC.

CRMMP
1996 Cultural Resources Mitigation and Management Plan for Snoqualmie Falls Project, FERC No. 2493. FERC online, Accession Number 19961008-0063.

Culin, Stewart 1907 Games of the North American Indians. BAE –AR

Curtis, Edward
1913 *The North American Indian*, being a series of volumes picturing and describing the Indians of the United States, the Dominion of Canada, and Alaska. Written, Illustrated, and Published By Edward S Curtis. Frederick Webb Hodge, ed. Volume 9.

Dalquest, Walter W
1948 *Mammals of Washington.* Museum of Natural History Publications, Volume 2, University of Kansas, Lawrence.

Daniels, Annie
1951 North Wind. Told to Leon Metcalf at Muckleshoot, June 28. Transcript on file, Lushootseed Research Archives, Seattle, Washington.

Davenport, William
1959 Nonunilinear Descent and Descent Groups. *American Anthropologist* 64 (4):557-572.

Davis, Ed
1983 Interview at Fall City, February 19. Manuscript on file, Lushootseed Research Archives, Seattle.

Davis, Henry
2012 E mail of Friday, 04 May 06, 12PM.

Denny, Arthur A
1895 *Pioneer Days on Puget Sound.* CB Bagley Printer, Seattle.

Denny, Emily Inez
1909 *Blazing the Way*: True Stories, Songs and Sketches of Puget Sound and Other Pioneers. Rainier Printing Company, Seattle.

Desmond, Gerald
1952 Gambling Among the Yakima. *The Catholic University of America Anthropological Series* #14. The Catholic University of America Press, DC.

De Sola, Ralph, ed.
1946 *American Wild Life Illustrated.* Compiled by WPA-NYC. William H Wise & Co, New York.

Donald, Leland
1997 *Aboriginal Slavery on the Northwest Coast of North America.* University of California Press, Berkeley.

Dorpat, Paul
1984 *Seattle Now and Then*, Volume I. Tartu Publications, Seattle.
1986 *Seattle Now and Then*, Volume II. Tartu Publications, Seattle.
1989 *Seattle Now and Then*, Volume III. Tartu Publications, Seattle.

Drucker, Philip
1937 Diffusion in Northwest Coast Culture in the Light of Some Distributions. PhD Dissertation, University of California at Berkeley.
1951 The Northern and Central Nootkan Tribes. Bureau of American Ethnology, Bulletin 141.

Duff, Wilson
1964 The Indian History of British Columbia. Volume 1: The Impact of the White Man. Provincial Museum of British Columbia: Anthropology in British Columbia, Memoir 5.

Durlach, Teresa
1928 The Relationship Systems of the Tlingit, Haida, and Tsimshian. American Ethnological Society, Volume #11. NY.

Edmonson, Munro
1958 Status Terminology and the Social Structure of North American Indians. American Ethnological Society, Monograph 30.

Eggan, Fred
1955 The Cheyenne and Arapaho Kinship System. *Social Anthropology of North American Tribes*: 33-95. Fred Eggan, ed. University of Chicago Press.

Elmendorf, William Welcome
1946 Twana Kinship Terminology. *Southwestern Journal of Anthropology* 2: 420-432.

1960 *The Structure of Twana Culture* ~ with Comparative Notes on the Structure of Yurok by Alfred Kroeber. Washington State Research Studies, Monographic Supplement 2, Washington State University, Pullman.

1961a System Change in Salish Kinship Terminologies. *Southwestern Journal of Anthropology* 17 (4): 365-382.

1961b Skokomish and Other Coast Salish Tales. Washington State University Research Studies 29 (1): 1-37, (2): 84-117, (3): 119-150.

1971 Coast Salish Status Ranking and Intergroup Ties. *Southwestern Journal of Anthropology* 27: 353-380.

1989 Skokomish Sorcery, Ethics, and Society: 147-182. *Systems of North American Witchcraft and Sorcery*. Deward Walker, ed. 1970, Anthropological Monographs of the University of Idaho 1, University of Idaho, Moscow.

1993 *Twana Narratives*: Native Historical Accounts of a Coast Salish Culture. University of Washington Press, Seattle

Farwest Lithographing and Printing
1932 *Seattle 1856*. Farwest Lithographing and Printing Company, Seattle.

FERC
2008 Memorandum of Agreement between the Federal Energy Regulatory Commission and the Washington State Department of Archaeology and Historic Preservation Regarding the Proposed Modifications to the Snoqualmie Falls Hydroelectric Project (FERC #2493), King County, Washington. FERC Online, Accession Number 20081209-0108.

FERC
2009 127 FERC 62,174 United States of America Federal Energy Regulatory Commission Order Amending License 1 June 2009. http://pse.com/aboutpse/HydroLicensing/ Documents/ snoqualmie/docs/SnoqualmieAmendmentOrder.pdf

Fleisher, Mark
1984 Hesquiat Kinship Terminology: Social Structure and Symbolic World View Categories. *Anthropos* 79 (1/3): 243-248.

Foster, Michael
1996 Language and the Culture History of North America. Handbook of North American Indians. Ives Goddard, ed. *Languages* 17: 64-110.

Freeman, John
1966 *Guide* to Manuscripts Relating to the American Indian in the Library of the American Philosophical Society. The American Philosophical Society, Memoir 65, Philadelphia.

Fried, Morton
1967 *The Evolution of Political Society*. NY

Galloway, Brent
1977   A Grammar of Chilliwack Halkomelem. PhD Dissertation, University of California at Berkeley.
1980.   Upper Halqemeylem Grammatical Sketch and Classified Word List.   Coqualeetza Education Training Centre, Sardis, BC.
1984   Samish Fieldnotes from Victor Underwood and Lena Daniels.

Garfield, Leonard, with Kenneth Tollefson
1992   National Register of Historic Places Form for Snoqualmie Falls (45-KI-508) 23pp.

Gibbs, George
1877   Tribes of Western Washington and Northwestern Oregon. United States Geographical and Geological Survey of the Rocky Mountain Region, Part II: 157-241. Department of the Interior, Washington DC.
1970   Dictionary of the Niskwalli (Nisqually) Indian Language, Western Washington. Reprinted The Shorey Book Store, Seattle. Originally published 1877, Contributions to North American Ethnology 1: 285-361.

Gifford, Edward
1922   Californian Kinship Terminologies. University of California Publications in American Archaeology and Ethnology 18: 1-285.

Gill, John Kaye
1909   Dictionary of the Chinook Jargon. JK Gill Company, Portland.

Goodenough, Ward
1970   *Description and Comparison in Cultural Anthropology.* Aldine Publishing, Chicago.

Graburn, Nelson
1971   *Readings in Kinship and Social Structure.* Harper and Row, New York.

Gramly, RM   2004   Part III ~ The Richey Clovis Cache." *The Amateur Archaeologist* 10 (1): 5-30. 1993
     Part IV ~ Blood Residues upon Tools from East Wenatchee Clovis Site. *Ohio Archaeologist* 41 (4): 21, 23.

Gunther, Erna
c1930-1940   Field Notebooks. Manuscript on file, Burke Museum, Seattle.

Haeberlin, Herman K
1916-1917   Puget Salish, 41 Notebooks. Microfilm #2965 on file, National Anthropological Archives, Washington, DC.
1918   SbEtEtda'q, A Shamanic Performance of the Coast Salish. *American Anthropologist* 20 (3): 249-257.
1924   Mythology of Puget Sound. *Journal of American Folklore* 37 (143-144): 371-438.

Haeberlin, Herman, and Erna Gunther
 1930 The Indians of Puget Sound. *University of Washington Publications in Anthropology* 4
    (1): 1-84.

Halverson, Matthew
 2013 Bad Blood: 54-63. *Seattle Metropolitan.* January.

Harbor Line Commission
 1891 First Report of the Harbor Line Commission of the State of Washington. OC White,
    Olympia, Washington.

Harmon, Alexandra
 1995 A Different Kind of Indians. Negotiating the Meanings of "Indian" and "Tribe" in the
    Puget Sound Region, 1820s-1970s. Ph.D. dissertation, Department of History, University
    of Washington, Seattle.
 1999 *Indians in the Making*: Ethnic Relations and Indian Identities around Puget Sound.
    University of California Press, Berkeley.

Harrington, John Peabody
 1910 Field and Class Notes, University of Washington, Seattle. Manuscript on file, Folders 36,
    37. Microfilm reel 015, National Anthropological Archives, Washington DC.

Hess, Thom
 1971 Prefix Constituent With /x^w/. *Studies in Northwest Indian Languages*: 43-69. James Hoard
    and Thom Hess, eds. Sacramento Anthropological Society, Paper #11.
 1976 *Dictionary of Puget Salish.* University of Washington Press, Seattle.
 p.c Kinship terms: Saanich from Ernie Olsen, Ahousaht from Peter Webster, and Nitinat from
    John Thomas.

Hilbert, Vi taq^{w}šəblu
 1976 Recording in the Native Language. *Sound Heritage* IV (34): 39-42.
 1979 *Yehaw.* Lushootseed Press, Seattle.
 1980a Ways of the Lushootseed People: Ceremonies and Traditions of the Northern Puget
    Sound Indians. United Indians of All Tribes Foundation, Daybreak Star Press, Seattle.
 1980b Haboo. Lushootseed Press, Seattle.
 1985 *Haboo*: Native American Stories From Puget Sound. University of Washington Press,
    Seattle.
 1996 *Haboo* ~ Lushootseed Literature in English. Lushootseed Press.

Hilbert, Vi taq^{w}šəblu, Jay Miller, and Zalmai Zahir
 2001 *Puget Sound Geography.* Revised Thomas T Waterman Ethnogeography. Lushootseed
    Press, Seattle.

Hoebel, Adamson
 1939 Comanche and H3kandika Shoshone Relationship Systems. *American Anthropologist* 41
    (3): 440-457.

Indian Claims Commission
   1974a Commission Findings. Docket No. 109, the Duwamish Tribe of Indians. Coast Salish and Western Washington Indians V: 29-51. David Agee Horr, ed. Garland Series, New York.
   1974b Commission Findings. Docket No. 98, the Muckleshoot Tribe of Indians. Coast Salish and Western Washington Indians V: 101-132. David Agee Horr, ed. A Garland Series, New York.
   1974c Commission Findings. Docket No. 132, the Suquamish Tribe of Indians. In Coast Salish and Western Washington Indians V: 620-644. David Agee Horr, ed. A Garland Series, New York.

Jacobs, Melville
   1932 Northern Sahaptin Kinship Terms. *American Anthropologist* 34 (4): 688-693.

Jenness, Diamond
   1955 The Faith of a Coast Salish Indian. Anthropology in British Columbia, Memoir 3. British Columbia Provincial Museum, Victoria.

Jilek, Wolfgang
   1982 *Indian Healing*: Shamanic Ceremonialism in the Pacific Northwest Today. Hancock House, Surrey, British Columbia.

Johnson, Lawrence
   2001 Hand Game ~ The Native North American Game of Power and Chance. Jacqueline Peterson. VisionMaker Video.

Kamb, Lewis
   2004 Tribe Longs for a Longhouse. *Seattle Post-Intelligencer*, 29 March 2004: B3.

Kellog, George Albert
   1934 A History of Whidbey's Island. Oak Harbor.

Kenyon, Susan
   1980 *The Kyuquot Way*. A Study of a West Coast (Nootkan) Community. Mercury Series, Canadian Ethnology Service, Paper #61. National Museums of Canada.

Kielland, Alfred
   1907 Report of an Investigation by a Board of Engineers of the Means of Controlling Floods in the Duwamish-Puyallup Valleys and Their Tributaries in the State of Washington. Lowman & Hanford, Seattle.

King County
   1886 King County Tax Assessment Roll. Seattle.

King, Thomas
  1998 *Cultural Resource Laws and Practice*: An Introductory Guide. AltaMira Press, Walnut Creek.

Kinkade, Dale
  1981 Dictionary of the Moses-Columbia Language. Nespelem: Colville Confederated Tribes.
  p.c Kinship Terms: Upper Chehalis and Moses-Columbian from his own fieldnotes, Klallam and Thompson from the notes of Laurence Thompson, and Sechelt from Ronald Beaumont elicited from Jennie Erickson.

Kinkade, M Dale, William Elmendorf, Bruce Rigsby, and Haruo Aoki
  1989 Languages. Handbook of North American Indians. Deward Walker, ed. *Plateau* 12: 49-72.

Kinkade, MD and JV Powell
  1978 Language and the Prehistory of North America. *World Archaeology* 8 (1): 83-100.

Klingle, Matthew
  2007 *Emerald City* ~ An Environmental History of Seattle. Yale University Press, New Haven.

Koch, Augustus
  1891 Birds-Eye-View of Seattle and Environs King County, Wash. Hughes Litho. Co., Chicago. Electronic document, http://hdl.loc.gov/loc.gmd4s.pm009750, accessed May 15, 2003. Digital ID g4284spm009750, Library of Congress Geography and Map Division Washington, D.C.

Kroeber, Clifton, and Bernard Fontana
  1986 *Massacre on the Gila*. An Account of the Last Major Battle between American Indians, with Reflections on the Origin of War. University of Arizona Press, Tucson.

Kruckeberg, Arthur
  1991 *The Natural History of Puget Sound.* University of Washington Press, Seattle.

Kuipers, Aert
  2002 Salish Etymological Dictionary. University of Montana, *Occasional Papers in Linguistics* #16. Missoula.

Lane, Barbara
  1973 Political and Economic Aspects of Indian-White Culture Contact in Western Washington in the Mid-19th Century. Assembled for law case U.S. v. State of Washington, 384 F. Supp. 312, resulting in the Boldt Decision. Manuscript on file, University of Washington, Seattle.
  1975 Identity, Treaty Status and Fisheries of the Snoqualmie Tribe of Indians, 15 October.

Larson, Lynn L
 1987 Ethnographic Background. In The Duwamish No. 1 Site 1986 Data Recovery: 2-1-2-34.
    URS Corporation, Seattle. Contract No. CW/F2-82. Submitted to METRO, Municipality
    of Metropolitan Seattle.

Levi-Strauss, Claude
 1982 *The Way of the Masks*. Sylvia Modelski, translator. UW Press, Seattle.

Lewellen, Ted C
 1983 *Political Anthropology.* Bergen & Gurvey, South Hadley, Massachusetts.

Liu, Martin
 22 August 2010 Mukle-Te-Oh Gathering. *Seattle Times*: pages A-1, A-7.

Longenecker, Julia, Darby Stapp, and Angela Buck
 2002 The Wanapum of Priest Rapids, Washington: 137-15. *Endangered Peoples of North
    America ~ Struggles to Survive and Thrive.* Tom Greaves, ed. Greenwood Press,
    Westport.

McClure, Richard, and Nathaniel Reynolds
 2015 Making the List: Mount St Helens as a Traditional Cultural Property, A Case Study in
    Tribal/Governmental Cooperation. *Journal of Northwest Anthropology* 49 (2): 117-142.

McDonald, Lucile
 1958 Susie Sampson Peter, Oldest of the Kikialus. *The Seattle Times*, 2 November. Seattle.

McConaghy, Lorraine
 2009 *Warship Under Sail* ~ The USS *Decatur* in the Pacific West. UW Press, Seattle.

Mangum, AW
 1911 Reconnaissance Soil Survey of the Eastern Part of the Puget Sound Basin, Washington.
    US Department of Agriculture, Bureau of Soils, Washington DC.

Mapes, Lynda
 6 May 2012 We Go Back to Time Immemorial. *Seattle Times*: pages B-1 and B-7.
 27 May 2012 Stalemate Puts Snoqualmie Tribe at Risk of Federal Takeover. *Seattle Times* 8PM.

Martin, Watson
 1933 Legal Deposition. Duwamish et alia v USA. US Court of Claims, R-275, RC 123. US
    National Archives I, DC.

Meany, Edmond
 1924 Chief Patkanim. *Washington Historical Quarterly* 15: 187-198.

Meeker, Ezra
1980 *Pioneer Reminiscences of Puget Sound.* Reprinted, The Printers, Everett. Originally 1905, Lowman and Hanford, Seattle.

Meeker, Jerry
1948 Notebooks A, B, C recorded by Alfred John Smith. Special Collections, University of Washington Libraries, Seattle.

Miller, Bruce Subiyay
1999 From the Time of Our Ancestors. Volumes 1 & 2. Ten Wolves Audio.
2006 Teaching of the Tree People ~ The Work of Bruce Miller. Katie Jennings & Tracy Rector. Islandwood DVD, Bainbridge Island, WA.

Miller, Bruce, and Daniel Boxberger
1994 Creating Chiefdoms: The Puget Sound Case. *Ethnohistory* 41 (2): 267-293.

Miller, Jay
1976 The Northwest Coast of What? Paper presented at the Conference on Northwest Coast Studies, Burnaby, BC.
1980 High-Minded High Gods in North America. *Anthropos* 75: 916-919.
1981 The Matter of the (Thoughtful) Heart: Centrality, Focality, or Overlap. *Journal of Anthropological Research* 36 (3): 338-342.
1985a Salish Kinship: Why Decedence? 20th International Conference on Salish and Neighboring Languages: 213-222. August 15-17, University of British Columbia.
1985b Art and Souls: The Puget Sound Salish Journey to the Land of the Dead. Paper presented at the 5th Conference of the National Native American Art Studies Association, Ann Arbor.
1988 *Shamanic Odyssey*: The Lushootseed Salish Journey to the Land of the Dead, in terms of Death, Potency, and Cooperating Shamans in North America. Ballena Press Anthropological Papers 32, Menlo Park, CA.
1990 *Mourning Dove ~ A Salishan Autobiography.* University of Nebraska Press, Lincoln.
1992a Native Healing in Puget Sound: Portrayal of Native American Health and Healing: 1-15. *Caduceus* ~ A Museum Journal for the Health Sciences. Winter.
1992b A Kinship of Spirit: Society in the Americas in 1492: 305-337. *America in 1492.* Alvin Josephy, ed. Alfred Knopf, New York.
1992c North Pacific Ethno-Astronomy: Tsimshian and Others: 193-206. *Earth and Sky*: Visions of the Cosmos in Native American Folklore. Claire Farrer and Ray Williamson, eds. University of New Mexico Press, Albuquerque.
1992d Society in America in 1492. America in 1492. Selected Lectures from the Quincentenary Program. Harvey Markowitz, ed. The Newberry Library, D'Arcy McNickle Center for the History of the American Indian, Occasional Papers in Curriculum Series 15: 151-169. Chicago.
1994 The Wisdom of Aunt Susie Sampson Peter, A Skagit Elder (Lushootseed~English).
1995a The Wisdom of Ruth Shelton, A Tulalip Elder (Lushootseed~English).
1995b The Wisdom of Isadore Tom, A Lummi Elder.

1996 Seattle (si'ał): 574-576. Encyclopedia of North American Indians. Frederick E. Hoxie, ed. Houghton Mifflin Company, Boston.

1997 Back to Basics: Chiefdoms in Puget Sound. *Ethnohistory* 44 (2): 375-387.

1998 Middle Columbia River Salishans. Smithsonian Handbook of North American Indians. *Plateau.* Deward Walker, ed. Volume 12: 253-270.

1999 *Lushootseed Culture and the Shamanic Odyssey*: An Anchored Radiance. University of Nebraska Press, Lincoln.

2000 Inflamed History: Violence Against Homesteading Indians in Washington Territory. *North Dakota Quarterly* 67 (3/4): 162-173.

2004 Winds, Waterways, and Weirs. Ethnographic Study of the Central Link Light Rail Corridor. Sound Transit, Contract Rta/Lr 69-00. Boas Project No 20005.D (Astrida Blukis Onat, PI). Seattle.

2014 Elders Dialog ~ Ed Davis and Vi Hilbert Discuss Native Puget Sound Language, Culture, and Heritage. (Lushootseed~English). 4Culture, King County Lodging Tax.

2015 Evergreen Ethnographies ~ Hoh, Chehalis, Suquamish, and Snoqualmi of Western Washington. Amazon.

2016a Herman Haeberlin Regained ~ Anthropology And Artifacts Of Puget Sound 1916-17, Amazon.

2016b Old Lukh ~ Native Puget Sound in Daily Life, Places, and Stories. Amazon.

2016c Pacific Plateau Portrayals ~ People, Places, Ponderings. Amazon.

2016d Leschi in Love ~ . Amazon.

2017a Minter Bay ~ Land, Lore, Loss, and Lucre in the South Salish Sea. Amazon.

2017b Native Met how ~ Improving Posterity. Amazon.

2017c George Gibbs Northwest Array ~ Full Reports, Place Names, Word List, Artifact Names, and Guide. Amazon.

2017d Herstory NW ~ Women Upholding Native Traditions

Miller, Jay, and Vi taqʷšəblu Hilbert

1993 Caring for Control: A Pivot of Salishan Language and Culture: 237-239. *American Indian Linguistics and Ethnography in Honor of Laurence C. Thompson.* Anthony Mattina and Timothy Montler, eds. Occasional Papers in Linguistics 10. University of Montana, Missoula.

1996 Lushootseed Animal People: Mediation and Transformation from Myth to History: 138-156. *Monsters, Tricksters, and Sacred Cows*: Animal Tales and American Identities. James Arnold, ed. New World Studies, University of Virginia Press, Charlottesville.

Miller, Jay, with Warren Snyder

1999 Suquamish Traditions. *Northwest Anthropological Research Notes* 33 (1): 105-175.

Minnis, Paul, and Wayne Elisens, eds.

2000 *Biodiversity & Native America.* University of Oklahoma Press, Norman.

Mitchell, Donald

1990 Prehistory of the Coasts of Southern British Columbia and Northern Washington. Handbook of North American Indians. Wayne Suttles, ed. *Northwest Coast* 7: 340-358.

Morgenstein, Maury E., and Astrida R. Blukis Onat
2003   Geoarchaeological and Paleontological Assessment, Central Link Light Rail Project. Report No. 20005.A1 BOAS, Inc, Seattle.   Submitted to Sound Transit, Contract No RTA/LR 69-00. Seattle.

Morse, Eldridge
1880 Notes on the History & Resources of Washington Territory Furnished to HH Bancroft. Berkeley: BANC MSS P-B 30-53.

Munsell, David
1968 The Ryegrass Coulee Site (KT88). Approved 29 November 1967. UW: Anthropology MA thesis, Seattle.

Murdock, George Peter
1949 *Social Structure*. New York: Macmillan Co. 387pp.
1965. Algonkian Social Organization. *Context and Meaning in Cultural Anthropology*: 24-35. Melford Spiro, ed. Free Press, New York.

Nelson, Charles M
1969 The Sunset Creek Site (45 KT 28) and Its Place in Plateau Prehistory. Washington State University, Laboratory of Anthropology, *Report of Investigations* 47.
1973 Prehistoric Culture Change in the Intermontane Plateau of Western North America: 371-90 in *Explanations of Culture Change: Models in Prehistory*. Colin Renfrew, ed. Gerald Duckworth, London.
1990 Prehistory of the Puget Sound Region. Handbook of North American Indians. Wayne Suttles, ed. *Northwest Coast* Volume 7: 481-484.   Smithsonian Institution Press, Washington DC.

Nelson, Margaret A
2000 Addendum: Draft Technical Memorandum on Cultural Resources, Light Rail Alternative E-4. Northwest Archaeological Associates. Submitted to Sound Transit, Seattle.

Newell, Gordon R
1977 *Westward to Alki*: The Story of David and Louisa Denny. Superior Publishing Company, Seattle.

Nies, Judith
1996 *Native American History. A Chronology of a Culture's Vast Achievements and Their Links to World Events*. Ballantine Books, NY.

Nordquist, Del
1963 Further Notes on Fish Weirs and Traps as Related to Site 45-SN-100. *The Washington Archaeologist* 7 (3): 2-20.

Norton, Helen H
 1980 Evidence for Bracken Fern as a Food for Aboriginal Peoples of Western Washington. *Economic Botany* 33 (4): 384-396.
 1990 An Inventory of Goods and Resources Marketed by Native Groups, Fort Nisqually, 1833-1849. *Northwest Anthropological Research Notes* 24 (1): 1-20.

NPS
 1990 Guidelines for Evaluating and Documenting Traditional Cultural Properties. Patricia L Parker and Thomas F King. US Department of the Interior, National Park Service, Interagency Resources Division, National Register Bulletin 38. Washington, DC.

NRHP
 2009 Snoqualmie Falls National Register of Historic Places Registration Form. Originally determined eligible and submitted in 1992, with a 2009 update. http://focus.nps.gov/nrhp/GetAsset?assetID=88f12c2b-db08-4c31-9c59-36acf64e305e (accessed on 11/12/15).

Page, Jake, ed.
 2001 Let the Spirit Flow: 82-93. *Sacred Lands of Indian America*. Photography by David Muench. Text by Charles Little, Jake Page, Ruth Rudner, Paula Gunn Allen, Rennard Strickland, James Parks Morton. Liveoak & Harry N Abrams, Inc, NY.

Panton, Blake
 1996 Seattle 1894. Electronic document, http://www.geoimages.com/cart/cart.htm, accessed July 21, 2002.

Parker, Patricia L, and Thomas F King
 1998 Guidelines for Evaluating and Documenting Traditional Cultural Properties. US Department of the Interior, National Park Service, Interagency Resources Division, National Register Bulletin 38. Washington, DC. Revised

Peter, Susie Sampson
 1995 x̌əč̓usədəʔ ʔə gʷəqʷulc̓ə ~ *The Wisdom of a Skagit Elder*. Transcribed by Vi Hilbert, translated by Vi Hilbert and Jay Miller, recorded by Leon Metcalf. Lushootseed Press, Seattle.

P-I ~ Post-Intelligencer
 1992a Prayers for Snoqualmie Falls. State Ponders Placing Them on National Historic Register. 28 February: B1, B6.
 1992b Local/Region: Puget Power Blocks Plan for Historic Falls Site. 22 May: B10.

Pullum, Geoffrey and William Ladusaw
 1996 *Phonetic Symbol Guide*. Second edition. University of Chicago Press, Chicago.

Rand, McNally & Co.
 1895 Rand McNally & Co's New 11 x 14 Map of Washington. Rand, McNally, & Co., Chicago.

Ray, Verne
1932 The Sanpoil and Nespelem ~ Salishan Peoples of Northeastern Washington. *University of Washington Publications in Anthropology* 5: 1-237.
1933 Sanpoil Folktales. *Journal of American Folklore* 46: 129-87.
1936 Native Villages and Groupings of the Columbia Basin. *Pacific Northwest Quarterly* 27: 99-152.
1939 *Cultural Relations in the Plateau of Northwestern America.* Southwest Museum, Los Angeles.
1960 The Columbia Indian Confederacy: A League of Central Plateau Tribes: 177-89. *Culture in History*: *Essays in Honor of Paul Radin.* Stanley Diamond, ed. Columbia University Press.

Reinartz, Kay F
1991 *Tukwila*: Community at the Crossroads. The City of Tukwila, Tukwila.

Relander, Click
1956 Drummers and Dreamers. Caxton, Idaho.

Richen, Marilyn Claire
1974 Legitimacy and the Resolution of Conflict in an Indian Church. Ph.D. Dissertation, University of Oregon, Eugene. University Microfilms, Ann Arbor.

Rigsby, Bruce, and Michael Finley
2009 Priest Rapids: Places, People, and Names. *JONA* 43 (1): 57-86. Spring.

Roberts, Helen, and Herman K. Haeberlin
1918 Songs of the Puget Sound Salish. *Journal of American Folklore* 31 (122): 496-520.

Roberts, Natalie Andrea
1975 A History of the Swinomish Tribal Community. PhD Dissertation, Department of Anthropology, University of Washington, Seattle.

Roblin, Charles
1919 M1343, Roll 6: Applications for Enrollment & Allotment – Washington Indians, 1911-9 Snoqualmie Squaxin Island Steilacoom Stillaguamish Suquamish Swinomish Tulalip-Spusam Wynookie {Originals in Box 7 NARA A1, DC}
1920 M1344 5 microfilmed reels, Records Concerning Applications for Adoption by the Quinaielt Indians, 1910–1919, Report of Special Agent [Charles] Roblin; Dr. Otis O. Benson, superintendent.

Ruby, Robert, and John Brown
1965 *Half-Sun on the Columbia*: A Biography of Chief Moses. University of Oklahoma Press, Norman.
1989 *Dreamer-Prophets of the Columbia Plateau*: Smohalla and Skolaskin. University of Oklahoma Press, Norman.

1996 *John Slocum and the Indian Shaker Church.* University of Oklahoma Press, Norman.

Sahlins, Marshall
1968 Poor Man, Rich Man, Chief: Political Types in Melanesia and Polynesia: 20-27. *Peoples and Cultures of the Pacific.* Andrew Vayda, ed. Natural History Press, NY.

Sapir, Edward
1916 Terms of Relationship and the Levirate. *American Anthropologist* 18 (3): 327-337.
1918 Kinship Terms of the Kootenay Indians. *American Anthropologist* 20 (4): 141-418.
1919 Corrigenda to 'Kinship Terms of Kootenay Indians'. *American Anthropologist* 21 (1): 98.

Scheuerman, R. and Clement, J.
2003 *Palouse Country*: A Land and Its People. Walla Walla.

Scheuerman, Richard, and Michael Finley
2008 *Finding Chief Kamaiakin* ~ The Life and Legacy of a Northwest Patriot. WSU Press, Pullman.

Schuster, Helen
1975 Yakima Indian Traditionalism: A Study in Continuity and Change. PhD Dissertation, University of Washington, Seattle.

Sercombe, Laurel
2001 And Then it Rained: Power and Song in Western Washington Coast Salish Myth Narratives. PhD Dissertation, Department of Music, University of Washington, Seattle.

Service, Elman
1962 *Primitive Social Organization.* Random House, NY. 1971

Smith, Allan
2006 *Takhoma* ~ Ethnography of Mount Rainier National Park. WSU Press, Pullman.

Smith, Edgar
1947 Indian Tribal Cases Decided in the Court of Claims of the United States, briefed and Compiled to 30 June 1947. General Accounting Office, Washington, DC.

Smith, Marian Wesley
1940 *The Puyallup-Nisqually.* Columbia University Contributions to Anthropology 32, New York.
1941 The Coast Salish of Puget Sound. *American Anthropologist* 43: 197-211.

Smith, Marian Wesley, ed.
1949 *Indians of the Urban Northwest.* Columbia University Contributions to Anthropology 36, New York.

Snoqualmie Falls Preservation Project
2004 Snoqualmie Falls Preservation Project, Richard M. Briggs, MD, Ann Cross Eschenbach, Attorney. http://www.sacredland.org/snoqualmie-falls/#sthash.6VjQmbhP.dpuf. http:// www.sacredland.org/snoqualmie-falls/

Snoqualmie Valley Reporter
1993 Advice To Feds: Stop Project. 11 August: A8-A9.

Snyder, Sally
c1964   Folktales of the Skagit.   Manuscript on file, Manuscripts, Special Collections, University of Washington Libraries, Seattle.
1964   Skagit Society and Its Existential Basis: An Ethnofolkloristic Reconstruction.   PhD Dissertation, Department of Anthropology, University of Washington, Seattle.
1975 Quest for the Sacred in Northern Puget Sound. *Ethnology* 14 (2): 149-161.

Snyder, Warren
1968   Southern Puget Sound Salish: Texts, Place Names, and Dictionary.   *Sacramento Anthropological Society*, Paper 9, Sacramento State College, Sacramento.

Solland, Sonja
1967 Proposed Quantitative Definitions of the Sunset Canyon and Crescent Bar Components of the Sunset Canyon Phase. Approved 28 November 1967. UW Anthropology MA thesis, Seattle.

Sound Transit
1999 Final Environmental Impact Statement. Central Link Light Rail Transit Project, Seattle, Tukwila and SeaTac, Washington. Central Puget Sound Regional Transit Authority (Sound Transit) and US Department of Transportation, Federal Transit Administration, Seattle.
2000 Programmatic Agreement among the Federal Transit Administration, Washington State Historic Preservation Officer, and the Advisory Council on Historic Preservation, Regarding Development of the Central Link Light Rail Transit Project in the State of Washington. Photocopy of signed document. 17 pp. included with Request for Qualifications/Proposals, Traditional Cultural Properties/Ethnographic Study for the Central Link Project, RFQ/RFP No.RTA/LR 84-00, May 2000. Sound Transit, Central Puget Sound Transit Authority, Seattle.
2001a Final Supplemental Environmental Impact Statement, Tukwila Freeway Route. Central Link Light Rail Transit Project: Seattle, Tukwila and SeaTac, Washington. Central Puget Sound Regional Transit Authority (Sound Transit) and US Department of Transportation, Federal Transit Administration, Seattle.
2001b "North Link'' Light Rail Study, Environmental Scoping Information Report. Central Puget Sound Regional Transit Authority (Sound Transit), Seattle.
2002a Central Link Southern Terminus, Central Puget Sound Regional Transit Authority (Sound Transit). Electronic document, www.soundtransit.org/stbusiness/facts/factsheets/ stbusinessSouthernTerminus.htm. accessed May 3,2002.

2002b   Central Link Light Rail Transit Project Initial Segment, NEPA Environmental Assessment. Central Puget Sound Regional Transit Authority (Sound Transit) and US Department of Transportation, Federal Transit Administration, Seattle.
2002c North Link Light Rail Alternatives. Map 1 July 2002. Central Puget Sound Regional Transit Authority (Sound Transit), Seattle.

Speidel, William C
1967 *Sons of the Profits*: Or There's No Business Like Grow Business. The Seattle Story 1851-190I. Nettle Creek Publishing Company, Seattle.
1978 *Doc Maynard*: The Man Who Invented Seattle. Nettle Creek Publishing Company, Seattle.

Spier, Leslie
1925   *The Distribution of Kinship Systems in North America.* University of Washington Publications in Anthropology 1 (2): 69-88.

Stanley, HA
1995   Rex Wayland's Fortune: 25-63. *Images of Angeline*: Two Views of Chief Seattle's Daughter from the Nineteenth Century. Steve Heinzen, ed. Lowell Printing & Publishing, Everett. [1898]

Stern, Theodore
1993 *Chiefs & Chief Traders.* Indian Relations at Fort Nez Perces, 1818-1855. Volume 1. Oregon Historical Society, Portland.

Suttles, Wayne
1955   Katzie Ethnographic Notes. British Columbia Provincial Museum, *Anthropology in British Columbia*, Memoir #2. Victoria, BC.
1958   Private Knowledge, Morality, and Social Classes Among The Coast Salish. *American Anthropologist* 60: 497-507.
1965 Linguistic Means for Anthropological Ends on the North West Coast. *Canadian Journal of Linguistics* 10: 156-166.
1987 *Coast Salish Essays*. University of Washington Press, Seattle.

Suttles, Wayne, ed.
1990 *Northwest Coast.* Handbook of North American Indians, Volume 7. Smithsonian Institution Press, Washington DC.

Suttles, Wayne, and William Elmendorf
1963 Linguistic Evidence for Salish Prehistory: 41-52. *Symposium on Language and Culture.* Viola E Garfield and Wallace Chafe, eds. Proceedings of the 1962 Annual Spring Meeting of the American Ethnological Society. University of Washington Press, Seattle.

Suttles, Wayne, and Barbara Lane
1990 Southern Coast Salish. Handbook of North American Indians. Wayne Suttles, ed. *Northwest Coast* Volume 7: 485-502. Smithsonian Institution Press, Washington, DC.

Suttles, Wayne, and Aldona Jonaitis
1990   History of Research in Ethnology.   Handbook of North American Indians.   Wayne Suttles, ed. *Northwest Coast* Volume 7: 73-87. Smithsonian Institution Press, Washington DC.

Swadesh, Morris
1954 Time Depths of American Linguistic Groupings. *American Anthropologist* 56: 361-362.

Teit, James   1928   The Middle Columbia Salish. *University of Washington Publications in Anthropology* 2 (4): 83-128.

Thom, Brian   2005   Coast Salish Senses of Place: Dwelling, Meaning, Power, Property and Territory in the Coast Salish World. PhD, Toronto.

Thompson, Laurence C and M Dale Kinkade
1990 Languages. Handbook of North American Indians. Wayne Suttles, ed. *Northwest Coast* Volume 7: 30-51. Smithsonian Institution Press, Washington DC.

Thompson, AH, RH McKee, JG Hefty, and CF Eberly
1908 Seattle, Washington quadrangle. USGS, Denver, Colorado

Thrush, Coll-Peter
2002   The Crossing-over Place: Urban and Indian Histories in Seattle. Ph.D. Dissertation, Department of History, University of Washington, Seattle
2007   *Native Seattle* ~ Histories from the Crossing-Over Place. University of Washington Press, Seattle.

Tollefson, Kenneth Dean
1982 Northwest Coast Village Adaptations: A Case Study. *Canadian Journal of Anthropology* 3 (1): 19-30.
1987a Duwamish Cultural Continuity Study. Petition of Federal Acknowledgement.
1987b The Snoqualmie: A Puget Sound Chiefdom. *Ethnology* 26 (2): 121-136.
1989a Religious Transformation among the Snoqualmie Shakers. *Northwest Anthropological Research Notes* 23 (1): 97-102.
1989b Political Organization of the Duwamish. *Ethnology* 28 (2): 135-149.
1992   The Political Survival of Landless Puget Sound Tribes. *American Indian Quarterly*. Spring: 213-235.
1995a Potlatching and Political Organization among the Northwest Coast Indians. *Ethnology* 34 (1): 53-73.
1995b Duwamish Tribal Identity and Cultural Survival. *Northwest Anthropological Research Notes* 29 (1): 103-116.
1996a In Defense of a Snoqualmie Political Chiefdom Model. *Ethnohistory* 43 (1): 145-171.
1996b Tribal Estates: A Comparative And Case Study. *Ethnology* 35 (4): 321-338.
1997 Tlingit: Chiefs and Present. *Portraits of Culture*. Ethnographical Originals. Melvin Ember, C Ember, D Levinson, eds. North America I: 267-292.

2015a interview 7 January 2015, 2-3pm. TCP ~ National Register for Historic Preservation for Snoqualmie Falls. Conducted by Jay Miller.
2015b Tribal Trio of the Northwest Coast. Jay Miller and Darby Stapp, eds. *Journal of Northwest Anthropology*, Memoir #10.

Tollefson, Kenneth, and Martin Abbott
1993 From Fish Weir to Waterfall. *American Indian Quarterly* 17 (2): 209-225.
1998 Snoqualmie Ethnicity: Community and Continuity. *American Indian Quarterly* 22 (4): 415-431.

Turner, Nancy J
1975 Food Plants of British Columbia Indians. *British Columbia Provincial Museum Handbook* #34. Victoria, BC.

Turney-High, HH
1941 Ethnography of the Kutenai. American Anthropological Association, Memoir #56.

Tweddell, Colin
1950 The Snoqualmie-Duwamish Dialects of Puget Sound Salish. *University of Washington Publications in Anthropology* #12. Seattle.

Underhill, Ruth
1965 *Red Man's Religion*. University of Chicago Press.

US Court of Claims
1933 The Duwamish, Lummi, Whidby Island, Skagit, upper Skagit, Swinomish, Kikiallus, Snohomish, Snoqualmie, Stillaguamish, Suquamish, Samish, Puyallup, Squaxin, Skokomish, upper Chehalis, Muckleshoot, Nooksack, Chinook and San Juan Islands tribes of Indians, claimants, vs. the United States of America, defendant. Consolidated petition No. F-275. Argus Press, Seattle.

US Department of the Interior, General Land Office.
1856 Plat of Township 25 North, Range 4 East. Washington, DC.
1862 Plat of Township 24 North, Range 4 East. Washington, DC.

Vizenor, Gerald, ed.
2008 *Survivance* ~ Narratives of Native Presence. University of Nebraska Press, Lincoln.

Walls, Robert E
1987 *Bibliography of Washington State Folklore and Folklife*. University of Washington Press, Seattle.

Waterman, Thomas T and Geraldine Coffin
1920 Types of Canoes on Puget Sound. *Indian Notes and Monographs*, Miscellaneous Series #5. Museum of the American Indian, Heye Foundation, New York.

Waterman, Thomas and Ruth Greiner
1921 Indian Houses of Puget Sound. *Indian Notes and Monographs*, Miscellaneous Series #9. Museum of the American Indian, Heye Foundation, New York.

Waterman, Thomas T and collaborators
1921 Native Houses of Western North America. *Indian Notes and Monographs*, Miscellaneous Series 11. Museum of the American Indian, Heye Foundation, New York.

Waterman, Thomas T
c1920 Native Place Name in Puget Sound and Western Washington State. Microfilm #1864 on file, National Anthropological Archives, Washington, DC.
1922 The Geographical Names Used by the Indians of the Pacific Coast. *The Geographical Review* 12 (2): 175-194.
1924 The Shake Religion of Puget Sound. Smithsonian Report for 1922: 499-507. Smithsonian Institution Press, Washington DC.
1930 The Paraphernalia of the Duwamish 'Spirit-Canoe' Ceremony. *Indian Notes* 7 (2): 129-148, 295-3 12, 535-561. Museum of the American Indian, Heye Foundation, New York.
1973 Notes on the Ethnology of the Indians of Puget Sound. *Indian Notes and Monographs*, Miscellaneous Series 59. Museum of the American Indian, Heye Foundation, New York.

Watson, Kenneth Greg, ed.
1996 The Legacy of Snoqualmie Falls. Special Issue. Snoqualmie Valley Historical Museum *& Snoqualmie Valley Reporter*. Wednesday, 28 February.
1999 *Mythology of Southern Puget Sound* by Arthur Ballard. Snoqualmie Valley Historical Museum, North Bend, Washington.

Watt, Roberta Frye
1931 *Four Wagons West*: The Story of Seattle. Metropolitan Press, Portland.

Webster, Lawrence
1982 Interview by Jay Miller. December. Transcript on file, Suquamish Tribal Archives, Suquamish, Washington.

Whitaker, John O, jr.
1980 *The Audubon Society Field Guide to North American Mammals*. Alfred A Knopf, New York.

White, Ellen, and Peter Wilson
1975 The History of Where You Come From – What You Call One Another. 10th International Conference on Salishan Languages: 155-171. Robert St. Clair, ed. LEKTOS, Interdisciplinary Working Papers in Language Sciences, Special Issue, University of Louisville, Kentucky.

White, Richard
  1980 *Land Use, Environment, and Social Change: the Shaping of Island County, Washington.* University of Washington Press, Seattle.

Wickersham, James
  1896 Pueblos on the Northwest Coast. *American Antiquarian* 18 (1): 21-24.
  1898 Nisqually Mythology, Studies of the Washington Indians. *Overland Monthly* 32 (109): 345-351.
  1899 Notes on the Indians of Washington. *American Antiquarian* 21 (6): 269-375.

Wike, Joyce A
  1952 The Role of the Dead in Northwest Coast Culture: 97-103. *Indian Tribes of Aboriginal America.* Sol Tax, ed. Proceedings of the 29th International Congress of Americanists. University of Chicago Press, Chicago.

Williams, Johnson
  1916 Black Tamanous, the Secret Society of the Clallam Indians. *Washington Historical Quarterly* 7: 296-300.

Wright, Robin K, ed.
  1991 *A Time of Gathering*: Native Heritage of Washington State. University of Washington Press, Seattle.

Yesler, Henry Leiter
  1995 The Daughter of Old Chief Seattle: 11-23. *Images of Angeline*: Two Views of Chief Seattle's Daughter from the Nineteenth Century. Steve Heinzen, ed. Lowell Printing & Publishing, Everett WA. [Originally 1881]

thanks

Acknowledgements

Thanks are on-going as we unfold and unravel truth. Friends at Puyallup, Skokomish, Swinomish, Sauk, and elsewhere among both Lushootseeds urge me on. At UW Special Collections are Karyl Winn, Carla Rickerson, Janet Ness, Sandra Kroupa, Diana Shenk, Lisa Scharnhorst, Avril Madison, Jennifer Evans, Linda DiBiase, Steve Eichner, Andrew Popochock, John Medlin, Dr Louis Hieb, and, most especially, Gary Lundell. Elsewhere are Fred and Joan Eggan, Elaine Miller, Lynette Miller, Joy Werlink, Sherrie Maljkovic, Valerie-Anne Lutz, Marilyn Graf, and Gary Fuller Reese.

Help with kinship terms from Lushootseed Elders in a language class at Swinomish, Washington, during the winter of 1983-4. Laura Wilbur, Lawrence Webster, and Vi Hilbert went over coastal terms with me, and Isabel Arcasa went over interior ones. Linguists who rallied and shared include Dale Kinkade, Thom Hess, Brent Galloway, Pam Cahn, and, indirectly, Ann Bates, Larry and Terry Thompson, Ron Beaumont, Jay Powell, and others.

For technical and emotional support, we are grateful to Warren Caldwell, Herb and Natalie Shippen, Tom Steinburn, Ellen Lowe, Astrida Blukis Onat, Lona, Jim, and Claude Wilbur, Brent Galloway, Celia Celffalo, Sarah Campbell, Carolyn Marr, Marge Coale, Ann Chi'en, Ken Tollefson, Coll-Peter Thrush (mostly), Alexandra (Sasha) Harmon, Alan Stay, Catherine Schrup, Harry Chesnin, David Secord, Amy Adams, Charles Roth, Barbara Efrat, Barbara and Robert Lane, James Hirabayashi, Ray Fogelson, John Bower, Jeff Schuster, Laurel Sercombe, Janet Pollak, William Seaburg, Dale Kinkade, Harvey Markowitz, Pamela Amoss, Sam and Janet Stanley, Wayne and Shirley Suttles, Sara Steel, Lucy Steelman, Jorge Villarreal, Rahmi Aiken, Bill Holm, Roger Ernesti, Jay Ellis Ransom, Marilyn Richen, Tammy Jackson, John and Marcia Winterhouse, Greg Watson, both Bruce Millers, and Vi Hilbert.

Closer to home, Mary Laya, Julian Baumel, John Adams, Sally Anderson, Robert Keyes-Bach, Ann Richel Schuh, Patt O'Flaherty, Geoff Keyes, Kurt Reidinger, Holly Taylor, Andy de los Angeles and family, Zalmai Zeke Zahir, Lushootseed Research, and, always, Monday Nite.

index

Index

1

1953, 3f, 10, 79, 87f, 112

A

Adams, John, 58f, 62
Adams, Ron, 8
Aeneas, 23f, 33
Alderton, 62
Alki Point, 28, 57
alpine, 4
Anishinaabe, 4
Ant & Bear, 94
apology, 7f, 87
Auburn, 42f
awxay ~ Owhi, 32f, 99

B

-b-, 82
Ballard, Arthur, 13, 36, 60f, 66, 81f, 119
Ballard Locks, 47
BAR ~ Bureau of Acknowledgement and Research, 3, 125
basket trap, 67
berries, 4, 36, 42, 51f, 69, 94, 113
bishops, 7
Bishop, Thomas, 104f
-bix^w, 49
blankets, 29, 45, 51f, 58, 73; dog ~ goat wool, 53, 71f
blood, 20, 25, 49, 68, 70f, 77f, 83f, 107, 113, 119f, 126
Bokwab, 1, 113
Boldt 1974 Decision, 20
Bolon, AJ, 33
Borst, JW, 25
-bsh, 49, 77f
"Bostons", 20f
Buchanan, Charles, 88, 106
bunks, 27, 45

C

Campbell, Joseph, 8
capsizing, 57
Carnation, 3, 6, 16, 88, 113
carpenters, 53, 74, 109
Cascades, 1, 21f, 30f, 70, 88, 102f
casino, 1, 3f, 11, 79, 88f
Catholics, 23, 27f, 74, 87, 106, 116
cattails, 39f, 45, 51f, 64
Changer, 6, 39, 92f
Cherokee, 1
Cheshiahud, John, 36f
Chief Seattle, 1, 28, 54f, 59, 104f
Chinook, 3, 11, 73, 108f
Chinuk Wawa Jargon, 13, 28f, 58, 67, 117f
Chowitshoot, 28
clams, 15, 42, 52f, 61f, 67f, 113
Clovis, 24
CNN, 8
Constitution, 1, 3, 10, 24f, 87f, 111f
Coupeville, 27
Cowlitz, 3, 11, 32, 87, 102, 108f
Cross family, 74f
Culin, Stewart, 24

D

d^{z}ak^w, 38
Davis, Ed, 13, 18, 25, 41f, 87, 106
Decatur warship, 28
Delaware, 1
Denny, Arthur, 25f, 36, 87
Denny, David, 36f, 41f, 87
Derrida, Jacques, 4
Desmond, Rev Gerald, 34
Diaper Boy, 6, 92f
Dickens, Walter, 22
dicta, 72, 93 #88
dip net, 66
Dog Eaters, 56
Dombrowski, Linda, 10

Dr Bills, 12f, 52
drainage, 1, 5, 38, 45f, 49f, 58f, 70f, 118
dualities, 5, 20, 79, 90
Duwamish, 1f, 24, 36, 40f, 54f, 64, 74, 87, 104f

E

earlobes, 54
Eddie Bauer's clothing store, 42
electric chair, 19
Eliade, Mircea, 8
Elliott Bay, 60
Entwistle, Jas, 26

F

Fall City, 13, 17, 30f, 106
FERC, 9f
ferns, 4f, 65, 68, 92
Filipinos, 27
fires, 4, 15f, 45f, 52f, 63, 67f, 96
"fish-eating tribes", 108
fish weirs, 6, 51, 75, 92
fish-sticks, 53
Ft Nisqually, 28

G

Garfield, Leonard, 7 #6
George, Ellen, 51
George, Jennie, 24
George, Wilson, 46, 56f, 62f
Gibbs, George, 71f, 87, 118
Gig Harbor, 74
Gilman, 40
Glasgow, Thomas W, 9 #9, 27 #22
Glencove, 74
glottal, 116
glottis, 116
Gold, Raelene, 11
Goliah, 28
Good Will Games, 10
Griffin, Arthur, 22f
Griffin Creek, 16, 113
Griffin's Prairie, 26
Gross, FA, 22

H

habitats, 4, 79
Hawaii, 118
Hawaiian kinterms, 86
hemp, 66f
Hess, Thom, 82, 115
Hibulb Museum, 89
hides, 27f, 59, 68
Hilbert, Vi taq^{w}šəblu, 87, 115, 151
Hill, Nathan, 22f, 28, 99f
Holmes Harbor, 22, 99f
house, 1, 14f, 27f, 41, 44f, 73f, 81f, 110
households, 23, 42, 49, 67, 84
houseposts, 45, 73
Hudson Bay Company ~ HBC, 48, 73

I

iišəd = 'feet near', 71
Indian Hill, 88
Indian Homestead Act of 1875, 40
Indian Shaker Church, 42, 48, 55, 73
Indien Civil Rights Act of 1968, 88
International Salish Conference, 115
Iroquois, 1
Ishi, 4
Issaquah, 12, 15, 40f

J

Jacobs, Julia, 64
Jefferson Head, 64
Jenness, Diamond, 76
Jimmicum, 28

K

Kamayakin, 23, 32
Kanim, 1, 13, 28f, 90, 114f
Kanim, Jerry, 3, 13, 23f, 30f, 88f
Karuk, 81
Kassass, 28
Keeper of the National Register, 10
kekule = pithouse, 102
Kennedy, Dorothy, 74
Key Peninsula, 74
kindreds, 5, 50, 70f, 84f
Kinkade, Dale, 92 #85
Kitsap, 54f

Kittitas, 1, 18, 27, 31f

L

Lakes, 1, 4f, 36f
Louie, Mary ~ Mali, 12
Lushootseed, 1, 4 #3, 20 #11, 32, 47f, 61f, 70f, 115f

M

Madrona Point, 8
Magnuson, Rev John, 8
Mamlukes, 89
mammals, 4, 53, 67, 75
mammoth, 25
Martin, Watson, 1, 22f, 113
Marysville, 13, 29, 105, 113
Mason, Charles, 22, 28
mastodon, 25
Medicine Creek, 5, 109
Meeker, Ezra, 36, 88
Miller, Bruce ~ UBC, 87
Miller, Bruce Subiyay, 23f
milt, 92
Mink, 93
Mission Beach, 3
mists, 6f, 87
*-mix^w = life force, 78
Mohegan Sun, 3
Monohan, 11, 15, 36, 40f, 87
Montlake, 37
Moon, 6, 13, 89, 93
Moons, 61f
Moon People, 13
Moses ~ Renton, 11
Moses ~ Chief, 32f, 104
Moses ~ Indian Hill, 88
Mt Si, 6f
Mt St Helens, 11, 87
Muckleshoot, 3f, 25, 42f, 60, 74, 87, 111f
Mukilteo, 9, 25
Museum of the American Indian, 11
Mutton, 71

N

nasal septum, 54
Natches Pass, 102
National Indian Gambling Commission, 90

National Register of Historic Places, 7f
Nelson, 30
Nesmith, JW, 20
nets, 53, 66; aerial, 69; gill, 69
NW Federation of American Indians, 104f

O

Ordinance # 5, 37
OSC = order to show cause, 90

P

P'na ~ Priest Rapids, 33
Pat Kanim, 3, 14, 22f, 30f, 99, 113
patkadəb, 23f, 35, 87, 103, 103
Patkanim, 1f, 9, 20f, 27f, 87f, 103
penstocks, 7f
Pentecostals, 13, 48
piupiumoksmoks ~ Peopeomoxmox ~ Yellow Swan, 33
Point Elliott Treaty, 1f, 23f, 105f
Portage Bay, 36f, 48
Portages, 16, 47f
prerogatives, 76
PSE ~ Puget Sound Energy, 8f
Pshwanwapum, 31 #30
Pskwaws ~ Wenatchee, 24, 32f
Puget Power. *See* Puget Sound Energy PSE

Q

-qən/-qəd = head, 54
q̓ʷu'šəd = 'feet together', 71
Qualawort, 28
Qualchan, 33
Quetalican ~ One Blue Horn, 33
Quinault ~ Quinaielt, 107f

R

ramages, 72
Rat, 17 #37, 93
Raven, 92f, 117
Return to Mukle-Te-Oh, 23
Richmond Beach, 64
RICO = racketeering & organized crime, 89
Roblin Roll, 24f, 87
Roblin, Charles, 3, 25, 104f
Ross, John, 26, 30
Ross, Samuel, 21

Ross, William, 11
Ryegrass Coulee Site (KT88), 31 #28

S

Saddle Mt, 33
Saduwa ~ Saniwa, 1, 20f, 30f, 87f
Sahaptian, 34, 85, 94, 104
Sahaptin, 27f
salmon, 4f, 16, 41f, 52f, 61f, 65, 75, 115
Salmon Tyee, 34
Salmon women, 6
šalqəb, 54f
Sammamish, 1, 11f, 40f, 87, 106
Sandhill Fort, 30f
Saniwa ~ Saduwa ~ Son-a-wa, 1, 20f
sdᶻixʷqs = "one + nose", 54
Sdohobsh, 3
səq̓ʷuʔq̓ʷuʔ, 18, 102
Seattle, John, 58, 105
Seattle Pacific University ~ SPU, 7, 23, 87
shawaway ~ Showaway, 32f
Shuwapso ~ swapc'a = Fast Runner, 33
siblings, 45f, 61, 71f, 80f, 120
Siddle, Julia & Lyman, 42f
Simmons, Michael, 20f
Skookum George, 22
Skykomish, 1, 15, 22f, 74, 113, 126
Slahal family, 1, 5, 24, 79, 87f
slaves, 27f, 30f, 45, 50f, 64, 71f, 84, 99
Slocums, John & Mary, 55, 73
Smith, Alfred John, 60f
Smith, Marian, 49, 61f
Smohalla ~ smoxala ~ šmuxala, 32f
snares, 68f
Snkyuse, 20 #18, 27, 33
Snohomish, 1, 18, 22f, 32f, 74, 82, 102f
Snoqualmie Falls, 1, 5f, 20f, 31, 79, 87f, 102
Snoqualmie Falls Preservation Project, 8
Snoqualmie Valley Historical Museum, 10
Snoqualmoo, 9 #9, 27 #22
Snuqualmie Jim, 3
Sotaiakum, Charles, 60
spədak, 11, 38, 56f, 64, 87
Split Sun ~ Suktalkosum ~ səq̓taɫk̓ʷusm, 32
sqʷəd = Snoqualmie Falls, 6, 17, 113
Star Child, 6, 92

Stockaders, 55
Sun & Moon, 6, 61, 93
Suquamish, 5, 24, 36, 42f, 51f, 74, 82, 102f
survivance, 4f, 70f, 80f, 87f
Syowin winter dancing, 44, 57f, 79

T

TCP ~ Traditional Cultural Place ~ Property, 7f, 87
Tecumsia, 104
Thornton Creek, 47f
Tibbets Creek, 15
Tibbetts, George, 40f
tiyayaš ~ Teias, 32
Tollefson, Kenneth, 7f, 23f, 35, 87f
Tolowa, 81 #81
Tolt, 3, 6, 13f, 16, 23f, 30f, 87f, 105f, 113
totems, 18, 74, 79
TRO = temporary restraining order, 90
Tulalip Reservation, 1f, 8f, 22, 29, 87f, 106f
Twin Peaks, 11
(t)xʷləšucid, 115
Tyee George, 74

V

Vantage, 31f
Vashon Island, 43
Victoria, BC, 59
Vizenor, Gerald, 4

W

Waashat, 34
Wallace, Leander, 28, 71 #44
wapato, 4, 65, 75
Washington Department of Archaeology and Historic Preservation ~ WA DAHP, 10f
Washington State Advisory Council, 10
Waterman, Thomas T, 11f, 37, 42f, 48, 87
watershed, 24, 49f, 70
Watson, K Greg, 10
Webster, Lawrence, 64, 82, 106, 151
Webster, Peter, 135
weirs, 6, 51, 60, 65f, 75, 92
Whahalchu, Jacob, 57
Whale House ~ *saɫuɫtxʷ*, 75
Whulshootseed, 5, 38, 47f, 64, 73, 115f
Whyeeka, 28

William, Mary, 13
Williams, Lucy, 60
Wiyawiikt ~ Weowich, 20 #18, 32f

X

xalalʔtxʷ, 14, 16, 18, 30, 113
x̣ačuʔabš, 6, 17, 43, 47
Xot, John, 27, 30

Y

Yelm, 62
yiʔduʔad ~ swing, 6, 17 #37, 93

Z

Zakuse, Amelia, 11
Zakuse, Jim, 36f

Please help defeat Typo Gnomes!

Report Offenses!

Sold @ Amazon.com

ACCULTURATING AMELIA ~ Round Valley 1937 California
ALASKA EDGE ISLAND ~ Siberian Yupiks of St Lawrence Island
ALLIED MOUNDS ~ Touching the Earth, Modeling the World, Reaching the Sky
ANIMAL PEOPLE ADVENTURES ~ Native North American Tribal Stories
AT BAY ~ Cultures Converging through Southwest Washington > 5
BALLARD BULWARK ~
CHACO ECHOES ~ Pervasive Keresan Priesthoods
CHACOKIA ~ Chaco, Cahokia, Cities & Ceremonies ~ Bundles & Blood Lines Centuries Ago
CHINOOK CONCERNS ~ Emma Millett Luscier, Isabella Bertrand, Verne Ray
CIRCLING FOUR CORNERS ~ Re-Viewing Native American Indiens > 10
CROSSING ~ LINES: An Educational Memoir of Native North America
DEL-AWARE ~ Lenape Legacies
DELAWARE INTEGRITY ~ Rituals, Removals, Reforms by Lenape Indiens
DISCLAIMING TREATIES I ~ Puget Tribes 1927 Testimonies
DISCLAIMING TREATIES II ~ Puget Tribes 1927 Testimonies > 15
ELDERS' DIALOG ~ Ed Davis & Vi Hilbert Discuss Native Puget Sound Language, Culture, & Heritage
EVERGREEN ETHNOGRAPHIES ~ Hoh, Chehalis, Suquamish, and Snoqualmi of Western Washington
FEDERAL FISH FILES ~ Swindell 1942 Treaty Rights Report
GEORGE GIBBS NORTHWEST ARRAY ~ Full Reports, Place Names, Word List, Artifact Names, and Guide
GRASSROOTS JANET ~ Advancing Salish and Traditional Cultures > 20
HERMAN HAEBERLIN REGAINED ~ Anthropology and Artifacts of Puget Sound 1916-17
HERSTORY NW ~ Women Upholding Native Traditions
INDIEN ~ ETHNOGRAPHY: Cultural Traditions of Native North America
INDIEN ~ ETHNOLOGY: Grounded, Gendered, Meaningful Cultural Traditions
LESCHI IN LOVE ~ A Novel of Native Puget Sound > x2 > 25
MARCO MUCK MASKS ~ Frank Cushing on Marshes and Mounds
MINTER BAY ~ Land, Lore, Loss, and Lucre in the South Salish Sea
NATIVE MET HOW ~ Improving Posterity
OLD LUKH ~ A Novel of Native Puget Sound Daily Life, Places, and Stories
OVER THE FALLS ~ Sdokwalbixw Survivance Surrounding Seattle > 30
PACIFIC PLATEAU PORTRAYALS ~ People Places Ponderings
RAY'S ARRAY ~ Raymond D Fogelson's Works
RIGHTING NATIVE PLACES ~ Adventures in Northwest Geography
SAHAPTINS STUDIES ~ Columbia River Plateau, Cora Du Bois, Homer Garner Barnett, Gerald Raymond Desmond
SDOQWALBIXW > 35
SOUND SALISH STRAITS ~ Central Salish Sea Cultures
UNSETTLING SEATTLE ~ Arresting Local Talent and Academic Illiteracy
WRITING WORDS IN WARY WORLDS ~ World Wide Improved Spellings of Native America
    Languages

JONA Memoirs

RESCUES, RANTS, & RESEARCHES ~ A Re-View of Jay Miller's Writings on Northwest Indien
    Cultures ~ #9
TRIBAL TRIO of the Northwest Coast by Kenneth D Tollefson ~ #10 > 40
INTERWEAVING COAST SALISH CULTURAL SYSTEMS ~ Collected Works of Pamela Thorsen
    Amoss ~ #14

University of Nebraska Press

ANCESTRAL MOUNDS ~ Vitality and Volatility Crossing Native North America 2015
HONNE ~ The Spirit of the Chehalis 2015